"RUN IT!
AND LET'S GET
THE HELL OUT OF HERE!"

The 100 Best Plays in Pro Football History

JONATHAN RAND

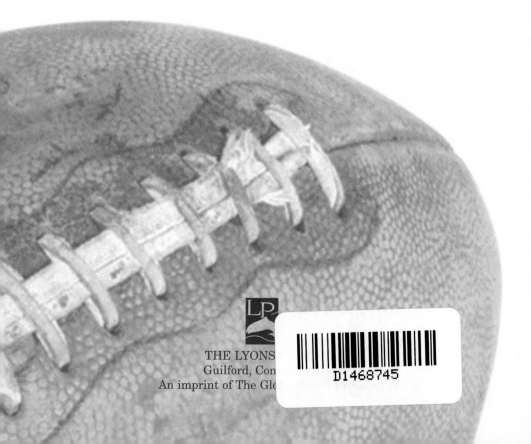

THE LYONS
Guilford, Con
An imprint of The Gl

The Lyons Press is an imprint of The Globe Pequot Press.

10 9 8 7 6 5 4 3 2 1

Printed in the United States of America

Designed by Mimi LaPoint

Library of Congress Cataloging-in-Publication Data

Rand, Jonathan, 1947-
     Run It! and Let's Get the Hell Out of Here!: 100 Football Plays
     that Shook the World / Jonathan Rand.
          p. cm.
     Includes bibliographical references and index.
     ISBN-13: 978-1-59921-187-9
     1. Football—United States—Anecdotes. 2. National Football
     League—Anecdotes. 3. National Football League—History. I. Title.
     GV954.R35 2007
     796.332'64--dc22
                                        2007012318

CONTENTS

INTRODUCTION

It's hard to imagine that, after writing about pro football for nearly four decades, my appreciation for those who play the game could possibly become any greater. Researching this book, however, was a stunning reminder of how many fantastic athletic feats we've come to take for granted.

I suppose we could blame the players for this. There are so many gifted players making so many great plays, you could easily compile a credible list of the one hundred greatest plays for each NFL franchise. Or the one hundred greatest plays from Super Bowl games. Or Jerry Rice's hundred greatest catches. Or Barry Sanders's hundred greatest runs.

There's such a smorgasbord of great plays that no two people would come up with identical lists. You could ask a hundred experts to name their one hundred greatest plays, and it would be surprising if any had more than two-thirds in common. Few NFL weekends pass without a great play, even if it doesn't result in a touchdown or decide the outcome.

I will consider every play since the 1958 season, which climaxed with the NFL championship game between the Baltimore Colts and New York Giants. This game is celebrated as the launching pad for the NFL's emergence as America's dominant professional sports league and considering that we are about to celebrate the fiftieth NFL season since that game, what better time to compile a list of the one hundred greatest plays? What are my criteria? I chose plays that helped turn the tide of big games, especially Super Bowls; plays of historical significance; plays that ended games in spectacular fashion; plays that involved great players; and plays that were unique.

A play that won a Super Bowl might not rate top-one-hundred consideration had it been made in October. Our list includes the tackle by St. Louis Rams linebacker Mike Jones that stopped Tennessee Titans wide receiver Kevin Dyson just short of a potentially tying touchdown on the final play of the January 2000 Super Bowl. That play is elevated to greatness because it came at such a dramatic moment and provides a snapshot of two fierce competitors locked in a tug-of-war of willpower.

Three Lynn Swann catches in the January 1976 Super Bowl each could have merited a chapter. In the interest of including as many plays as possible, all three have been grouped together. For the same reason, two great plays from the same game often are placed in the same chapter.

While my mission is to pick the one hundred greatest plays—not the hundred greatest games or hundred greatest players, those three categories are sometimes impossible to isolate. So often, we see that great players make great plays and great plays make great games.

When I undertook this project, I thought it might become drudgery to pore over tapes and piece together incomplete accounts of great plays. Instead, it became a treat to watch these plays over and over. Perhaps I shared the enjoyment of art lovers who study a painting from various angles and notice another exquisite detail with each viewing.

These plays may not all make your list of personal favorites. But you've got to admit, these one hundred are all worth celebrating.

#100
SECOND CHANCE
KENNY KING'S SUPER BOWL ROMP
JANUARY 25, 1981

THE OAKLAND RAIDERS for decades prided themselves on being the team of last resort. Talented players who didn't fit in elsewhere found a home with the Raiders and usually helped them win.

Nobody made more of his second chance in Oakland than quarterback Jim Plunkett. The New England Patriots made him the first overall pick of the 1971 draft, but he was beaten up and beaten down by high expectations and weak supporting casts. Plunkett became another Raiders reclamation project and was almost thirty-three when he began the 1980 season as the backup to Dan Pastorini.

The Raiders dropped to 2–3 in a game in which Pastorini suffered a fractured leg. Plunkett stepped in and led the Raiders to thirteen wins in fifteen games, including a 27–10 Super Bowl victory over the Philadelphia Eagles at New Orleans. He threw for 261 yards and three touchdowns, including an 80-yard pass to fullback Kenny King that broke the game open.

If the Raiders expected to win, they had to protect Plunkett. He was sacked eight times in a 10–7 loss to the Eagles in November, the main reason the Eagles were favored in the Super Bowl. Plunkett was sacked just once in the rematch, and when his protection faltered, he was still nimble enough to throw on the run.

Plunkett made the scramble of the game with time running out in the first quarter. The Raiders led 7–0 and faced third-and-4 from their 20-yard line. Cliff Branch, who caught two touchdown passes that day, lined up left. Bob Chandler, the primary receiver on a deep crossing pattern, lined up right. King was the outlet receiver.

Plunkett stepped up in the pocket to avoid the rush but couldn't find anybody open and scrambled to his left. King, seeing the opportunity for a big play, headed down the left sideline, and Plunkett hit him at the Oakland 39. Cornerback Herm Edwards leaped but could only get a fingertip on the ball.

"Plunkett rolled out of the pocket, and Kenny King's right behind me," Edwards recalled. "I was going toward the line of scrimmage; I thought he was going to run the ball. He stepped up and threw it over my head. I was backing up, trying to make a play. I could've made it . . . but didn't make it that day."

King ran 80 yards, the longest scoring play in the first fifteen Super Bowls. "The play wasn't designed for me to go deep," he said. "I'm supposed to go 6 yards up field and cut for the sidelines, but when I saw Plunkett scramble, I took off. The linebacker dropped me when he saw Plunkett scrambling, and Jim got me the ball.

"The most memorable part of that was catching the ball, running down the sideline and having Bob Chandler come across the field and make the last block to spring me to the end zone and going on to set a Super Bowl record that lasted sixteen years. I didn't hear any footsteps behind me, and Chandler kept up with me stride for stride. I didn't know he was that fast."

King, who came to the Raiders that season in a trade with the Houston Oilers, scored with nine seconds left in the quarter to give the Raiders a 14–0 lead. That lead seemed likely to hold up because the Raider defense was smothering the Eagles. Quarterback Ron Jaworski avoided throwing at the area with two Raider standouts—left outside linebacker Ted Hendricks and left cornerback Lester Hayes. But the Eagles' strategy backfired when right outside linebacker Rod Martin made three interceptions.

King still owned the longest touchdown reception in Super Bowl history until Antonio Freeman made an 81-yard catch from Brett Favre in January 1997. King still got an awful lot of mileage from a play that was designed to get him 6 yards.

#99
MERLIN THE MAGICIAN
OLSEN'S TIP LEADS THE RAMS
DECEMBER 22, 1974

LOS ANGELES RAMS defensive tackle Merlin Olsen was near the end of his Hall of Fame career when he forced the play that knocked the Washington Redskins out of the 1974 playoffs. Olsen broke in during an era in which defensive stars went unnoticed and, thanks partly to him, retired in an era in which defensive stars were dominant.

The Redskins visited Los Angeles for a divisional playoff game—and a grudge match. Redskins coach George Allen coached the Rams to five straight winning seasons before he was fired in 1970. Olsen, leader of the Rams defense, was among Allen's old players. Now the same defense that made Allen a winner was making him miserable. The Rams recovered three fumbles and forced three interceptions against the Redskins.

"George Allen always said that if you can get six turnovers in a game, you'll win it," Olsen said after the Rams' 19–10 victory.

This was a defensive tussle in which each team scored just one offensive touchdown. Finally, the Redskins' sixth turnover broke their backs. The Rams led 13–10 in the fourth quarter as quarterback Sonny Jurgensen tried to get the Redskins into field-goal position. As he dropped back, Olsen got penetration up the middle and hit Jurgensen's arm. The pass wobbled and was intercepted by weak-side linebacker Isiah Robertson, who weaved 59 yards for the touchdown that clinched the victory.

Olsen was a thorn in Allen's side all day. The Redskins led 10–7 in the third quarter when Olsen forced Larry Brown to fumble, setting up a 37-yard field goal by David Ray. Ray also made a 26-yard kick to put the Rams ahead in the fourth quarter, but their lead remained shaky until Robertson's interception.

The Rams couldn't reach the Super Bowl, however. They lost a week later, 14–10 at Minnesota, in an NFC championship game that featured a controversial illegal procedure penalty on Rams guard Tom Mack inside the Vikings' 1-yard line. The Vikings lost the Super Bowl 16–6 to the Pittsburgh Steelers in a matchup of the "Steel Curtain" defense and "Purple People Eaters," the Vikings' front four. Olsen, who was enjoying a string of fourteen straight Pro Bowl berths, was voted the league's Most Valuable Player. Defense, clearly, was ruling the roost in the NFL.

But defense wasn't so popular when Olsen joined the Rams in 1962. That began to change when the Rams assembled the "Fearsome Foursome"—tackles Olsen and Roosevelt Grier and ends Deacon Jones and Lamar Lundy. That group terrorized quarterbacks, and Jones, arguably the best pass rusher ever, coined the term "sack."

Defenses became so dominant in the 1970s that NFL rules makers worried about losing their audience. They made major rules changes in 1977 and 1978 to open up the passing game. The Rams had plenty of talent on both sides of the ball when Allen returned to them as head coach in 1978. But he was fired before the season started. Players rebelled at his personality quirks, including his obsession with tidiness.

The last straw for Rams players came when Allen insisted a player pick up a paper cup from the practice field. That player was Robertson, who for the second time in his career ended a season for Allen.

#98
MORE HEARTBREAK
LEON LETT STRIPS THURMAN THOMAS
JANUARY 30, 1994

THE BUFFALO BILLS finally were poised to win a Super Bowl after losing the championship game three years in a row. They led 13–6 at halftime over the Dallas Cowboys, who'd thrashed them 52–17 in the previous year's Super Bowl. Bills quarterback Jim Kelly was stinging the Dallas defense, and Cowboys quarterback Troy Aikman was still battling symptoms of a concussion he'd suffered the week before.

As the second half began in the Georgia Dome, the Bills were on the march and on the verge of shoving the Cowboys against the ropes. Then, in just one play, the redemption of the Bills turned into a repetition of their annual nightmare.

Cowboys defensive tackle Leon Lett had been embarrassed a year earlier when Bills wide receiver Don Beebe knocked the ball out of his hands for a touchback as Lett was showboating before he reached the end zone on a fumble return. Lett was all business, however, when Thurman Thomas carried on the third play of the third quarter. On first-and-10 from the Bills' 43-yard line, Thomas got 3 yards, but Lett slapped the ball loose. Reserve safety James Washington recovered the fumble and returned it 46 yards for a touchdown that tied the score and brought the Bills' momentum to a screeching halt.

Bills coach Marv Levy called Thomas's fumble "the most de-moralizing moment of his great career." Thomas wasn't the only Bill demoralized, though. The Bills never regained their spark. On the first play of the fourth quarter, with the Cowboys ahead 20–13, Washington intercepted a pass intended for Beebe and

5

returned it to the Buffalo 34-yard line. That set up a 1-yard touchdown run by Emmitt Smith, his second scoring run of the day, which assured the Cowboys' 30–13 victory.

Thomas also fumbled in the first half when, with the score 3–3, he caught a Kelly shovel pass and was nailed by Washington. Thomas was a key ingredient in the Bills' glory years of the 1990s, yet on Super Bowl Sundays he seemed cursed.

He had a big game in his first Super Bowl, against the New York Giants. But his Super Bowl fortunes went downhill from the moment he misplaced his helmet and missed the first series of a 37–24 loss to the Washington Redskins. In his last three Super Bowls, Thomas gained 69 yards on 37 carries, including 37 yards on 16 carries in the fourth straight loss.

"I fumbled," he said. "I cost us the game."

Bills general manager John Butler tried to console Thomas in the locker room. "I love him dearly, and I always will," he said. "Thurman Thomas got us to four Super Bowls. If he's a goat, I'd like to have a whole herd of them."

There was little for the Bills to say after their thirty-five-point loss to the Cowboys, except that it could have been even worse. The 30–13 loss, however, was a game the Bills were controlling and might have won had Thomas held on to the ball. And the Bills had to realize their odds of reaching a fifth straight Super Bowl were pretty long.

"This one is the worst," wide receiver Andre Reed said. "We should have won. They came up with twenty-four unanswered points. That last fumble was one in a million. Those things always happen to the Bills."

#97
LONG ARM OF THE LAW
TY LAW STARTS AN UPSET
FEBRUARY 3, 2002

NEW ENGLAND PATRIOTS cornerback Ty Law was fed up hearing about "The Greatest Show on Turf." That was the star-studded, league-leading offense of the St. Louis Rams and the reason they were fourteen-point Super Bowl favorites over the Patriots. So you can imagine how satisfied Law felt when he jump-started one of the biggest Super Bowl upsets ever by intercepting a Kurt Warner pass and returning it 47 yards for a touchdown.

The Rams led 3–0 when Law stepped in front of wide receiver Isaac Bruce and ran untouched down the left sideline with 8:49 left in the second quarter. It was the first of three turnovers that led to seventeen points. They negated the Rams' 427–267 edge in yardage and fueled the Patriots' 20–17 victory in New Orleans.

"[Linebacker] Mike Vrabel put the pressure on Warner," Law recalled. "We were in man coverage. Bruce did the out cut. I waited on it and it came right to me and then it was me on the sidelines and hoping a lineman or the quarterback didn't catch me.

"I made plenty of interceptions in my career in big games, but when you do it in the Super Bowl and change the momentum, especially with the play of the game, that's always going to stick out like a sore thumb. A lot of people will probably remember me by that because it was on the grand stage. To hear everybody tell it, we weren't even supposed to show up."

The Patriots forced their next turnover late in the first half. Warner completed a 15-yard pass to wide receiver Ricky Proehl, who fumbled after a hit by safety Antwan Harris. Five plays later, Brady hit wide receiver David Patten for an 8-yard touchdown

7

pass and a 14–3 lead. The Patriots made it 17–3 in the third quarter on an Adam Vinatieri field goal, set up by cornerback Otis Smith's return of an interception to the Rams' 33-yard line. The Rams rallied and tied the score on a Warner run and a touchdown pass to Proehl. Nobody actually expected they could be kept out of the end zone all day.

The Rams led the NFL during the regular season with 6,930 yards and 503 points behind Warner, the league MVP. Considering their defense also ranked among the NFL's best, the twice-beaten Rams appeared even stronger than their championship team of two years earlier.

The Patriots, meanwhile, were a surprising worst-to-first team led by a pup of a quarterback, Tom Brady. Who could have guessed this heavy underdog was about to join the Dallas Cowboys as the only teams ever to win three Super Bowl games in four years?

The Patriots took pride in their relative anonymity and skipped the traditional individual-player introductions. Instead, they came out on the field together. "We came out as a team, which was the first time it's ever been done in the Super Bowl," Law said. "But we had some big plays as individuals."

No play was bigger than Vinatieri's 48-yard field goal on the final play. Without that kick, Law's interception might be just a Super Bowl footnote. "You have to win the Super Bowl to realize what it means—that was big," Law said. "You go out there to make a play like that and give your team the opportunity to win that game. With the help of Adam, that could put me in the history book of great plays."

#96

MUD BOWL
A. J. DUHE PICKS OFF A BIG WIN
JANUARY 23, 1983

LINEBACKER A. J. DUHE didn't seem to belong in the Miami Dolphins' standout defense of 1982. That unit was nicknamed the "Killer Bs" because six starters had last names beginning with "B." They were linemen Doug Betters, Bob Baumhower, and Kim Bokamper; linebacker Bob Brudzinski; and safeties Glenn and Lyle Blackwood. Duhe, of course, was two letters off.

And Duhe wasn't even supposed to be a linebacker. He was a defensive end from Louisiana State when the Dolphins picked him in the first round of the 1977 draft. Duhe was quick with excellent range and was an immediate starter. But he was light for a defensive lineman. Consequently, a Palm Beach beat writer, Chuck Otterson, asked coach Don Shula if he'd considered making Duhe a linebacker. This was the first time Shula was known to seriously consider a journalist's suggestion.

Duhe was starting at left inside linebacker when the New York Jets came to Miami for the 1982 AFC championship game on the Orange Bowl's mud-soaked Prescription Athletic Turf. The Dolphins and Jets survived an eight-team AFC playoff tournament in the wake of a strike-torn season that included only nine regular-season weekends.

But the Jets couldn't survive Duhe's three interceptions of Richard Todd passes. He returned his last interception 35 yards for a touchdown, to clinch a 14–0 victory. The Dolphins were headed to the Super Bowl for the first time in nine years.

The Dolphins took full advantage of Duhe's versatility that day and lined him up at six different positions. He literally had a hand in both Miami touchdowns.

"That was the Mud Bowl," Shula recalled. "That was one of the best games I ever saw a linebacker play."

The game was scoreless at halftime before Duhe intercepted Todd in the third quarter and set up the Dolphins at the New York 48-yard line. An unsportsmanlike-conduct penalty helped the Dolphins move to the 7, from where Woody Bennett scored on a run up the middle.

For the clinching touchdown, Duhe didn't need anyone else to hit the end zone. Lined up at left end early in the fourth quarter, he was rushing Todd but spotted running back Bruce Harper waiting for a screen pass. Duhe alertly moved into the passing lane and jumped to make the interception, though he bobbled the ball twice before hauling it in and scoring. He held the ball high in the end zone to celebrate the win and his banner day. The Dolphins held the Jets to 139 yards, the lowest total ever in an AFC championship game.

Duhe made another interception a week later in the Super Bowl, at the Washington Redskins' 47-yard line, with the Dolphins ahead 17–13 in the third quarter. The Redskins got the ball back with their own interception, then three plays later quarterback Joe Theismann was horrified to see his pass batted, and almost intercepted, by Bokamper. Before the defensive end could gain control of the ball and head for the end zone, however, Theismann knocked it out of Bokamper's hands. The Redskins won 27–17.

"That was the biggest play of the game," Theismann boasted. "I had visions of Duhe last week, and I didn't want to be in Richard Todd's shoes."

#95
CHAMP DETHRONES THE CHAMPS
BAILEY PUTS AWAY PATRIOTS
JANUARY 14, 2006

THE DENVER BRONCOS were ahead 10–6 in a divisional playoff game, but their slim lead didn't mean much because New England's Tom Brady was knocking at the door.

Brady, the winning quarterback in the two previous Super Bowls, moved the Patriots to a third down at the Broncos' 5-yard line in the last minute of the third quarter in Denver. He had no idea that cornerback Champ Bailey was about to turn the game around with a 100-yard interception return.

Brady wanted to throw, but cornerback Nick Ferguson was pressuring him. Brady rolled right and spotted wide receiver Troy Brown in the corner of the end zone. With a touchdown, the Patriots would grab the lead and perhaps be on their way to an eleventh-straight postseason victory. Bailey read the play, however. He stepped in front of Brown a yard deep in the end zone and intercepted the pass.

"They were blitzing; I thought I had Troy," Brady said after the Broncos' 27–13 victory. "I threw it, and Champ wheeled back and made a great play. That's basically a ten-point swing, and that's kind of the way the game went. Poor execution . . . bad throw. What else can you say?"

For the Broncos, it was a great defensive play and a great return. What else can you say? "It was a great play by me," said Bailey.

Once he grabbed the ball, Bailey saw nothing but daylight down his left sideline. He seemed sure to be gone unless a defender sprouted wings. Kevin Faulk, a speedy running back, almost caught up with Bailey past midfield only to see him slip through his fingers. Bailey was alone now but couldn't see tight end Ben Watson rushing diagonally across the field. Watson was every bit as determined as Buffalo's Don Beebe was in his Super Bowl pursuit of the Cowboys' Leon Lett twelve years earlier.

"I never saw the guy coming, but I was going as hard as I could," Bailey said. Yet he slowed near the goal line and let the ball hang at his hip. Watson tackled him and knocked the ball loose. The ball was ruled out of bounds at the 1, for a Broncos' first down. Bailey was still on his back, breathing hard, when Patriots coach Bill Belichick issued a replay challenge. He claimed the ball crossed the goal line, causing a touchback, which would've given the Patriots a first down at the 20-yard line.

Referee Jeff Triplette ruled the play would stand. Bailey was credited with a 100-yard return, the longest nonscoring interception return in postseason history. Unlike offensive plays, which are measured from the line of scrimmage, returns are measured from the spot they started. Running back Mike Anderson scored on the next play to give the Broncos a 17–6 lead and put them in charge the rest of the way.

Bailey's interception was one of five turnovers forced by the Broncos, and a four-yard touchdown pass from Jake Plummer to wide receiver Rod Smith midway through the fourth quarter made the score 24–6. For just the second time in five years, the Patriots were not going to reach the Super Bowl, much less win it again.

Broncos coach Mike Shanahan inevitably had been second-guessed for trading franchise running back Clinton Portis to the Washington Redskins for Bailey in March 2004. That second-guessing officially ended when Champ knocked out the champs.

#94
A BIG BLOCK
VERNON PERRY'S PLAYOFF PARTY
DECEMBER 29, 1979

THE HOUSTON OILERS were going to San Diego for a divisional playoff game, and it was hard to see how they'd have much of a chance to win. Their playmakers were all sidelined. Running back Earl Campbell and quarterback Dan Pastorini were out with groin pulls, and wide receiver Ken Burrough was out with a tailbone injury.

The Chargers of 1979 were the strongest team of the Air Coryell era, named for coach Don Coryell's quick-strike offense. For the Oilers to stay in the game, their defense would have to carry a big load. The Chargers were eight-point favorites, yet strong safety Vernon Perry turned into a one-man wrecking crew and led the Oilers to a 17–14 upset.

"Those were our key guys!" Oilers coach Bum Phillips said, referring to his injured stars. "But then Vernon Perry, who wasn't a widely known player, intercepted four passes and blocked a field goal. That was the contribution of one guy! That was the thing that amazed me most that day. You don't see one guy do that very many times.

"Vernon was a free agent who played some Canadian ball. He was in the right place at the right time against San Diego. He got a tipped ball or two that helped him with the interceptions. But it was amazing that we could come back and beat the Chargers. Overall, San Diego was a better football team than we were, but not that day."

While there were better defensive backs than Perry, there were none in the league that day. He enjoyed a career's worth of postseason highlights, most notably his blocked kick, because that changed the game's momentum. Mike Wood attempted a 26-yard field goal in the second quarter that could have put the Chargers ahead 10–0. Perry blocked his attempt, picked up the ball, and ran 57 yards to the San Diego 28-yard line. That set up Toni Fritsch's 26-yard field goal, which meant the blocked kick caused a six-point swing.

The Chargers' Dan Fouts came out throwing after the ensuing kickoff. Perry made his second interception and gave his offense the ball at the San Diego 38-yard line. Gifford Nielsen kept the drive going with a first-down pass to running back Rob Carpenter, who was so sore from a sprained ankle that he literally crawled back to the huddle. A Nielsen scramble set up a 1-yard touchdown run by Boobie Clark, and a stunned San Diego crowd saw the Oilers lead 10–7 at halftime.

"Being fair, I think the Chargers were a little bit overconfident and didn't think they were going to have to play hard," Phillips said.

The lead changed twice more, and the Oilers led 17–14 in the fourth quarter. Fouts moved his offense to the Houston 35-yard line and threw short for tight end Bob Klein. Linebacker Robert Brazile closed quickly, though, and deflected the ball into the air, where it was grabbed by Perry for his third interception. Little more than a minute remained when the Chargers got one last chance. Fouts threw deep, but Perry made his fourth interception, an NFL playoff record that still stood nearly three decades later.

Oilers defensive coordinator Eddie Biles claimed he'd been stealing offensive signals. "We pretty much knew ahead of time when they were going to pass," he said.

That didn't explain how, against the Pittsburgh Steelers in the AFC championship game a week later, Perry intercepted Terry Bradshaw's first pass and returned it 75 yards for a touchdown. But the Oilers couldn't score an offensive touchdown and lost 24–13. On that day, there was only so much that even Perry could do.

#93
BEAUTY OF A THROW
LEN DAWSON TO OTIS TAYLOR
JANUARY 4, 1970

IT WAS AS FINELY THREADED a pass as you'll ever see, and it propelled the Kansas City Chiefs to a Super Bowl. Wide receiver Otis Taylor was pinned to the right sideline between Oakland Raiders defensive backs George Atkinson and Willie Brown, and it appeared Len Dawson would need a guided missile to hit his target.

It also was as gutsy a pass as you'll ever see—and in an AFL championship game no less. The Chiefs faced third-and-14 at their own 2-yard line, and the score was 7–7. An interception would have set up the Raiders for the go-ahead score. Instead, Dawson completed a pass that, he said, "was where it had to be."

Taylor reached out and made a one-handed catch for a 35-yard gain. Six plays later, running back Robert Holmes ran 5 yards for the decisive touchdown in a 17–7 victory that gave the Chiefs the chance to beat the Minnesota Vikings in the Super Bowl.

Dawson was understandably worried that the Chiefs' poor field position could cost them the game. On the play before the critical pass, the Chiefs had fumbled at the 6 and were fortunate to recover.

"That was a defensive battle, and if we don't get a first down and punt the ball away, that gives them great field position," Dawson recalled. "Otis wasn't the primary receiver. I was looking for Robert Holmes coming across the middle, but he got banged.

"I was rolling out of the pocket because I knew they'd be flying after me. I got outside, and I couldn't wait much longer, so I threw it, and it would have gone out of bounds if he didn't catch it. It was a great catch.

"I was looking not just to get a few yards. I was looking to get it all. It's a throw you work on all the time in practice and hope when you release the thing it's the good release and hope it's the right distance. There's a lot of hoping going on."

Dawson's hopes always had a better chance of materializing when his receiver was Taylor. He was tall and strong and could outjump defenders. As nearly perfect as that pass was, Taylor was among the few receivers who could have caught it.

"I had to catch the ball as it came in—reaching out and one-handing it," he said. "I pulled it in and covered up. It was one of my better catches, especially considering the pressure of the situation and game."

The Chiefs had lost two close regular-season games to the Raiders. They were incensed when they arrived at the Oakland Coliseum and saw the Raiders carrying their luggage for a post-game departure to New Orleans, site of the Super Bowl that year.

"They assumed they were going to win the game," Chiefs coach Hank Stram recalled. "It gave us a boost. Everyone was upset."

The Chiefs got an even bigger boost when Dawson and Taylor connected. "That play was really significant," Dawson said, "because when you get right down to it, it was the season, it was the championship and the reason we're all wearing Super Bowl rings."

#92
A SHOCKING HIT
LAWRENCE TAYLOR'S GRISLY SACK
NOVEMBER 18, 1985

LAWRENCE TAYLOR'S bone-snapping tackle of Washington Redskins quarterback Joe Theismann was the goriest scene ever on an NFL telecast. Theismann's face was contorted with pain, and a snapped bone protruded from his skin. New York Giants linebacker Lawrence Taylor, who usually took pride in his intimidating persona, was visibly distraught as soon as he saw the damage he'd inflicted, and he called for help.

It was the second quarter of a *Monday Night Football* game in Washington, and the Redskins ran one of their favorite gadget plays. Theismann handed off to running back John Riggins, who faked a run, then pitched the ball back to Theismann, who tried to pass. But the Giants' defense wasn't fooled. Linebacker Harry Carson and nose tackle Jim Burt chased Theismann to his left, and he never saw Taylor coming from his blind side. Taylor tackled Theismann and rolled over his right leg, breaking his tibia and fibula.

Taylor jumped up and frantically motioned to the Redskins bench to bring out their medical staff. The Redskins' orthopedic surgeon, trainer, and coach Joe Gibbs were on the field in seconds. Theismann's leg was placed in a cast, and he was put on a stretcher and taken off the field for the last time. He underwent surgery that night and said he never watched a replay of the injury.

"I remember handing the ball to John, getting it back, and then looking downfield," Theismann told the *Washington Post*. "I couldn't find [Art] Monk deep, and then I looked to my right for

Donnie [Warren, the tight end]. At that point, I was feeling some pressure, and the next thing I knew, I heard what sounded like a shotgun going off—pow! pow!—and felt this excruciating pain. Then I was on the ground."

Theismann, who'd been with the Redskins since 1974 and led them to two Super Bowls, received a huge ovation as he was wheeled off the field. To the *Post*, he described the crowd reaction as one that "I'll never forget as long as I live. The big Longines clock at RFK Stadium was at 10:05. Everything is so vivid in my mind."

He was replaced by Jay Schroeder, who completed thirteen of twenty-one passes for 221 yards and a touchdown and led the Redskins to a 23–21 win. The Giants and Redskins were marquee teams of that era and would win four of the next seven Super Bowls. A Taylor-led defense would carry the Giants to championships in the 1986 and 1990 seasons. Gibbs added Super Bowl wins with Doug Williams and Mark Rypien, giving him three Lombardi trophies with three different quarterbacks.

Theismann actually expected to play again, because he had played only eight weeks after suffering a broken right leg in 1972 in the Canadian Football League. He seemed so confident he could make another successful comeback that Theismann kept seeking NFL tryouts, even though the 1985 injury left his right leg slightly shorter than his left. Anyone who saw his injury would have been flabbergasted to see him return, and Theismann finally retired.

"People break legs all the time in football," said Dan Dierdorf, a Hall of Fame offensive tackle who later became a *Monday Night Football* analyst. "It involves the cracking of a bone, but most times, you can't see it. That night, what you saw was so graphic, and when you watch something that's so far out of the normal, you just gag, but you almost can't help watching it again and again."

#91
RECORD BREAKER
PEYTON MANNING'S FORTY-NINTH TD PASS
DECEMBER 26, 2004

PEYTON MANNING'S record-breaking touchdown pass meant more than just a record. He threw his forty-ninth touchdown pass of the 2004 season with a game on the line.

Indianapolis Colts fans were getting restless for Manning to break Dan Marino's twenty-year-old record of forty-eight touchdown passes in a season. They actually booed when Manning took a knee at the end of a home victory over the Baltimore Ravens when he was at number forty-seven and counting. Manning had just two games left and had never thrown more than thirty-three touchdown passes in any of his six previous seasons. Who knew if he'd ever get another chance this good to eclipse Marino, the Miami Dolphins legend?

The next game, at home against the San Diego Chargers, made everybody happy. Colts fans saw Manning enter the record books, and he did it his way, in a game-deciding situation. He tied the record with a 3-yard shovel pass to running back James Mungro in the third quarter, but the Colts trailed 31–23 when they reached the San Diego 21-yard line with a minute left in the fourth quarter.

Manning didn't care for the play that was called for him. He walked over to wide receiver Brandon Stokley and said quietly, "Run a post." The Colts hadn't run this play in a game and had practiced it only in one-on-one drills. Manning, famous for waving his arms behind center like an orchestra conductor, pretended he was signaling for Stokley to run a corner route.

That ploy fooled Chargers safety Terrence Kiel so badly that he fell down when Stokley cut to the middle. The pass arrived just as he turned his head. "It says a lot about Peyton that here we are, the game on the line, and he calls a play we've never run before," Stokley said. "I just didn't want it to hit me in the face."

What that play also said about Manning is that beneath all his professionalism and success lies a kid throwing a football around a sandlot. "You think the NFL is real complex," he said. "But it turns into street ball real quick."

Manning didn't have the luxury of basking in the record right away because the Colts, down 31–29, needed a two-point conversion. Edgerrin James's run tied the score. Manning had asked that the game not be stopped if he broke Marino's record, and after the conversion he went to the sidelines, where he was mobbed by teammates.

Mike Vanderjagt's 30-yard field goal in overtime gave Manning's day the perfect ending. A 34–31 victory clinched home-field advantage for the Colts throughout the AFC playoffs, and Manning barely played in the last regular-season game.

Soon after Vanderjagt's kick, Manning was hooked up by phone with Marino, his childhood hero. "I was getting all emotional talking to him; I can't believe it," Manning said. "Dan, besides my father, was always my favorite player. I would have been content if I would have stayed tied. I would have shared that record."

Archie Manning and his wife, Olivia, didn't arrive at the RCA Dome until almost midway through the fourth quarter because of winter-travel delays. Colts owner Jim Irsay sent his private plane to pick them up in Memphis, where they had missed their connecting flight to Indianapolis.

"I don't care how long you played and how many touchdowns you throw, you'll always remember your comeback wins," said Archie Manning, who preceded Peyton as an NFL quarterback. "You remember this day and breaking the record of a great player. It was a very special day."

#90
JET IN THE WIND
JOE NAMATH TAMES THE ELEMENTS
DECEMBER 29, 1968

IT WAS THE DAY that Joe Namath tore a hole in the wind. Even when Shea Stadium was cold and gusty, the New York Jets quarterback was seldom discouraged from throwing deep. And this was the AFL championship game against the Oakland Raiders.

Namath completed only nineteen of forty-nine passes in the Jets' 27–23 victory. He also threw for three touchdowns, yet made a costly mistake when a fourth-quarter pass for wide receiver Don Maynard was intercepted by cornerback George Atkinson and returned to the 5-yard line. Namath knocked him out of bounds, but Pete Banaszak ran into the end zone on the next play, and the Jets trailed 23–20. With the fourth quarter nearly halfway finished, Namath couldn't afford another critical misfire.

Earl Christy's return of the ensuing kickoff put the Jets at their 32-yard line; then Namath threw to wide receiver Pete Lammons for 10 yards. On the next play, Namath sent Maynard deep down the right sideline, a route that would require a tremendous throw because Namath was setting up at the left hash mark and throwing into the wind.

Namath led Maynard perfectly for a 52-yard gain to the 6, and this time Atkinson could do nothing except shove the receiver to make sure he was out of bounds. The ball traveled at least 75 yards in the air.

"It was the greatest catch I ever made," said Maynard, who caught six passes that day despite a sore hamstring. "I mean, the greatest in my career. There's no doubt about it. I remember earlier in the game, I said, 'Joseph, I got a long one in me when you

need it.' So when we got in the situation of being behind, I remember Namath saying in the huddle, 'No penalties, we're going
to go for it.'

"And the wind was blowing really tough. Joe's pass was coming to me around the ten o'clock area. All of a sudden the wind
catches it and my hands and head begin to go around. I turned
completely and caught the ball around the two o'clock area. After
the catch, my momentum carried me out of bounds."

Namath on the next play hit Maynard for a 6-yard touchdown. That pass, too, was impossible to defend. "When Joe called
the play in the huddle, I was the number one receiver," Maynard
said. "As the play started, because of the coverage, immediately I
became the number four receiver. So Joe first looked at [George]
Sauer, then Lammons, then [running back] Billy Mathis, and
was pumping his arm. Each guy was covered, and I was doing a
delayed route that I'm supposed to. I turned back in, and Joe
drilled it about three feet high off the ground, and I caught it
away from the defender."

The victory was especially sweet for the Jets. Not only were
they headed for the Super Bowl—they also avenged a 43–32 loss
at Oakland in the *Heidi* game that fall. The Jets were upset with
themselves for giving up two touchdowns in the last 1:05 of that
game and also with the officiating, particularly the ejection of
safety Jim Hudson.

Perhaps the calls evened out in the AFL title game. The
Raiders on their last drive moved to the Jets 12-yard line. Daryle
Lamonica threw a swing pass for Charlie Smith, who had caught
the winning pass in the *Heidi* game. But this pass was thrown
behind him and fell to the ground. Jets linebacker Ralph Baker
pounced on the ball, which was ruled a recovered lateral. The
Jets took over, and Namath finally could give his arm a rest.

#89
BREATHING ROOM
WILLIE WOOD'S SUPER PICKOFF
JANUARY 15, 1967

FOR THE GREEN BAY PACKERS, the first Super Bowl was too close for comfort—until free safety Willie Wood broke the game open in the third quarter.

The Packers were favored by seventeen-and-a-half points over the Kansas City Chiefs and were feeling pressure from NFL partisans, who couldn't bear the thought of their champions losing to an AFL team in the first championship game between the leagues. The Packers led only 14–10 at halftime.

"I told the defense to stop being so cautious and go after the Chiefs' offense," Packers coach Vince Lombardi recalled. "Early in the third quarter, we called our first blitz."

It couldn't have come at a better time for the Packers. The Chiefs faced third-and-5 at their 49-yard line, and Len Dawson threw for tight end Fred Arbanas in the flat. Weak-side linebacker Lee Roy Caffey pressured Dawson into throwing a wobbly pass, which Wood intercepted and returned 50 yards to the 5-yard line. He was tackled by running back Mike Garrett, but running back Elijah Pitts scored on the next play. The Packers now had some breathing room and went on to win 35–10.

Wood called it "my legacy play." It was one of the biggest plays of the Lombardi era and probably helped Wood get elected to the Hall of Fame.

"Dawson had to hurry the pass," Wood recalled. "It didn't have any velocity on it. It was an outside route. I was in coverage. It was just a routine play. It wasn't anything spectacular. It gave us a little impetus."

Lombardi had lectured his defense for its first-half lapses. They included a 31-yard pass to wide receiver Otis Taylor, who beat Wood and set up a touchdown that tied the score 7–7. "We got the message," Wood said. "I was stung by the pass Otis Taylor caught against me, so I was sort of waiting for a chance. We were all anticipating a sideline chance on a third-and-5 situation."

Dawson was anticipating a first-down pass and moving down the field to grab the lead. "That was the play that killed us," he recalled. "We didn't have anybody to pick up that linebacker, and I was trying to get it to the tight end. It wasn't so much they were much better than us—they guessed right on a particular play. I knew we couldn't get behind by a large margin and have to throw because they had a heck of a defense. You can't imagine how many times I wanted to have that pass back."

Probably no more often than Chiefs coach Hank Stram would have liked to have had that play back. "That interception was the key play of the game," he said. "It changed the personality of the game. Before that play and touchdown, we were doing the things we wanted to do. You don't like to think that one play can make that much difference, but it seemed to. From that point, we had to play catch-up. We had to pass more and do things we don't normally do best. They knew we had to pass."

Dawson learned from his mistake and helped the Chiefs beat the Vikings in the Super Bowl three years later. Still, nobody let him forget the loss to the Packers. His brother, Jack, a retired minister, once asked Len to autograph a football for a charity auction. The Hall of Fame quarterback signed his name and added, "MVP of Super Bowl IV."

"He said, 'Why didn't you put Super Bowl One on there?'" Len Dawson recalled. "I told him, 'Super Bowl One? I'm trying to forget that.'"

#88

TOO TIRED TO SCORE
AHMAD RASHAD'S 98-YARD CATCH
DECEMBER 10, 1972

AHMAD RASHAD was still Bobby Moore, the Arizona Cardinals were still in St. Louis, and the St. Louis Rams were still in Los Angeles. Times have changed in the NFL, though not as quickly as a Cardinals rookie weaved through the Rams defense late in the 1972 season.

Rashad, a wide receiver from Oregon, was the fourth overall pick in the 1972 draft and led the Cardinals in touchdown catches with three that year. But his best catch that season, in a 24–14 victory over the Rams, didn't produce a score. He went 98 yards with a Jim Hart pass, the longest nonscoring pass play in NFL history.

The Cardinals were at their own 1-yard line in Busch Stadium when Hart dropped back deep in the end zone and threw for Rashad on the left sideline. He outran cornerback Gene Howard and caught the ball at his 39-yard line. Rashad stumbled after the catch but regained his balance. Cornerback Jim Nettles came flying over and had the angle on Rashad but overran him, and Rashad cut inside him.

That's when Rashad started making detours. He ran completely across the field, then down the right sideline until he finally was dragged down at the 1-yard line by cornerback Al Clark's one-handed tackle. Rashad's effort was not in vain, though. Running back Donny Anderson scored on the next play.

"I ran about 200 yards on that play," Rashad recalled. "It was a great catch. It was one of those cold days, and it just stuck to my hands. By the time this guy caught me from behind, I fell on my back—that's how tired I was. He barely touched me."

His teammates gave Rashad a good razzing. "We gave him a ration of [grief] that somebody actually caught him at the 1-yard line," recalled Conrad Dobler, a rookie guard who went on to enjoy a Pro Bowl career. "Then we got ticked off [and said], 'Why didn't you score? Now we to have to run all the way down the field to run another play.' We could say that because he was a top-shelf guy—a nice guy.

"When you have all that open field and you run that far, you're going to get tired. Ahmad could run ten of those doing wind sprints. But it's like the first time deep-sea diving. You use up a tank of air real fast. It was quite amazing."

The Cardinals had an additional reason for not wanting to run a play from the 1-yard line. That end zone was a health hazard. "That was the game when they put chemicals on the field to melt the ice," Dobler recalled. "It was just in that one end zone, and the teams spent a little bit of time in that end zone when the Rams were scoring. Their offense and our defense wound up with all these blisters, burns, and stuff. It tore up their skin. I don't think our offense ever got any of those. That was the only time we were going in. That's why we didn't get damaged; we only ran one play."

Dobler also suggests the field conditions might have aided Rashad. "You get it wet and icy, who's to say if on a dry field the guy would've missed the tackle?" he asked. "We were totally shocked. To cover those many yards, that quickly, it's the best play I've ever been involved in."

Hart needed excellent protection to avoid a safety. "When you're blocking down there, you'd better make sure there's no off-sides, no holding, and that you do not get beat," Dobler said. "You know they're going to bring the linebackers, so everybody on the line has to get his man covered, and you hope the tight end and blocking back pick up their responsibilities. I think because it was such a long pass, we caught them with their pants down."

Rashad didn't know he'd set a league record until after the game. "I've never been interested in records," he said. "But I thought that was pretty neat. That's a record that will never be broken."

#87
THE TACKLE
BEN ROETHLISBERGER SAVES THE DAY
JANUARY 15, 2006

COACHES USUALLY DON'T like having their quarterbacks making tackles. Some coaches even tell their quarterbacks to run off the field if a fumble or interception is being returned. Why get your most important player hurt to perhaps save one touchdown?

But sometimes that touchdown can end a season, which is why Pittsburgh Steelers quarterback Ben Roethlisberger went after Indianapolis Colts cornerback Nick Harper near the end of an AFC divisional playoff game. Harper had recovered a fumble, and there was nobody between him and the goal line except Roethlisberger. The quarterback dived at Harper, reached out a hand, and tackled him at the Colts' 42-yard line. That play, revered in Pittsburgh as "The Tackle," kept the Steelers' Super Bowl drive alive.

Had Roethlisberger missed that tackle, the Colts would have gone to Denver for the AFC championship game, and the Steelers-Colts game would have gone down as one of the most controversial in playoff history. A bad call against the Steelers could have cost them the game.

The Steelers led 21–10 and appeared to have the game wrapped up when safety Troy Polamalu picked off a Peyton Manning pass with under six minutes left and fell to the turf. Colts coach Tony Dungy made a replay challenge, however, and referee Pete Morelli ruled that Polamalu didn't control the ball. The NFL office acknowledged that Morelli made a mistake, but the call almost changed the outcome.

The Colts made the most of their second chance. Edgerrin James scored on a 3-yard run with 4:24 left, and Manning's two-point conversion pass to Reggie Wayne made the score 21–18. The Colts got the ball back at their 18-yard line with 2:31 left but seemed doomed when Manning was sacked on fourth down at the 2 with 1:27 left.

The Steelers gave the ball to fullback Jerome Bettis, who was going to retire at the end of the season. A sure-handed runner, he hadn't fumbled on 136 previous carries during the 2005 regular season and playoffs.

This time, though, linebacker Gary Brackett got his helmet on the ball, knocking it out of Bettis's hands and into the air. Harper grabbed the ball and seemed on his way to a game-winning play. It took an extraordinary effort by Roethlisberger to stop him. Yet Colts fans were left to wonder whether Harper might have broken free had not his wife, Daniell, punctured his right knee with a knife during an argument the day before.

"Once in a blue moon, Jerome fumbles," said Roethlisberger, who threw two touchdown passes against the Colts. "Once in a blue moon, I make a tackle. They just happened to be in the same game."

The Colts still had a chance to tie, but Mike Vanderjagt missed badly on a 46-yard field-goal try with twenty-one seconds left. "It went from an all-time high to an all-time low back to an all-time high," said Steelers wide receiver Hines Ward.

Bettis said he never could have retired if his season ended with a fumble that lost a playoff game. "I was frustrated," he said. "That shouldn't happen. I'm supposed to take care of the football. I was upset that it happened. My defense bailed me out. I can leave here with my head up high."

It was, actually, Roethlisberger who bailed him out the most.

#86
THE FUMBLE
EARNEST BYNER'S INFAMOUS PLAY
JANUARY 17, 1988

CLEVELAND BROWNS fans were still stewing over "The Drive," John Elway's 98-yard masterpiece that denied the Browns the AFC championship the year before. But here was sweet revenge on the way, as running back Earnest Byner headed for the end zone with the Browns seven points down and 1:12 left in the AFC championship game at Denver. Instead, Browns fans received yet another dose of bitter disappointment.

The Browns trailed 21–3 at halftime but tied the score 31–31, only to see Elway strike again with a 20-yard touchdown pass to Sammy Winder with 4:01 left. Browns quarterback Bernie Kosar took the Browns right down the field, however. On second down from the 8-yard line, Byner got the call on a trap play and cut outside when he saw a big hole.

"The play was supposed to go inside," Byner said, "but I saw that [linebacker Karl] Mecklenburg was plugging up the hole, so I slid to the outside. And I had daylight, too. There was no doubt in my mind that we were going to score."

But he didn't score, even though Byner's momentum carried him into the end zone. He no longer had the ball because cornerback Jeremiah Castille rushed up and stripped it from Byner's left arm inside the 3, then made the recovery. The Broncos intentionally took a safety, wrapping up the victory. "This doesn't hurt any more than last year," Browns coach Marty Schottenheimer said. "When you lose, they all hurt."

This game became known as "The Fumble," and Byner was considered the goat. He remained a villain in Cleveland long after Castille was a forgotten hero in Denver, which speaks to the passion and frustration that Browns' fans experienced with that 38–33 loss. Yet Byner had a terrific performance, with 67 yards rushing, 120 yards receiving, and two touchdowns. Schottenheimer was so disturbed by fan and media criticism of Byner that he eventually pointed out that blame for the fumble rested at least equally with wide receiver Webster Slaughter. He was supposed to block Castille, who was covering him.

"The wide receiver is supposed to take ten steps, then block [Castille] to the outside," Schottenheimer said. "Instead, he wanted to watch the play. Earnest never saw Castille coming. Earnest was the reason we were still in the game at that point. He had several heroic runs and catches over the course of the second half that allowed us to have a chance to tie the game at 38. All of these heroics, unfortunately, were overshadowed by a single draw play from the 8-yard line."

Castille was playing so far off the line of scrimmage that Slaughter could have blocked his path to the ball merely by getting in front of him. Castille explained, "I was thinking, 'I got burned the last time I tried to bump-and-run this guy,' so instead I stepped back 6 to 8 yards before the snap, so I could better see the play unfold. I saw it was a draw play and Byner had the ball. I remember thinking that Byner ran all over us that entire second half, so there was no way I was going to tackle him. Instead, I went for the ball the whole time."

The Broncos were relieved that he did: "Last year I was elated at the end of the game," coach Dan Reeves said. "This year I'm just numb."

#85
MAKING THEM PAY
HUMPHRIES'S BOMB BURNS COCKY STEELERS
JANUARY 15, 1995

THERE MAY NEVER have been a cockier team in a conference championship game than the Pittsburgh Steelers before they met the San Diego Chargers.

How cocky were they? The Steelers were planning a Super Bowl rap video, reminiscent of the one made by the 1985 Chicago Bears. Defensive end Ray Seals predicted the Chargers wouldn't score. Some Steelers partied the night before the game. And the city of Pittsburgh, which prided itself on four Super Bowl victories during the 1970s, already was envisioning one ring for the thumb.

The Chargers sat and stewed as they read about the Steelers' remarks and antics. The visitors took smug satisfaction when Stan Humphries hit wide receiver Tony Martin with a 43-yard touchdown pass with 5:13 left for a 17–13 upset at Three Rivers Stadium.

The Chargers faced third-and-long, and the Steelers blitzed. The Chargers picked up the blitz, and Martin was one-on-one with cornerback Tim McKyer. Martin blew by him and caught the pass that left the Steelers in shock.

"The whole game went the way we wanted it to go, and we just gave them two big plays," said cornerback Rod Woodson, referring also to a 43-yard touchdown pass to tight end Alfred Pupunu. "That's all. They didn't do anything else. I don't care what anybody says. Two big plays in the passing game, and that won the game for them."

The Steelers lost their last regular-season game, 37–34, at San Diego but were resting key players after they clinched home-field advantage throughout the AFC playoffs. But the Steelers should have noticed that early in the season Humphries and Martin hooked up on a 99-yard touchdown pass.

"I think that fired up the offense when they said we wouldn't score," said linebacker Dennis Gibson, who knocked away a fourth-down pass from the San Diego 3-yard line on the Steelers' final play. "The Super Bowl video is another thing. Games are never won or lost off the field. They are won or lost on the field."

McKyer was so distraught by giving up the game-winning score that he appeared to collapse at game's end. Teammates carried him off the field. Once Neil O'Donnell's fifty-fourth pass, for running back Barry Foster, was knocked away by Gibson, it was the Chargers' turn to talk trash.

"I think they tried to rely too much on the Steel Curtain mystique, the days of old," said cornerback Darrien Gordon. "When it came down to crunch time, they didn't really want it. You could see it in their eyes out on the field.

"They started throwing the ball in the third quarter. We were like, 'These guys are scared.' The best running team in the league starts throwing the ball with a 13–10 lead at home? The defense is playing pretty good, and the fans are going crazy, and they start throwing the ball."

The Chargers, bound for their first Super Bowl, were entitled to woof a little. "The best thing that probably happened to us was we got here on Friday, and we got to hear about how good their defense was, and we were never mentioned," said linebacker Junior Seau.

Seau made sixteen tackles. The Steelers' rap video wasn't made at all.

#84
THANKSGIVING FEAST
WALTER STANLEY ENDS A SHOOTOUT
NOVEMBER 27, 1986

THE DETROIT LIONS in 1934 started an annual tradition of playing host to a Thanksgiving Day game, and from 1951 through 1963, the Green Bay Packers were the guests. That game usually brought out the best in both teams, especially after Vince Lombardi took over the Packers in 1959, and both teams boasted hellacious defenses.

The Packers' only loss in 1962 was a 26–14 drubbing on Thanksgiving in which the Lions sacked Bart Starr eleven times. "After that game [and a 13–13 tie in 1963], Lombardi refused to come and play us every year," recalled Don Shula, the Lions defensive coordinator before he became a Hall of Fame head coach.

The Packers didn't return to Detroit for Thanksgiving until 1984, then again in 1986 for one of the rivalry's most memorable games. The combatants from the 1960s would have barely recognized the surroundings. The Lions had long moved out of the Detroit Tigers' ballpark for the Silverdome in suburban Pontiac, and Thanksgiving was featuring shootouts instead of defensive struggles.

The Lions, ahead 40–30, seemed well on their way to a victory before Packers quarterback Randy Wright threw an 11-yard touchdown pass to running back Paul Ott Carruth with 3:31 left. The Lions couldn't move the ball after the ensuing kickoff, and Jim Arnold punted to Walter Stanley, a wide receiver and kick returner who'd already caught touchdown passes for 21 and 36 yards.

Stanley fielded the ball at the 17-yard line, then started to his left but saw two defenders closing in. He tried to put on the brakes but slipped, then steadied himself with one hand and reversed his field. Now he was picking up blocks along the right sideline, one from Eddie Lee Ivery near the Packers bench and the last block from Mossy Cade, who took out Arnold near the Detroit 30-yard line. Stanley now had clear sailing and once inside the 20 began pointing a forefinger in celebration. He scored with forty-one seconds left for a 44–40 lead. Lions quarterback Joe Ferguson, who'd thrown three touchdown passes, got the ball back but was intercepted as the Packers nailed down the victory.

The Packers, given their desperate situation, tried to block Arnold's punt. Stanley, consequently, didn't have much blocking when he caught the ball.

"I wasn't supposed to run," he said. "It was set up for a block, and I was supposed to fair catch. But I decided not to because I wanted to get something going. The thing is, I'm expecting to make big plays. Not all the time, but if you want to be better than average, you're going to have to make the big plays, and that's exactly what I try to do every chance I get."

Once Stanley reversed his field, the Lions were in trouble. "He made a spin move, and I was about two steps away from him," linebacker Paul Butcher said. "I've got to contain on the left side, but he got away from me."

Packers coach Forrest Gregg voiced no complaints about Stanley's decision to forget about a fair catch. "All I know is the guy is a good athlete and has a lot of heart," Gregg said. "I think they probably underestimated his ability a little bit. Nobody will be guilty of that again."

#83
WHITE SHOES
BILLY JOHNSON DAZZLES 'EM
OCTOBER 16, 1977

ONE PUNT RETURN was all you needed to appreciate why Billy "White Shoes" Johnson was picked as the punt returner for the NFL's seventy-fifth anniversary team in 1994. Johnson was in his fourth season with the Oilers when he fielded a punt from Greg Coleman of the Cleveland Browns in the Houston Astrodome.

Johnson took the kick at the 13-yard line, near his left sideline, and started to his right. Defensive back Ron Bolton got a good jump getting downfield but overran the play and grabbed air instead of Johnson. In a flash, Johnson darted to the right sideline and began picking up blocks. The Browns, clearly, were now in trouble. Johnson was a handful to tackle even in tight spaces, but now he was in the open field.

Brian Duncan had an angle on Johnson but was cut down as Johnson picked up steam down the sideline. Dick Ambrose was the next defender knocked out of the play. Johnson got another sideline block, on Coleman, then cut to the middle and toward the left sideline. He'd started from his left and crossed the field twice.

Bolton, having recovered from his initial whiff, sprinted downfield and got in front of Johnson at the 20-yard line. But he was completely turned around by Johnson's last move and had barely recovered when Johnson reached the end zone. He handed the ball to lineman Ernest Kirk, who spiked it gleefully.

Oilers coach Bum Phillips, wearing a live microphone, thoroughly enjoyed the show. He was never one of those stoic coaches who took pride in concealing his emotions. As Johnson headed for the end zone, Phillips kept throwing his arms in the air and held his head in his hands, feigning disbelief. He yelled, "Whoo . . . ho-ho-ho . . . whoo . . . wow!" Phillips slapped hands with an assistant coach, went over to a winded Johnson on the bench, and said, "Super job, man! You looked 10 foot tall going down that field."

Phillips's recollection of the return was even more colorful than the actual event. "He kept runnin' . . . kept runnin," Phillips said. "I was standing on the sidelines, and every once in a while I'd say, 'Hi, Billy,' and then he'd come back, and he'd come back by again. They couldn't touch him."

The Oilers lost that game 24–23, but Johnson was a key contributor to Phillips's revival of the Oilers. As a kick returner and third-down specialist, he scored nineteen touchdowns during his first four seasons with the Oilers—five on punt returns, two on kickoff returns, ten on receptions, two on runs. But Johnson suffered a severe knee injury in 1978 that curtailed his game-breaking days.

Johnson picked up his nickname in high school in Boothwyn, Pennsylvania. He played in white shoes to separate himself from teammates wearing black shoes, which, many athletes claim, make them appear slower. When he began catching touchdown passes in his rookie season with the Oilers, Johnson celebrated by dancing the "Funky Chicken," which was based on a popular song. That was one of the NFL's earliest touchdown celebrations and set the stage for many more to come.

Other touchdown makers, such as Terrell Owens and Chad Johnson, have since come up with more flamboyant touchdown celebrations. But nobody has figured out how to match Johnson when it comes to dancing through kick coverage.

#82
THE CHRISTMAS KICK
GARO YEPREMIAN ENDS A MARATHON
DECEMBER 25, 1971

IT DOESN'T SEEM like an impressive kick in the game summary—a 37-yard field goal by the Miami Dolphins' Garo Yepremian. Actually, it was a huge kick. It ended a 27–24 playoff victory over the Kansas City Chiefs in the longest game ever played—eighty-two minutes and forty seconds. It also ended one dynasty and started another.

Had the Chiefs won, Ed Podolak's 78-yard kickoff return to the Dolphins 22-yard line would've been the greatest play of this game. Jan Stenerud's 31-yard field-goal attempt went wide right with thirty-five seconds left, however, and forced overtime on Christmas Day. It was the last game ever played in Kansas City's Municipal Stadium.

Overtime became a grim struggle, with linebacker Nick Buoniconti blocking Stenerud's 42-yard attempt in the fifth quarter and Yepremian missing from 52 yards. Finally, in the sixth quarter, fullback Larry Csonka broke loose for 29 yards, setting up Yepremian's game-winning kick. Until then, the Dolphins never led, and don't try telling Yepremian that he made a routine kick.

"It was the last game in that old stadium, and the field was a complete mess," he recalled. "There were spots where there was no grass, and the dirt was painted green so it would look good on television. I watched as Jan Stenerud missed three field goals earlier in the game. I know how bad he felt, and I didn't want to feel that way.

"As the game kept going on, the goal posts got narrower and narrower. I knew I had to focus and prepare. It was a 37-yard kick, but in the sixth quarter it seemed a lot longer."

That kick brought joy to the Dolphins and heartbreak to the Chiefs. They wouldn't experience another playoff game for fifteen years. The Dolphins, in just their second season under Don Shula, would be propelled to their first of three straight Super Bowl games.

"Kansas City was sitting on top of the world," Shula recalled. "They were the football power, and we were the upstarts. To wind up winning was one of the things that really turned us around. Garo was such a unique individual; he was the same all the time. He never showed any pressure at all. His personality always remained calm and confident. So when you put a kicker out there like that, you have all the confidence in the world, and he came through for me."

Yepremian also may have prevented Podolak from scoring on his kickoff return. The kicker was the last man in his way and forced Podolak to slow down, just long enough for cornerback Curtis Johnson to force him out of bounds.

Stenerud felt every bit as crushed as Yepremian suspected he would. "I have the worst feeling anyone could have," he said. "I have no idea what I'm going to do now. I feel like hiding. I don't feel like playing football. It's a shame guys play like hell, like our team did, and lose because of a missed field goal. It's unbearable. It's totally unbearable."

The Dolphins lost 24–3 to the Dallas Cowboys in the Super Bowl but a year later completed the NFL's first perfect season by beating the Washington Redskins, 14–7. Yepremian, for all his big kicks, is most famous around the nation for a feeble pass attempt that gift-wrapped the Redskins' only touchdown in the Super Bowl. In Miami and Kansas City, however, he's most famous for making or breaking a Christmas celebration.

#81
THE SECOND CATCH
ERIC WRIGHT'S FORGOTTEN TACKLE
JANUARY 10, 1982

IF THERE'S ANY DRAWBACK to savoring the NFL's greatest plays, it's that they often obscure the plays that made them possible or allowed them to stand up. Cornerback Eric Wright's tackle of wide receiver Drew Pearson in the final minute of the NFC championship game is one of those overlooked plays. San Francisco fans who appreciate its significance refer to it as "The Second Catch."

Everybody remembers "The Catch"—Joe Montana's touchdown pass to a leaping Dwight Clark that gave the San Francisco 49ers a 28–27 victory over the Dallas Cowboys. Fewer remember that the Cowboys had the ball with fifty-one seconds left and just needed a field goal to break the 49ers' hearts.

"[The Catch] is the play that gets the most publicity when people look back at it, but as a defense we knew the game wasn't over," Wright said. "There was still enough time for them to come back. The Cowboys had a lot of respect around the league with their winning reputation."

From his 25-yard line, Danny White hit Pearson at midfield on a post pattern. Cornerback Ronnie Lott and safety Dwight Hicks, who should've covered Pearson, collided. Suddenly, there was nothing but daylight between Pearson and the end zone. He seemed primed, at the very least, to sprint into field-goal range.

Wright was a step behind Pearson, however, and grabbed him by the inside of his jersey, between his neck and shoulder pads. Pearson dragged Wright but was brought down at the San Francisco 44-yard line. "Luckily, I couldn't react to the man I was supposed to cover as Pearson was going by and just happened to be in the right place at the right time," Wright recalled.

The 49ers sewed up the win when Lawrence Pillers sacked White and forced a fumble, which was recovered by defensive end Jim Stuckey. "If Eric doesn't tackle Pearson at that moment, he scores a touchdown for Dallas without much time left and who knows what would have happened?" Stuckey asked.

It's only fitting that Wright's tackle played second fiddle to The Catch because an underappreciated defense was a key to the 49ers' success. Coach Bill Walsh had the best quarterback of all time, yet his defense had much more talent than his offense in 1981. Without that unsung unit, the 49ers couldn't have reached the NFC championship game.

Walsh showed his ingenuity with the passing game as soon as he took over the 49ers in 1979. Steve DeBerg set an NFL record with 347 completions. But without much of a running game or defense, Walsh totaled just eight wins in his first two seasons. He then orchestrated one of the greatest one-season defensive turn-arounds in league history.

He drafted three defensive backs—cornerbacks Lott and Wright and safety Carlton Williamson—in the first three rounds in 1981 and made them all starters. He acquired Fred Dean, one of the NFL's top pass rushers, from the San Diego Chargers. And he signed Jack Reynolds, a valuable linebacker whom the Los Angeles Rams mistakenly considered over the hill. Walsh now had a championship defense and never needed it more than against the Cowboys in the final minute.

"Without Eric's play," Montana said, "there's no telling if we would have gotten the ball back again."

#80
THE SHORTEST OT
DAVID WILLIAMS WRAPS IT UP
NOVEMBER 27, 1980

SUDDEN-DEATH OVERTIME had never been as sudden as on Thanksgiving Day in Detroit once Chicago Bears kick returner David Williams got his hands on the ball. It took him just twenty-one seconds to take the overtime kickoff and return it 95 yards for a 23–17 victory over the Lions. At the time, that was the NFL's shortest overtime game ever.

The Bears were underdogs in this traditional matchup in the NFC Central, also known as the "Black-and-Blue" division. The Bears stood 4–8 and were mired in an early-1980s rut. The Lions stood 7–5 and were contending for the division title.

The Lions, ahead 17–3, seemed to have the game in hand. But the Bears, behind Walter Payton's 123 yards rushing, stormed back and tied the score on the last play of regulation. The Bears won the overtime coin toss, and Williams, who was averaging 21 yards per kickoff return, awaited Eddie Murray's kick.

The kick was low and taken by Williams at the 5-yard line. He headed up the middle, broke a tackle by one defender who was partially blocked, and was gone. No other Lion touched Williams as he cut to the left side and sprinted into the end zone.

"End of the day—we're out of here," said Bears tackle Dan Jiggetts. "Just so fast that we didn't even have to go back out on the field and deal with any more of the Lions."

Teammates mobbed Williams and backed him against the wall behind the end zone. Players were leaping on each other's shoulders and slapping Williams's helmet. Somebody accidentally broke his nose.

Jiggetts claimed the Bears had a poor first half because they were underutilizing Payton. "At the start of the second half, " he said, "I looked up at the scoreboard, and somebody in the Lions' organization thought it would be a good idea to put a comment up there that said, 'Walter Who?'

"We were in the huddle, and Walter goes, 'Did you see that?' And he proceeded to gain about 120 yards in the half."

That loss cost the Lions a playoff spot, because they lost a tie breaker for the division title to the Minnesota Vikings. The Bears got a lift from that win, though, and a week later pounded the Green Bay Packers 61–7. That was sweet revenge for a 12–6 overtime loss in the opener that ended with place kicker Chester Marcol scoring with the deflection of a blocked field-goal attempt.

Williams's record for the shortest overtime game stood for seventeen years, until the New Orleans Saints defeated the Seattle Seahawks 20–17 in 1997. Seahawks quarterback Warren Moon was intercepted by linebacker Winfred Tubbs, whose return to the 20-yard line set up Doug Brien's 38-yard field goal after just seventeen seconds.

In 2001 Bears safety Mike Brown intercepted a pass from San Francisco 49ers quarterback Jeff Garcia in overtime and returned it 33 yards for a touchdown and a 37–31 victory. That took just sixteen seconds.

The next year Chad Morton returned the overtime kickoff 96 yards to give the New York Jets a 37–31 victory at Buffalo. That took only fourteen seconds.

Williams may have lost his spot in the record books but not in Bears lore. Fans in Chicago still remember what he did long after they've forgotten how long it took.

#79
SPEED VS. SPEED
GREEN RUNS DOWN DORSETT
SEPTEMBER 5, 1983

DALLAS FANS remember this game as one of the most stunning comebacks in Cowboys history. Washington Redskins fans remember it as an unforgivable collapse. Most everybody can agree this was the game that announced the arrival of a cornerback who had speed to burn.

By resuming one of the league's most bitter rivalries in the season's first Monday night game, the NFL was hoping to help expunge fan apathy and anger after the 1982 players' strike. Redskins cornerback Jeris White was staging his own strike over a contract dispute, which forced the defending Super Bowl champions to start rookie Darrell Green, their first-round draft pick.

Green stood only 5 feet, 9 inches, weighed 170, and came from a small school, Texas A&I. But he had world-class speed, and once 1977 rules changes restricted defenders to one chuck on a receiver, speed became more important than strength for a cornerback. An entire nation was about to appreciate just how fast Green could run.

The Cowboys' Tony Dorsett was the league's fastest back and given one good block, he might be gone. During the first half, the Cowboys were at their 17-yard line when Dorsett got a block from fullback Ron Springs, found a hole, and cut to the left sideline for what appeared a sure touchdown. Cornerback Vernon Dean and linebacker Mel Kaufman gave chase.

Then, all of a sudden, Green, who'd lined up on the opposite side of the field, sprinted between his teammates and knocked Dorsett out of bounds at the 6-yard line. Dorsett picked up 77 yards on that run, but the Cowboys settled for a field goal, their only points as they trailed 23–3 at halftime. Dean gave Green the nickname "Ten-Speed."

"Nobody ever thought anybody could catch Tony," recalled Redskins quarterback Joe Theismann. "Darrell's legacy and reputation sort of asserted itself in that game. There was no way I thought Darrell would catch him. Darrell has run sub-4.3s [for 40 yards] forever. He took a great angle and managed to catch him. It's really one of the great highlights of Darrell's career and established him as an incredibly quick and fast defensive back."

Green's tackle must have been spectacular to stand as the top highlight of one of the best Cowboys-Redskins games ever. Cowboys quarterback Danny White threw bombs for 75 and 51 yards to Tony Hill, and his 1-yard run early in the fourth quarter put the Cowboys ahead, 24–23. Theismann was then intercepted by cornerback Ron Fellows, whose 33-yard return set up White's 1-yard touchdown pass to Doug Cosbie that iced a 31–30 win for the Cowboys.

The 1983 Redskins regrouped quickly, however. They lost only one more game until they were trounced 38–9 by the Los Angeles Raiders in the Super Bowl.

Other NFL teams quickly began looking for speed-burning cornerbacks, with Deion Sanders, drafted by the Atlanta Falcons in 1989, the prime example. Offenses answered with receivers who could fly, too, which explains why today's NFL sometimes resembles a track meet. This all started the night Green chased down Dorsett.

#78
LOOK WHAT I FOUND
CHESTER MARCOL'S KICK AND RUN
SEPTEMBER 7, 1980

THERE WAS NO LOVE lost between the Chicago Bears and Green Bay Packers even before Chester Marcol showed up. A star kicker at Hillsdale College in Michigan, he was drafted by the Packers in the second round in 1972 and quickly became a Bears nemesis.

Marcol in his rookie year kicked a field goal with thirteen seconds left to beat the Bears 10–7 in an exhibition game. When the teams met during the regular season in Green Bay, he kicked two field goals, including a 37-yarder with thirty seconds left for a 20–17 victory. Five weeks later in Chicago, he kicked three field goals, including one with 1:46 left in a 23–17 Green Bay victory.

With thirty-three field goals that helped the Packers win a division title, Marcol made one of the greatest impacts of any rookie in franchise history. But who could've guessed his biggest play against the Bears was yet to come?

Bears coach Abe Gibron was so incensed by Marcol's heroics that he told special teams player Gary Kosins to rough up Marcol on kickoff returns. When the Packers complained about that tactic, Gibron said: "Who do they think he is, a Polish prince?"

Marcol's family had moved to Michigan from Poland, and he spoke no English when a high school teacher noticed his powerful soccer kicks and introduced him to place kicking. Marcol caught on quickly. He excelled as a college kicker and was drafted by the Packers because coach Dan Devine became exasperated with erratic kickers.

Gibron's nickname for Marcol, "the Polish Prince," endured. So did his penchant for beating the Bears. When the teams met in a 1980 opener, Marcol kicked field goals of 41 and 46 yards. Bob Thomas converted from 41 and 34 yards for the Bears, and the teams were tied 6–6 heading into overtime. Then the worst kick of the game turned into one of the greatest plays of all time.

The Bears won the toss but were forced to punt, and Fred Nixon returned the kick 16 yards. A 32-yard pass from Lynn Dickey to James Lofton set up a 34-yard field-goal attempt by Marcol. The kick never stood a chance because defensive tackle Alan Page made a strong push up the middle, leaped, and blocked the kick.

The ball bounced off Page's face mask, right back into the arms of Marcol. He bolted for the left corner of the end zone as the Packers' Jim Gueno blocked the only Bear in the area. Marcol scored six minutes into overtime for a 12–6 victory and gave Packer fans a golden memory to help keep them warm on cold Wisconsin nights during their team's mostly dark days of the 1980s.

"Chester follows through, and just like a rifle shot, the ball went back to his chest, and he took off running like he had a loaf of bread," Dickey recalled.

Packers coach Bart Starr called this "the most dramatic win I've ever been part of." That was high praise from the quarterback of the Lombardi era, whose triumphs included the famous "Ice Bowl" game and two Super Bowls.

"The next day, when I picked up the papers," Dickey said, "the real interesting thing was seeing Alan Page's comments. In the huddle, he told everybody, 'Now I'm going to block this kick, and this is when you outside guys get up the field, and when you catch it in the air or on one hop, we're going to score a touchdown right here.' Unfortunately for them, the ball hits Chester, and their outside guys already had gone up the field. So Chester ran underneath them and around the left side."

Consequently, Page, a future Hall of Fame player who had a pretty good idea of what was about to happen, was defeated by a kicker who had no idea what was about to happen. Nobody ever said the NFL's greatest plays all turned out the way they were designed.

#77
A ONE-MAN GANG
KEITH LINCOLN'S 67-YARD RUN
STARTS A ROUT
JANUARY 5, 1964

THE CHARGERS of the early 1960s, more than any other team, exemplified what the new American Football League was all about. It was about wide-open offenses and former NFL coaches and players making the most of their second chances.

Sid Gillman, one of the most innovative offensive coaches of all time, had just been fired by the Los Angeles Rams when he was hired to take over the Chargers in 1960, their lone year in Los Angeles. When Gillman combined his wizardry with game-breaking personnel, the results were awesome. He had several playmakers each of whom on any given day could take over a game. When the San Diego Chargers met the Boston Patriots in the 1963 AFL championship game at Balboa Stadium, it was fullback Keith Lincoln's turn to shine.

Lincoln, a power runner, was Gillman's most versatile offensive player. "Keith could kick, pass, and run," said safety Bob Zeman. There was no need for him to kick as the Chargers rolled to a 51–10 victory, their only win in five championship games during the AFL's first six years.

Gillman went into the game respectful of a Patriots defense that held the Chargers to twenty-four points in two hard-fought San Diego victories during the regular season. Gillman's game plan, which he called "Feast or Famine," was designed in part to turn Lincoln loose. Gillman also had a standout halfback, Paul Lowe, but for this game Lowe repeatedly was sent in motion to make the Patriots hesitant to blitz and force much of the action away from Lincoln. Motion wasn't commonly used during that era.

Gillman's game plan, however, didn't anticipate Lincoln coming down with the flu. He threw up on the bench and, referring to his 325-pound teammate, said, "I felt like I would have trouble beating Ernie Ladd in a one hundred-yard dash. I believe I would have done a lot better if I felt better."

Considering that Lincoln totaled 329 yards from scrimmage—206 yards on 13 carries and 123 yards on seven catches—it's scary to imagine how he might've fared if healthy. On the first play from scrimmage, he turned a swing pass from Tobin Rote into a 12-yard gain. Lowe went in motion on the next play and created just the kind of confusion Gillman wanted. The Patriots were set up to blitz, but the motion caused end Bob Dee to nearly jump offsides and the linebackers to hesitate.

Lincoln broke loose on a trap play up the middle and ran 56 yards to the 4-yard line. Rote scored on a sneak two plays later, and the Chargers led 7–0. That set the stage for the run that broke the game open and was the most famous run of Lincoln's career.

On their second possession, the Chargers faced third-and-18 at their 33-yard line. By forcing a punt, the Patriots could have seized the momentum and perhaps tied the score. The defense braced for a pass by Rote and wasn't ready for what Gillman called next.

Gillman, recalled Ed Gruver of the Professional Football Researchers Association, liked to run his backs outside to stretch defenses horizontally and use his deep passing game to stretch them vertically. But who would have expected a fullback to run wide in a long-yardage situation?

Barely two minutes after his first long run, Lincoln circled around left end and caught the Patriots off guard. Only one defender was in position to prevent Lincoln from getting loose, and Lincoln, sickness and all, leaped over him and broke into the clear. He scored on a 67-yard run, which put him well on his way to the greatest all-around performance ever by a running back in a championship game.

"I think the key was we showed them motion, which was something we didn't show them earlier in the year," Lincoln said, "and I think that's what gave us the advantage. That's what froze the linebackers for a second and gave us the chance to hit 'em quick."

During championship games over the next four decades, no back topped Lincoln's total yardage, and only two backs rushed for more yards. Lincoln totaled 242 yards from scrimmage in the first half alone.

"I thought we were ready, but they just beat us at everything," Patriots coach Mike Holovak said. "I don't know how a back could be any better than Lincoln was against us."

Lincoln ran for a touchdown, caught a 25-yard touchdown pass from backup quarterback John Hadl, and even threw a 20-yard pass to Jacque McKinnon. He also completed a long pass to wide receiver Lance Alworth that was nullified by a penalty. Lowe, despite his decoy role, scored on a 58-yard run in the first quarter that gave the Chargers a 21–7 lead.

The tempo of the AFL championship game was dramatically different from that of the NFL championship game a week earlier. The Chicago Bears defeated the New York Giants 14–10 in a grim and brutal defensive struggle. As the Chargers celebrated their victory, some players shouted, "Bring on the Bears."

Gillman, in fact, challenged Bears coach and owner George Halas Jr. to play his team for the championship of professional football. Halas, an old-fashioned owner who had loathed the new league since its formation, predictably declined.

NFL diehards considered the Chargers merely the cream of an inferior league, but respected AFL coaches suggested Gillman's team could have given the Bears a run for their money. "Sid's team was like the 49ers [of the 1980s]," said Hank Stram, who coached the Kansas City Chiefs against the NFL champions in two of the early Super Bowl games. "Everybody talked about their offense, but they had a great defense, too."

The AFL still was struggling to succeed in 1963, but thanks to high-scoring teams like the Chargers, fans began to enjoy the new league. Nobody who watched Lincoln break loose for 67 yards against the Patriots could resist coming back for another look.

#76

A HUGE FIRST DOWN
MARK INGRAM KEEPS THE GIANTS ROLLING
JANUARY 27, 1991

THE NEW YORK GIANTS went into the Super Bowl against the Buffalo Bills with a simple offensive game plan. Because they were going with backup quarterback Jeff Hostetler, they would run the ball, throw short passes, and control the clock as much as possible. The Bills' quarterback was Jim Kelly, who led the NFL's quickest-striking offense. This was a matchup between the tortoise and the hare—and the tortoise won.

The Giants held the ball for 40:33, a Super Bowl record, in a 20–19 victory. To keep the ball for that long, the Giants needed some big first-down plays. None was bigger than the 14-yard catch that wide receiver Mark Ingram made in the third quarter.

The Giants were trailing 12–10 when they began one of four scoring drives that covered at least 58 yards and took at least ten plays. A 75-yard touchdown drive at the start of the third quarter chewed up 9:29, the longest drive in Super Bowl history. An extraordinary effort by Ingram kept the drive going.

After the Giants gained a first down at the Buffalo 29-yard line, tight end Mark Bavaro was penalized for holding, and the Giants faced third-and-13 at the 32. Hostetler, who replaced an injured Phil Simms late in the season, threw a pass over the middle to Ingram. The receiver didn't have any running room, so he created some.

Ingram made one improbable escape after another, and each tackle dodged or broken represented a knife to the heart of every Bills fan. "Tackle him!" they screamed as Ingram broke cornerback Kirby Jackson's tackle at the 30. "Tackle him!" they screamed as linebacker Darryl Talley failed to grab him well short of a first down at the 25. Jim Brown in his prime couldn't have been any tougher to bring down than was Ingram on that play.

He still had to avoid two more defenders before fighting for a first down at the 18-yard line. Nickelback James Williams pushed Ingram out of bounds, but anyone could see the game's momentum changing with that Herculean effort by a 190-pound receiver.

Ingram's play led to a 1-yard touchdown run by Ottis Anderson, the game's MVP, and gave the Giants a 17–12 lead in a nip-and-tuck game. It wasn't decided until Bills kicker Scott Norwood missed a 47-yard field-goal attempt with eight seconds left.

The Bills' inability to tackle Ingram, or running back Dave Meggett on an 11-yard first-down pass earlier on the drive, was a tip-off that the Giants were wearing down the Bills. "We had been on the field a long time, and we were starting to get tired," linebacker Cornelius Bennett said. "And when you get tired, you get away from your techniques and start reaching and grabbing instead of making clean tackles. We almost got him. We almost stopped their drive right then. But almost isn't good enough."

The Bills didn't lose because of Norwood's miss. They lost because they couldn't get their defense off the field. Seldom does a team execute an offensive game plan as flawlessly as did the Giants. They ran thirty-nine times for 172 yards, and Hostetler completed twenty of thirty-two passes for 222 yards and a touchdown. The Giants ran 71 plays and the Bills 55.

It was odd to see so little of the Giants' defense. Led by linebacker Lawrence Taylor, that unit was the backbone of a team that also won the Super Bowl four years earlier. But this day belonged to an offense that held on to the ball like a dog with a bone.

"It gets frustrating standing on the sideline, wanting to get in there and not being able to do anything about it," Kelly said. "We knew if we got the ball, we'd score a lot more. Give 'em credit. They did the only thing that could beat us: keep us off the field."

Ingram, who led Giants receivers with five catches for 74 yards, was a big part of the reason for that.

#75
KICK TO THE CLOCK
TOMMY BROOKER'S FACE-SAVING KICK
DECEMBER 23, 1962

DALLAS TEXANS kicker Tommy Brooker had a stiff wind at his back when he made the 25-yard field goal that won the 1962 American Football League championship game. It took a good deal of confusion to put Brooker in that position before he ended a 20–17 victory over the Houston Oilers after seventy-seven minutes and fifty-four seconds, the longest game ever in the AFL.

The confusion was caused by Abner Haynes, the Texans' star running back and team captain. With the score tied 17–17, Haynes went out for the overtime coin toss. Because there was a strong wind blowing toward the scoreboard end of Houston's Jeppesen Stadium, Texans coach Hank Stram wanted to kick off and force the Oilers to move into the wind. If Haynes won the toss, Stram explained, he was to elect to have the wind at his back. If the Oilers won and elected to receive, Haynes would elect to kick to the clock.

Haynes won the toss but became confused and said, "We'll kick to the clock." To the referee, that meant the Texans were electing to kick off. The Oilers had to receive and still got to take the wind at their backs. Haynes's mistake seemed to assure the Oilers their third straight AFL championship.

"He just didn't understand the option," Stram said. "It was a mistake you don't like to make, but there was no use crying over it."

The Oilers failed to press their advantage, and the Texans killed drives with two of their five interceptions of George Blanda. Defensive end Bill Hull made the last interception near the end of the fifth period and returned it 23 yards, putting the Texans at midfield with the wind at their backs for the sixth period. Len Dawson passed to running back Jack Spikes for 10 yards, and Spikes's 19-yard run put the Texans in field-goal range.

"Lenny told everyone to be quiet in the huddle because noise might make me nervous," Brooker said. "We called time-out so I could clean the mud from my shoe. I didn't want that as an alibi if I missed. Then I just waited and kept my eyes on the ground. I knew Lenny would place the ball right for me because he's the best at that."

Then Brooker told his teammates, "Don't worry about it. It's all over now."

Brooker's confidence was well founded, and the ball sailed straight and cleanly over the outstretched right arm of defensive tackle Ed Culpepper. Brooker's teammates carried him off the field to celebrate the Texans' first AFL title.

"I never took my eyes off the ground until after the kick," Brooker said. "Then I looked up and saw the ball going through the uprights."

Aside from Brooker, nobody could have been happier about that kick than Haynes. He scored twice as the Texans took a 17–0 halftime lead but until the end remained in danger of being the goat. "I've never seen a team fight for a win like this one did today," Stram said. "None of us will ever forget it."

#74
PAYBACK
STEVE LARGENT GETS EVEN
DECEMBER 11, 1988

OPPORTUNITIES FOR REVENGE seldom knock as they did for Seattle Seahawks wide receiver Steve Largent. In the 1988 opener at Denver, Dave Krieg threw a pass to Largent that was broken up by free safety Mike Harden's jaw-rattling hit.

Harden left his feet to deliver a forearm shot that mashed Largent's face mask, gave him a concussion, and broke two teeth. He remained on the ground, unconscious, for several minutes. Even without their star receiver, the Seahawks defeated the Broncos, two-time defending AFC champions, 21–14. Game officials didn't penalize Harden for his hit, but the NFL fined him $5,000 for "unnecessary viciousness."

Because the Seahawks didn't join the NFL until 1976, many assumed their AFC West rivalries weren't as bitter as those among the division's four other teams, which had been battling since 1960. But the Seahawks' division rivalries were intense and nasty, too, as underscored by Harden's hit on Largent.

Largent, 5 feet, 11 inches and 187 pounds, enjoyed a Hall of Fame career because of his precise patterns, sure hands, and acrobatic catches. The Seahawks were able to achieve a winning record in just their third season, 1978, thanks in no small part to having drafted Largent in the eighth round of their first draft.

Despite his average size, Largent was extremely durable. He missed only four games because of injuries until his final season, 1989, and played the week after Harden injured him. Two weeks after the knockout, in San Diego, Largent broke Charlie Joiner's all-time record of 12,146 career receiving yards. In his last season, Largent broke Don Hutson's record of ninety-nine career touchdown catches.

Harden's hit on Largent remained on everybody's front burner when the Seahawks and Broncos met again at Seattle late in the season. The week before, foot and thumb injuries caused Largent to miss his only game of the 1988 season. There was no way he was going to miss the rematch with the Broncos.

The Seahawks scored touchdowns on their first six possessions and won 42–14. But their biggest treat was Largent's payback. Harden intercepted a pass and began weaving his way up the field but never saw Largent coming from the side. Largent drilled his shoulder into Harden as fiercely as he could and watched Harden go down hard and lose control of the ball. Largent recovered the fumble, to the immense delight of the crowd at the old Kingdome.

"It wasn't meant to be a vindictive thing," Largent said. "But it sure felt good."

Seahawks coach Chuck Knox enjoyed the hit as much as anybody except, of course, Largent. "That was a great, great legal hit," Knox said. "Harden had hit him and really taken advantage of Steve. And Steve was a lot tougher person, mentally and physically, than a lot of people give him credit for."

The Seahawks have experienced dramatic changes since Largent's days. They've moved into a new stadium, changed divisions, and played in a Super Bowl. Yet one of the franchise's enduring moments is the time its first Hall of Fame player settled his score.

#73
PICKING OFF A LEGEND
DICK ANDERSON INTERCEPTS UNITAS
JANUARY 2, 1972

BLAME MIAMI DOLPHINS strong safety Dick Anderson for ruining John Unitas's last hurrah. The Baltimore Colts were defending Super Bowl champions but in 1971 were edged out for the AFC East title by the Miami Dolphins. Unitas, a legendary quarterback, was coming off an injury-filled and mediocre regular season.

The Colts rolled over the Cleveland Browns in their first playoff game and came to Miami for the AFC championship game with the old master at the controls. Unitas was facing one of his stiffest defensive challenges ever. The Dolphins defense was emerging as one of the best of all time, though it would not claim even one Hall of Famer until 2001. Hence its nickname, the "No-Name Defense."

A 75-yard pass from Bob Griese to Paul Warfield put the Dolphins ahead 7–0 at halftime. Unitas looked for a deep strike of his own in the third quarter and threw for wide receiver Eddie Hinton down the left side. But cornerback Curtis Johnson deflected the pass, which was grabbed by Anderson at the Miami 38-yard line.

Anderson, whose reputation as a thinking man's safety belied his terrific open-field running, headed down the right sideline. He used the entire field while weaving behind six blocks. "My eyes were popping as I ran," Anderson said. "I've never seen so many people land on their heads."

Running so gracefully that his gait appeared effortless, Anderson cut to the middle at the Baltimore 40-yard line, then glided to the left sideline. Unitas was in position to shove Anderson out of bounds but was flattened at the 7 by tackle Bob Heinz, and Anderson juked inside to complete a 62-yard touchdown return. The Dolphins now led 14–0 with 4:39 left in the third quarter.

That might once have been plenty of time for Unitas and the Colts to stage another stirring comeback, but this game was as good as over. A 50-yard pass to Warfield set up a 5-yard run by fullback Larry Csonka in the fourth quarter to wrap up a 21–0 victory. The Colts were shut out for the first time in ninety-eight games.

Anderson's return left coach Don Shula awestruck. "The interception by Dick and the runback and the way our defensive players became offensive players and the way Dick maneuvered across the field to set up those blocks . . . it's hard to practice something like that," Shula said. "The way he weaved his way into the end zone, it was all done by instinct. It had to be one of the greatest plays I was ever associated with."

That earned the Dolphins a Super Bowl date with the Dallas Cowboys, whose coach, Tom Landry, famously said of Miami's defenders: "I can't recall their names, but they are a matter of great concern to us."

With that remark, the "No-Name Defense" was christened, and it helped the Dolphins win Super Bowls in the 1972 and 1973 seasons. A major highlight of their 1973 season was Anderson's four interceptions in a 30–26 victory over the Pittsburgh Steelers. The *Monday Night Football* announcers and a prime-time audience were dazzled by the safety's ball-hawking and return skills. The Dolphins and Unitas had seen it all before.

#72
HALL OF FAME STOP
KEN HOUSTON BULLDOGS A COWBOY
OCTOBER 8, 1973

NFL COMMISSIONER Paul Tagliabue had a ringside seat for the game-saving tackle that Washington Redskins safety Ken Houston made against Dallas Cowboys fullback Walt Garrison.

"I'm sitting in the end zone, and he makes an unbelievable play," Tagliabue recalled. "A lot of people say that jarring tackle got Ken Houston in the Hall of Fame."

The Cowboys-Redskins rivalry was at peak intensity. The year before, the Redskins snapped the Cowboys' run of back-to-back NFC titles, and in 1973 the two teams were battling it out in the NFC East. The Monday night crowd at RFK Stadium was starting to celebrate as the Redskins led 14–7 and forced the Cowboys to punt with 2:00 left.

Marv Bateman's punt took a strange bounce, however. The ball touched an unsuspecting Redskin and was recovered by the Cowboys at the Washington 31-yard line. Five plays later, Craig Morton hit Garrison with a 10-yard pass for a first down at the 4-yard line, but the Cowboys were running out of time.

Morton threw again for Garrison on first down, but the pass was broken up by linebacker Dave Robinson. A pass for wide receiver Otto Stowe was low and incomplete. Another pass for Stowe was broken up in the end zone by cornerback Pat Fischer.

On fourth down, with twenty-nine seconds left, Morton threw for Garrison. He swung out of the backfield, drifted to the middle, and caught the ball at the 1-yard line. He seemed certain to score, but Houston arrived at the same time as the ball. He wrapped his arms around Garrison, turned him around, and wrestled him to the ground six inches short of the goal line. Redskins quarterback Sonny Jurgensen fell on the ball, and time expired.

"I was looking for that play," Houston said. "They had been trying to hit that flare all night. [Morton] made a pump, and I came up. As strong as [Garrison] is, I thought he should have scored. But I managed to keep him out. I knew exactly where he was and exactly where I was. They were on the four, so I lined up on the goal line and came up as he threw it."

Tackling Garrison was no mean feat. He was a 6-foot, 205-pound fullback renowned for his toughness. A cowboy in more ways than one, he competed on the amateur rodeo circuit in the off-season, and his specialty was bulldogging steers. Now Garrison, eight pounds heavier than Houston, was playing the steer.

"That's the biggest tackle I've made in my life," said Houston, the best safety of his era. "It was probably the most important game of my career. It was *Monday Night Football*, it was Howard Cosell, it was the Cowboys and the Redskins. And it couldn't have come at a better time because I had been traded [from the Houston Oilers] that off-season, and I really hadn't done anything out of the ordinary to prove myself to the players who were on that team.

"After that particular night, I felt I was accepted as a Redskin, and the rest of my career was easy. From that time on, my career kind of jump-started, and I had great years there. People are still stopping me on the street and mentioning that play. Everyone claims to have seen it."

#71
BRETT'S BOMB
FAVRE'S AUDIBLE BURNS PATRIOTS
JANUARY 26, 1997

GREEN BAY PACKERS quarterback Brett Favre was at the peak of his powers in 1996, when he won his second of three straight league MVP awards. When he led the Packers to their first Super Bowl in twenty-nine years, Favre had the opportunity to plant his flag at the summit. He did just that on the Packers' second play from scrimmage.

New England Patriots defensive coordinator Bill Belichick tried to throw Favre out of his rhythm early. On second-and-9 at the Green Bay 46-yard line, he sent six blitzers. But they never reached Favre until he burnt them with what he considered the smartest audible of his career.

Favre got some extra preparation earlier in the day while he was in his New Orleans hotel room, killing time by watching Super Bowl highlights. He saw the San Francisco 49ers' Joe Montana call an audible in almost the same situation against the Denver Broncos seven years earlier. When he looked over the Patriots' defense, it didn't take long for Favre's lightbulb to brighten.

"The [original] play was '322 Y Stick,' just a little dump-off to the tight end," Favre recalled. "I said, 'Black 78 Razor.' Black means he's changing it. Seventy-eight is the protection, meaning both backs go weak. Razor means Z runs a post."

The Z receiver was Andre Rison, a highly strung but talented wide receiver picked up late in the season. Lined up wide to the right, Rison eluded cornerback Otis Smith at the line of scrimmage, sprinted down the middle of the field, and hauled in a 54-yard pass for the first score of a 35–21 Packers victory. Rison caught the pass at the 21-yard line and scored easily because a defensive lapse left no safety in the area.

Favre, playing less than an hour away from his hometown of Kiln, Mississippi, then presented the image that's remembered best from that Super Bowl. He ripped off his helmet and held it triumphantly above his head as he sprinted joyfully down the field.

Packers coach Mike Holmgren, who considered his quarterback a thoroughbred he could barely rein in, gave Favre grudging approval to call audibles. "I told him, if he audibles, that's fine," Holmgren said. "But they have to work, and that one worked beautifully."

A second-quarter audible didn't work too badly for Favre, either. The Patriots were ahead 14–10 and still calling blitzes that put defensive backs in single coverage. Favre, at his own 19-yard line, saw wide receiver Antonio Freeman single-covered by safety Lawyer Milloy. "A safety on me, playing bump and run?" a surprised Freeman asked after the game. "I liked my chances."

Favre liked Freeman's chances, too. He called an audible for maximum pass protection, which meant he'd have fewer receivers. But he was only interested in throwing to one. Freeman easily beat Milloy and Willie Clay, the other safety, down the right sideline for an 81-yard touchdown pass, the longest play from scrimmage in a Super Bowl. Favre also scored on a 2-yard run for a 27–14 halftime lead.

Favre revealed after the win that he'd been running a high fever just a few nights before the Super Bowl and worried about being ill for the biggest game of his life. "I've done everything I possibly can," he said. "I hope too many people didn't bet against me because they're broke right now."

#70
SNAGGING A FLY
TOM BROWN SAVES THE PACKERS
JANUARY 1, 1967

IF STRONG SAFETY Tom Brown could've hit major-league pitching, the Dallas Cowboys, instead of the Green Bay Packers, might've represented the NFL in the first Super Bowl game. Instead, Brown was in a Packer uniform to make the interception that preserved a 34–27 victory in the NFL championship game.

Brown, who played football at Maryland, was the Packers' second-round draft pick for 1963. Because of the AFL-NFL signing wars, the NFL draft was held December 3, 1962, and coach Vince Lombardi invited Brown to stand on the Packers sideline at Lambeau Field for the NFL title game against the New York Giants. The Packers won the championship but lost a draft choice. Brown was miserable because the temperature was only 18 degrees at kickoff, and 25- to 40-mile-an-hour winds ripped through the stadium.

A gifted outfielder, Brown opted for a much worse franchise and better weather. He signed with the Washington Senators, who finished 60–101 in Brown's rookie season. He hit just .147 in thirty games and a year later was ready for whatever weather Green Bay might offer. Brown moved right into the lineup and was a savvy veteran by the time the championship game in Dallas rolled around. Yet for most of that day, Brown was getting beaten like a rookie.

The Packers, thanks mainly to four Bart Starr touchdown passes, led 34–20 when reserve wide receiver Frank Clarke beat Brown on a 68-yard touchdown pass from Don Meredith. The

Cowboys got the ball back with a chance to tie near the end, and as Brown recalled, "[Clarke] ran the same damn play to beat me again." The safety grabbed Clarke before he could score and was called for pass interference at the 2-yard line. Dan Reeves ran for 1 yard, then tackle Jim Boeke was penalized for illegal procedure, and the Cowboys were moved back to the 6.

The outcome was decided by a fourth-and-2 play. Meredith rolled to his right but soon was in the grasp of blitzing linebacker Dave Robinson. Before he was brought down, Meredith threw a high, desperate pass for wide receiver Bob Hayes in the back of the end zone. Brown, as if moving under a lazy fly ball, intercepted the pass with twenty-eight seconds left and sealed the win.

The Cowboys' final play failed partly because Hayes didn't carry out his assignment to block Robinson before releasing into the end zone. That mistake proved especially costly when Robinson blitzed, which he wasn't supposed to do. He took a chance by cutting inside guard Leon Donohue, who was looking for outside pressure. Had Meredith spotted the blitz in time, he could have run outside Donohue and maybe scored. Coach Vince Lombardi gave Robinson the lowest possible grade for that play because he freelanced.

"I should've fronted the guard," Robinson admitted. "Instead, I went behind him, and if Meredith gets in the end zone, it's because of me. Even though it was a great play, he gave me a minus two. He thought if you do things right every time, you win the war."

Robinson was accustomed by now to Lombardi's unforgiving opinions. He was the Packers' first-round pick the year they took Brown and eagerly awaited his first film session in Green Bay. Robinson had just played on a College All-Star team that defeated the Packers in an exhibition game and couldn't wait for

Lombardi's approval when the film showed him shedding the block of tight end Ron Kramer to make a tackle.

Instead, Lombardi berated Kramer. Then, failing to recognize Robinson on film, he barked, "That kid probably won't even make the team that drafted him!" Maybe Brown's decision to skip his rookie year with Lombardi wasn't such a bad idea, after all.

#69
MOVING THE FRIDGE
WILLIAM PERRY'S EARTH-SHAKING TD
OCTOBER 21, 1985

THE CHICAGO BEARS have had some of the greatest running backs in the history of professional football. They've also had one of the most unusual.

William "The Refrigerator" Perry was still trying to get his feet wet as a rookie defensive tackle when coach Mike Ditka decided he was ready for bigger and better things. Ditka would make Perry a fullback—partly out of revenge and partly because any coach had to like the idea of a quick 325-pounder opening holes for Walter Payton.

It stuck in Ditka's craw that San Francisco 49ers coach Bill Walsh had used guard Guy McIntyre as a blocking back on the goal line during a 23–0 victory over the Bears in the 1984 NFC championship game. When the Bears returned to San Francisco in 1985, Ditka let Perry make two short, thunderous carries. The Fridge was just warming up.

Perry had the perfect stage for his coming-out party—a *Monday Night Football* game against the Packers. On two plays near the goal line, Perry leveled linebacker George Cumby, allowing Payton to score twice. Cumby finally got under Perry's block to stop another goal-line run late in the game.

"I said I wanted to help the team any way I could," Perry said. "I only have one obligation and that's to block the linebacker. Whoever else got in the way, I took him out, too. Cumby didn't say anything. I think I rung his bell."

Payton was astonished to see the holes Perry opened for him. "I felt like I was stealing on the second touchdown," he said. "I walked into the end zone."

Perry's biggest moment, though, came when he scored on a 1-yard run that broke a 7–7 tie in a 23–7 victory. Before viewers were able to let that hilarious play sink in, Perry spiked the ball with a violence matched only by his unspoiled joy.

Bears right tackle Keith Van Horne was somewhat worse for wear because Perry landed on him while scoring. "I was saying, 'Pass it. Pass it,'" Van Horne said.

Payton was grateful for the holes opened by the rookie but didn't want Ditka to forget about regular fullback Matt Suhey. "He would do just as good," Payton said. "Maybe the hole wouldn't be so wide, that's all."

Suhey, asked what it would take for him to reclaim his goal-line responsibilities, replied, "Gain a hundred pounds or forget about it."

Perry, after just seven NFL games, was one of America's most popular athletes. Thirteen days after his Monday night heroics, he caught a touchdown pass against the Packers in a 16–10 victory at Green Bay. Perry climaxed his season with a 1-yard touchdown plunge in the Super Bowl as the Bears mopped up in a 46–10 victory over the New England Patriots. Perry also tried a run-pass option near the goal line in the first quarter but couldn't find a receiver and was tackled for a 1-yard loss.

Perry's Super Bowl score caused some hard feelings. Many suggested Ditka should've let Payton, the franchise icon, score his first Super Bowl touchdown. But awe was the popular reaction to Perry's performance at fullback. Bears linebacker Jim Morrissey, referring to suspensions being assessed by the NFL office, told him, "Fridge, you're knocking more guys out of the league than the drug policy."

#68
PREEMPTED
CHARLIE SMITH HIDDEN BY HEIDI
NOVEMBER 17, 1968

DARYLE LAMONICA'S 43-yard touchdown pass to halfback Charlie Smith is the only play in pro football history that's famous because of how many people did not see it. That pass provided the go-ahead score for the Oakland Raiders against the New York Jets in a showdown between the American Football League's top teams. While fans in the Oakland Coliseum were going berserk, NBC television viewers were wondering why the heck they were suddenly looking at a little pigtailed Swiss goat herder.

This was the *Heidi* game, memorable for wide-open AFL offenses, hard hits, and cheap shots in a matchup of bitter rivals. It's most memorable, however, as the stage for the biggest sports-broadcasting gaffe ever.

The lead changed five times. The Jets, led by Joe Namath's 381 yards passing, finally seemed in charge when Jim Turner kicked a 26-yard field goal for a 32–29 lead with 1:05 left. The game was scheduled for a three-hour slot on NBC but was so full of penalties and passes that its finish was headed past the expected end, 7:00 p.m., Eastern time. Then it was time for *Heidi*, a TV movie adapted from a children's book. Dick Cline, NBC supervisor of broadcast operation control, followed network policy and broke away from the game to start the movie on time.

It seemed like the perfect time to change programs. The game appeared decided, and after the field goal, NBC went to a commercial, then the movie. What followed in Oakland, however, was the best finish you never saw. A 20-yard pass by Lamonica and a 15-yard penalty moved the ball to the New York 43-yard line.

The game included 19 penalties for 238 yards, including a third-quarter penalty on Jets safety Jim Hudson that got him so angry, he mouthed off to an official and was thrown out of the game.

Smith was sent one-on-one with Hudson's replacement, flew by him, and hauled in Lamonica's fourth touchdown pass of the day. That put the Raiders ahead 36–32 with forty-two seconds left. Earl Christy fumbled the ensuing kickoff at his 10-yard line, and the ball bounced to the 2, where Preston Ridelhuber picked it up and scored to finish off a 43–32 victory.

By the time Ridelhuber was picking up that fumble, East Coast viewers, especially in New York, were picking up their telephones and angrily dialing NBC headquarters in Manhattan. The network's switchboard wasn't built to handle the volume of calls it received and crashed, preventing any more calls from going in or out.

NBC president Julian Goodman issued a public apology the next day. That episode dramatized just how passionate viewers were becoming about professional football. Ever since, the networks have stuck with games to their conclusions.

The Jets needed more time than the viewers to recover from Smith's touchdown. "The game in Oakland was devastating, the way we blew it in the last minute," fullback Matt Snell said. "But we got together and decided to hang out as a team more. We put our heads together and decided to go forward and move on."

The Jets got another crack at the Raiders in the AFL championship game at Shea Stadium. They turned the tables 27–23 and went on to upset the Baltimore Colts 16–7 in the Super Bowl. Jets fans wouldn't have stood for missing one second of that game.

#67
JUMBO-SIZED COMEBACK
ELLIOTT'S TACKLE-ELIGIBLE CATCH
NOVEMBER 11, 2000

THE NEW YORK JETS were trying to save an extraordinary comeback from going to waste. The visiting Miami Dolphins led 30–7 at the start of the fourth quarter, but the Jets mounted a furious rally and tied the score before the Dolphins regained the lead, 37–30.

A Monday night crowd that had mostly fled Giants Stadium after the third quarter was back in the stands now, stirred into a frenzy, as quarterback Vinny Testaverde brought his offense out of the huddle at the Miami 3-yard line with under a minute left. The Jets placed their fate in the hands of tackle Jumbo Elliott— literally. The officials were alerted that he'd be an eligible receiver, as is routine when a player with a lineman's number lines up at a receiver's position. What happened next was anything but routine.

Elliott was all by himself in the end zone as the play completely surprised the Dolphins. Testaverde threw a soft pass that would have been a piece of cake for any receiver. But for an offensive lineman? Elliott juggled the ball three times before grabbing it and falling with forty-two seconds left. That was Testaverde's fifth touchdown pass of the night and paved the way for the Jets' 40–37 victory in overtime.

"We were all on the sidelines like, 'Oh, come on, Jumbo, catch it,'" wide receiver Laveranues Coles told *ABC Sports Online*. "When he bobbled it, we were like, 'Oh, man.'"

"But he caught it, and then we looked at his face on the jumbo screen. His eyes were just wide open, and I think all the guys were like, 'Jumbo, did you catch it?' And he was like, 'Yeah.' So for us, it was very exciting. I mean, we just kept asking, 'You caught it, right? You caught it, right?' I think he was ignoring everybody. It was a big play for us. We had worked on it, and it came through for us at the end."

Though the Jets had practiced that play, they were probably almost as surprised as the Dolphins that it would be called at such a pivotal point. The next huge play for the Jets was cornerback Marcus Coleman's interception of a Jay Fiedler pass in overtime. That led to John Hall's 40-yard field goal after 6:47 of the fifth period.

That critical turnover capped a night that went from delight to disaster for Fiedler. After a touchdown run by Lamar Smith made the score 30–7 near the end of the third quarter, Fiedler told Dolphins defensive end Jason Taylor that the game was over. Those words would come back to haunt Fiedler, who didn't know Taylor was wearing a live microphone for *Monday Night Football*.

Jets fans agreed the game was over and walked out in droves. "It was like a high school game out there," Dolphins linebacker Zack Thomas said. "There was no one in the stands, and we really felt we had it won."

But in the next eleven minutes, Testaverde threw three touchdown passes, and Hall kicked a field goal. The score was 30–30, but the Dolphins seemingly rescued themselves from humiliation when Fiedler threw a 46-yard touchdown pass to Leslie Shepherd. But then, Kevin Williams's kickoff return set up the Jets at their 43-yard line, and Testaverde guided them down the field. On fourth-and-1 from the Miami 4, he completed a 2-yard pass to Richie Anderson.

Two plays later, the Jets called Elliott's number. Who would've thought that for one of the biggest plays in franchise history, that number would be 76?

#66
DEFYING GRAVITY
RANDALL CUNNINGHAM AS HOUDINI
OCTOBER 10, 1988

WHEN RANDALL CUNNINGHAM was a Philadelphia Eagles rookie quarterback in 1985, he was a backup who made amazing scrambles in cameo appearances. Gradually, he became a dangerous passer, and when he put his legs, arms, and agility together, Cunningham became one of the most exciting quarterbacks of all time.

He showcased all those assets on a touchdown pass to tight end Jimmie Giles against the New York Giants in a 24–13 Monday night victory for the Eagles. That Cunningham was able to release that pass defied the imagination, not to mention gravity.

Cunningham was rolling out from the Giants' 4-yard line. Linebacker Carl Banks had him in his sights and hit Cunningham hard in the midsection for an almost-certain sack. The quarterback twisted away in midair, yet still was falling down. But he stuck a hand down to balance himself and barely kept his knees off the ground. Then he scrambled to his feet and threw to Giles for one of his three touchdown passes that night. "Sometimes I amaze myself," Cunningham said after passing for 369 yards.

Banks, understandably, stared in disbelief. Soon, he would be getting used to this, because Cunningham saved some of his most athletic displays for the Giants. The next season, 1989, he led a late 81-yard drive against the Giants, which Cunningham ended by diving over the top for a 21–19 win. In the rematch that year, he clinched a 24–17 win at Giants Stadium by kicking a wind-propelled 91-yard punt.

"You have to be able to control his scrambling ability to where it doesn't beat you in a game," Giants coach Bill Parcells said.

"Most of the time when they've beaten us, it's come down to where he's made a few running plays that have continued drives and allowed them to score. When all around him appears to be breaking down, he's got you right where he wants you."

Defensive end Bruce Smith was poised to flatten Cunningham in the end zone for a safety as he came flying in from the passer's blind side during a 1990 game at Buffalo. Cunningham somehow managed to duck under Smith and, while off balance and throwing into the wind, hit wide receiver Fred Barnett 60 yards downfield for a 95-yard touchdown play in a 30–23 Bills victory.

Cunningham's prowess even forced the officials to watch him more carefully than other quarterbacks. As his escape from Banks showed, an official couldn't afford to be too quick on his whistle if Cunningham had the ball. Officials also had to be concerned that his scrambles might leave them woefully out of position.

Giants historian Jerry Izenberg described a pregame meeting of referee Gordon McCarter's crew before the 1989 game that featured Cunningham's long punt.

"We all know that this guy is the master of the broken play," McCarter said. "That means if we aren't very careful, somebody is going to wind up out of position. Now with this guy moving around so much, I don't have to remind you that we have to keep an eye on that line of scrimmage because the line is so fine, he could be across it, not know it, and still throw it.

"Another thing we have to make ourselves aware of is to pay special attention to the illegal chuck rule and when it's in and when it's out. Cunningham leaves that pocket, and he becomes a runner. That affects the rule. Once he moves, we've got to adjust."

If Cunningham prompted so much preparation from game officials, just imagine how much preparation was required for an opposing defense. As Banks found out the hard way, you could do everything right to bring down Cunningham, yet still find yourself clutching nothing but air.

#65
CLOCK PLAY
DAN MARINO FOOLS THE JETS
NOVEMBER 27, 1994

DAN MARINO threw for 61,361 yards and 420 touchdowns while winning 147 games for the Miami Dolphins during his Hall of Fame career. Isn't it odd that many remember him best for one act of trickery?

The Dolphins, losing 24–6 to the New York Jets at Giants Stadium, closed the gap to 24–21 before Marino led the game's last drive. He moved the Dolphins to a first down at the Jets 8-yard line with twenty-two seconds left. Then he signaled his teammates that he was going to spike the ball to stop the clock and shouted, "Clock! Clock!" But instead of spiking the ball, he dropped back and threw a touchdown pass to Mark Ingram, the wide receiver who was making his fourth touchdown catch of the second half.

Marino only slightly pretended he was going to spike the ball before taking a short drop, but his ploy created just enough hesitation that Ingram had little trouble beating cornerback Aaron Glenn. The play was suggested to Marino by backup Bernie Kosar during a preseason game. Marino decided to save it for a game that counted.

"It didn't work much on the practice field," Marino recalled. "We tried it in the fourth game of the year against Minnesota [a 38–35 loss], and it didn't work especially well then. But it alerted our linemen, and they saw, 'Hey, we could do that.' The Jets game was a perfect scenario, and it worked."

Dolphins coach Don Shula wasn't especially fond of trick plays but prided himself on preparing his team for almost every conceivable situation. The Dolphins, it turned out, needed that victory to edge the New England Patriots for the AFC East title.

"That's something we worked on when we practiced the two-minute drill," Shula recalled. "It was time to do it, and we did it. When you watch the way Dan did it, he didn't really fake throwing the ball into the ground. They were expecting a clock play, and Marino just hesitated and threw the quick out.

"It's all part of your two-minute package, and in practice you want to put them in every situation they're going to be faced with. You want to make sure they know what to do and they're able to handle it when the game's on the line."

Few quarterbacks could match Marino's ability to make big plays with a game on the line. He led thirty-seven fourth-quarter comeback victories, including three in the postseason. And because he was one of the best pure passers of all time, Marino didn't just win games. He also put on a show.

"When you start talking about him, you talk about excitement," Shula said. "Dan made practice exciting. He had that flair. He was just fun to watch. He just loved to throw the football, throw it into tight spots. You were never out of a ball game with Dan."

Marino proved that once more with his sleight of hand against the Jets. "To me, Dan is the greatest competitor among over two thousand athletes I have coached," Shula said. "His will and determination are legendary, and I've never been around someone who wants to win as much as Dan."

#64
BUTKUS'S FAVORITE PLAY
LINEBACKER'S EXTRA POINT A WINNER
NOVEMBER 14, 1971

FOR ALL HIS CRUSHING tackles, forced fumbles, interceptions, and sacks, it's hard to believe that Chicago Bears middle linebacker Dick Butkus singled out an extra-point conversion as his favorite play. Though he was, in anybody's book, the hardest-hitting linebacker of all time, Butkus also was proud of his versatility.

"It'd take me all day to run a hundred yards," he said. "But 30 yards sideways or on an obstacle course, I was pretty quick."

That was especially true before Butkus suffered a knee injury in 1970 that prematurely ended his career. He returned twelve kickoffs, gained 28 yards on a fake punt, and twice caught passes for extra points. One of his extra points was a game winner and holds a place in Bears lore, especially because it came after his knee injury.

The Bears were trailing the playoff-bound Washington Redskins 15–9 at Soldier Field early in the fourth quarter. Cyril Pinder took a handoff from quarterback Bobby Douglass on a quick trap up the middle and went 40 yards for a touchdown. The kicking unit came on with Gene Hamlin at center, Douglass holding, and Mac Percival kicking. But the snap was high, and the Bears had to scramble.

"Everyone was screaming and cheering because it tied the score at 15," Pinder said of his run. "But there was a mix-up on the snap. Douglass could only jump up and bat it down. He managed to get control of the ball and run around. There were Redskins all over the place and no way for him to run it in."

Butkus and linebacker Doug Buffone were blocking backs for Percival. Butkus still had blood streaming from a gash above his left eye, which he'd suffered on a punt return shortly before Pinder's touchdown. Butkus was still getting treated for his wound just before he went out for the extra point.

When he saw the high snap, Percival yelled to Douglass, "You're on your own." Butkus took off for the end zone and waved his hands. His 6-foot-3, 245-pound frame made him a big, if untested, target.

"It was too late to go back and block for Bobby," Butkus said. "I did the only thing possible. I didn't know how deep I was in the end zone. I just turned around and waved, hoping Bobby would see me."

Douglass scrambled left and lobbed the ball for the corner, where Butkus and a couple of defenders stood. "They all jumped for it, and when the bodies cleared there was Butkus with the ball and we had the extra point," Pinder said. "We won 16–15."

Butkus made an over-the-shoulder catch before falling to the ground. Still on his back, he triumphantly held the ball in the air. But an official, mistaking Butkus for an ineligible receiver, threw a penalty flag. Butkus quickly approached the official because, he said, "I wanted to make damned sure he knew I had reported in."

The flag was picked up, and the extra point counted. The Bears still had to keep reserve quarterback Sonny Jurgensen and the Redskins out of the end zone for another eleven minutes and sweat out Curt Knight's 46-yard field try, which sailed wide left.

"Now everybody remembers that extra point, and not many recall my run before it," Pinder said. "But one person did. When I went to the White House the next year as the Bear representative in the Athletes Against Drug Abuse Program, President

[Richard] Nixon, known to have been a dedicated Redskins fan, greeted me and told me he had lost a wager on that game because of me. We had a big laugh over it."

Bears fans had a good laugh three decades later when their team trailed at Washington and Paul Edinger lined up for a field-goal try. But the snap went to holder Brad Maynard, who stood up and threw a 27-yard touchdown pass to middle linebacker Brian Urlacher for a 20–15 victory over the Redskins. There's more than one reason why Bears fans describe Urlacher as the closest thing they've seen to Butkus.

#63

SLIP AND RUN
O. J. SIMPSON WON'T STAY DOWN
NOVEMBER 17, 1975

O. J. SIMPSON is best remembered in the NFL for becoming in 1973 the only runner ever to top 2,000 yards in a fourteen-game season. You could make a good case, however, that his 1975 season was even more impressive. He won the third of his four NFL rushing titles by gaining 1,817 yards. He also totaled 426 yards in catches while scoring twenty-three touchdowns, then the league record.

Simpson's seldom-matched speed and moves were highlighted in a 33–24 loss at Cincinnati on a Monday night. He ran for 197 yards, including 60 on arguably the most dazzling run of his career.

The Bills were at their 28-yard line when Simpson headed for the left side and cut inside a block from tackle Dave Foley and into the secondary. Defensive back Bernard Jackson and linebacker Al Beauchamp appeared to have Simpson sandwiched, but he burst between them as if barely avoiding a closing door. Then he cut completely across the field and down the right sideline. Safety Tommy Casanova and cornerback Lemar Parrish caught up with the play and waited for Simpson at the 25-yard line. He tried to cut left but slipped and slid a few yards. Both defenders fell with him as if they were part of a choreographed pratfall, and neither touched him.

Though Simpson wasn't down by contact, most backs would have been content to stay down and catch their breath. Not Simpson. He quickly jumped up and cut back to the middle of the field before he was finally buried in a pile of tacklers at the

12. Even the hometown fans were dazzled by what they had just seen.

"These Cincinnati fans are all on their feet," ABC announcer Frank Gifford said. "They're seeing O. J. Simpson at his very best."

Though Bengals quarterback Ken Anderson passed for 447 yards, Simpson's long run endures as the celebrated highlight of that game. Bills fans were by then accustomed to seeing Simpson's best runs serve as lonely highlights in dispiriting losses. He made just one playoff appearance, in 1974, during his eleven seasons and played for only three teams that won more than four games.

Rivals knew that if they stopped Simpson, they'd probably beat the Bills. And as the Bengals proved, teams often beat the Bills even when they couldn't stop Simpson. John Madden began coaching the Oakland Raiders in 1969, Simpson's rookie season, and saw plenty of him during the next decade.

"We knew we had to stop O. J.—or try to stop him," Madden said. "Our idea was to gang-tackle him as much as possible, but he would always glide by. Watching him from the sideline was never fun, especially when that jersey with "Simpson" and "32" was running unmolested. You knew he was gone.

"The only time I truly appreciated him was watching him do that to other teams on game films. Then it was fun. But when you were watching O. J. from the sideline, you kept thinking, 'Get him. Stop him. Don't let him get away.'"

Simpson had five straight 1,000-yard seasons before a knee injury in 1977 sidelined him for the second half of the season and prompted his trade to San Francisco. He had only one more 100-yard game. Madden last saw Simpson play when he was a TV analyst covering the 49ers and Los Angeles Rams in 1979, Simpson's final season.

"On a sweep, O. J. tried to get around the corner, but he couldn't cut," Madden recalled. "He still had his great vision. He saw the hole. But he couldn't plant his foot hard enough to cut sharply through the hole. When you plant a foot that hard, the shock doesn't go into the foot. It goes into the knee joint. On his sweeps against the Rams that day, O. J. had to run out of bounds. One tackler nailed him late, which annoyed me.

"'You shouldn't be hitting him late,' I remember thinking, 'because when O. J. was O. J., you couldn't have done it.'" The 1975 Bengals could have vouched for that.

#62
RAINING TOUCHDOWNS
JOE WASHINGTON'S WINNING RETURN
SEPTEMBER 18, 1978

BALTIMORE COLTS running back Joe Washington carried 240 times for 956 yards in 1978 without running for a touchdown. That should come as a shock to anyone who saw Washington turn into a touchdown machine against the New England Patriots on the third Monday night of the 1978 season. He produced a touchdown every which way but by running the ball.

Washington already had caught one touchdown pass and thrown one on the rain-soaked, slippery artificial turf at Foxboro, Massachusetts. Yet the Colts fell behind when the Patriots scored in the last two minutes.

Washington received the ensuing kickoff, which came to him on a hop at the 10-yard line. He seemed to be the only player on the field getting traction and was nearly untouchable. He burst straight ahead, then made a couple of feints to his left and kept cutting back to the middle for a 90-yard touchdown return and a 34–27 Colts victory.

"What a game this turned out to be!" exclaimed ABC announcer Howard Cosell as Washington scored with 1:18 left. Only one defender even got a hand on him. Washington made a big splash for the Colts with that return and another big splash when he spiked the ball in a puddle in the end zone.

That marked the last leg of Washington's scoring trifecta. The first leg came when he took a pitchout from quarterback Bill Troup and started running to his left, then stopped and threw for wide receiver Roger Carr. The Patriots' defense bit hard on the pitch, and Carr was all alone down the left sideline for an easy 54-yard touchdown catch.

Washington caught the Patriots flat-footed again when he raced out of the backfield as a receiver down the left sideline. Linebacker Rod Shoate came over late as Troup hit Washington in stride for a 23-yard touchdown pass.

"Joe Washington was a tremendous athlete," recalled Patriots quarterback Steve Grogan. "It was a back-and-forth game, a rainy night. We came back toward the end, and then he took the kickoff and ran it back to beat us. A very disappointing evening."

It also was a very entertaining evening, though not for Patriots fans. Both teams combined for forty-one points in the fourth quarter, and Washington gave one of the most versatile performances in league history. Though he played for two of the Washington Redskins' Super Bowl teams, the NFL would have seen even more of Washington's repertoire had it not been for knee injuries that disrupted three of his nine seasons.

He was the first-round draft pick of the San Diego Chargers in 1977 and, coincidentally, suffered his first knee injury in an exhibition game against the Patriots. It was played at Norman, Oklahoma, site of Washington's college heroics, and he was hurt in the first half. The injury diminished his role, and the Chargers gave up on him.

With the Colts Washington began to fulfill his first-round promise. He made the Pro Bowl in the 1979 season after leading the NFL with eighty-two catches and becoming just the second player, after the Redskins' Charley Taylor, to gain at least 750 yards both rushing and receiving in one season. But what he did on one rainy night was just as impressive.

#61
VICTORY LAP
AL HARRIS'S LOVE-IN AT LAMBEAU
JANUARY 4, 2004

GREEN BAY PACKERS fans will never forget cornerback Al Harris. He not only won a playoff game for them but gave them the sweetest revenge.

Emotions ran high for Packer fans any time their team played the Seattle Seahawks after the 1998 season. Coach Mike Holmgren, who'd brought the Super Bowl trophy back to Green Bay for the first time since the Vince Lombardi era, left for Seattle to coach and run the entire football operation. For fans in the hallowed football town of Green Bay, this represented a staggering desertion.

So you can imagine the passion among Packer fans when Holmgren brought the Seahawks to Lambeau Field for a first-round NFC playoff game after the 2003 season. Adding extra spice to this grudge match, Seahawks quarterback Matt Hasselbeck had been Brett Favre's backup in Green Bay before Holmgren traded for him.

Those expecting a hard-fought game weren't disappointed. The Seahawks tied the score 27–27 on Shaun Alexander's touchdown run with fifty-one seconds left. On the last play of regulation, Packers kicker Ryan Longwell missed a 47-yard field-goal attempt. The Seahawks won the coin toss for overtime, and Hasselbeck told the referee and the entire stadium, "We want the ball, and we're going to score."

He couldn't have made a worse prediction. The Seahawks punted on their first possession in overtime and lost the game on their second. Harris jumped on a Hasselbeck pass and returned it down the sideline, right past Holmgren and the Seahawks bench, for 52 yards and a touchdown. This marked the first time in NFL history that a defensive touchdown ended an overtime playoff game.

The Seahawks faced third-and-11 from their 45-yard line and brought in a fifth wide receiver, Taco Wallace. The Packers called a time-out, and defensive coordinator Ed Donatell switched their pass coverage from a zone to man-to-man. "He said, 'Go all out and go get 'em,'" safety Darren Sharper told the *Milwaukee Journal-Sentinel*.

Before play resumed, Holmgren replaced Wallace with Alexander. Hasselbeck saw the Packers crowding the line, stepped back and called an audible for hitch routes with him taking a three-step drop. "That check Hasselbeck made, Al remembered him doing that earlier," said defensive back Bhawoh Jue.

In single coverage were defensive backs Michael Hawthorne and Mike McKenzie on the Packers' left side and Jue and Harris on the right. They sat about 10 yards off the line as Hasselbeck threw short for Harris's man, Alex Bannister. Harris jumped in front of the receiver, intercepted the pass, and outran Bannister and Hasselbeck. Harris, clearly, didn't expect to get caught. Just 9 yards into his game-winning return, he raised his left forefinger in celebration.

"I was just praying that he did throw the ball because I was going to gamble on that play," Harris said. "I anticipated it, and I know the quarterback ain't going to catch me."

Harris could have been burnt for a touchdown had Bannister been running a stop-and-go and darted behind the secondary. Green Bay coach Mike Sherman, however, applauded Harris's gutsiness. "I told the guys that to win a [playoff] game, you have to be aggressive," he said. "We were very aggressive in our blitz on that play. You have to go get playoff games. They don't come to you."

The celebration at Lambeau Field was predictably wild. There was no Lambeau Leap by Harris because he was immediately tackled in the end zone and buried by ecstatic teammates. Though Harris was a newcomer with the Packers, he realized he owed the Packer faithful a personal touch. So he took a victory lap, slapping hands with countless fans as he ran.

That scene once would have warmed Holmgren's heart. Not anymore. "I'm dying inside," he admitted. "It hurts bad to lose this game."

Holmgren also watched Favre, the reckless young quarterback he groomed into an all-time great, set an NFL record by throwing a touchdown pass for the fourteenth consecutive playoff game. Favre's 23-yard pass to tight end Bubba Franks in the second quarter produced the game's first touchdown.

Favre threw for 319 yards, enhancing his reputation as a passer who thrived despite wicked Green Bay winters. The wind chill dropped to seven degrees at kickoff, but thanks to Harris, Favre didn't need a hot hand at the end.

"I'm not surprised by anything," Favre said. "And if you're around long enough, you lose games that you're supposed to win and you win games that you're supposed to lose."

#60
STOPPED SHORT
MIKE JONES'S CHAMPIONSHIP TACKLE
JANUARY 30, 2000

TENNESSEE TITANS wide receiver Kevin Dyson was oh-so-close to the touchdown that could have tied the Super Bowl . . . except that St. Louis Rams linebacker Mike Jones had Dyson's legs in his grasp and determination in his heart. Dyson reached with the ball as far as he could but came up about a foot short of the goal line. Time ran out, and the Rams celebrated a 23–16 victory.

"When you're an offensive player, you dream of making the touchdown run, throwing the winning score," Jones said. "Defensive guys think of maybe making an interception for a touchdown or forcing a fumble to win the game. You never really think about making the tackle at the goal line. But that's the way it happened."

The Titans battled back from a 16–0 deficit to tie the score. But a late 73-yard touchdown pass from Kurt Warner to Isaac Bruce left them climbing uphill again. The Titans' spirit was willing, but time was short. From the St. Louis 26-yard line, Steve McNair scrambled, escaped defensive end Kevin Carter, and hit Dyson with a pass at the 10 with six seconds left. The Titans used their last time-out, and coach Jeff Fisher conferred with offensive coordinator Les Steckel, who was in the coaches' booth.

Steckel called for "Gun Spear Right Open Zag Firm Silver Right Detroit." This told McNair to take the snap from the shotgun formation and send two receivers to each side. On the right were tight end Frank Wycheck and Dyson, key players in the "Music City Miracle" kickoff return that defeated the Buffalo Bills in a first-round playoff game.

Wycheck, split away from his right tackle, would run straight to the end zone. Dyson, outside him, would start in motion, taking five steps inside before returning to his original position and running a slant. "In the huddle, I don't think anybody had any doubt in their mind that we were going to score," Dyson told the *Sporting News* in a detailed recollection of the famous play.

The Rams defended Dyson's side with safety Billy Jenkins, cornerback Dexter McCleon, and Jones. When Wycheck ran for the end zone, Dyson went behind him to the area he vacated, expecting Jones to stay with Wycheck. McNair drilled the ball to Dyson at the 5-yard line. "It was a perfect ball—in the stomach, low, in front of me," Dyson recalled.

When he saw Jones running with Wycheck, Dyson said, he expected to score. Jones never took his eye off Dyson, though, and passed Wycheck on to Jenkins. Jones zeroed in on Dyson as soon he saw him looking back for the pass. Jones quickly closed in, reached out with his right arm, and at the 2-yard line grabbed Dyson's right leg, just below the hip. Dyson was outweighed 240 to 202, yet fought so fiercely that his momentum swung Jones completely around.

Now Jones was behind Dyson, who was trying to yank his leg free. Jones held on, however, then grabbed Dyson's left leg, just above the knee. Finally, he fell on the back of Dyson's left leg, exerting an iron grip. For Dyson, this was like a scene out of a movie when a desperate man on the side of a cliff gets a hand inches from the top, only to come up short and fall. "When he got his hands on me, I thought I was going to break the tackle," Dyson said. "But he got my foot, tripped me up, and wrapped up nicely."

All Dyson could use now were his arms. He rolled over and while on his back tried to put the ball across the goal line with his right arm. Still refusing to give up, Dyson rolled over again and tried to put the ball across with his left arm. But his knee was down, and this ferocious test of wills between two dogged competitors finally was over.

"I thought I was going to get a kill shot," Jones said. "Then the angle I had, I went from a kill shot to just making the tackle. I knew when I had my arms wrapped around him, he wasn't in the end zone. I knew he was about two yards away. I knew the only way he was getting in was if I missed the tackle, and I wasn't missing a tackle.

"It's something I do all the time. I was supposed to make that play. It wasn't like you come off the corner and beat somebody and sack him or pick it up and score. I never thought of that one play being as dramatic as it seems. Even after the game, it was just a tackle to me. It just happened to be the last play of that game."

At training camp the next summer, Jones said he didn't want his Super Bowl performance evaluated solely by that play. "I played pretty well to that point," he said. "Why worry about one play? What if I didn't make that one play?"

Then he answered his own question. "I probably wouldn't be in St. Louis," he said, laughing. "That's for sure."

#59
NOT SO SWEET
WALTER PAYTON'S FIERCE COLLISION
OCTOBER 13, 1985

WALTER PAYTON'S size—5 feet, 10 inches and 202 pounds—would suggest a running back who danced around tacklers. Payton preferred to take them on. No run of his was complete until he bounced off a tackler or clubbed him with a forearm.

"When you get the opportunity to hit somebody and nail somebody, this is what the game is all about," said Payton, who ran for 16,726 rushing yards, formerly the NFL career record. "I just don't want somebody having all the fun on defense, so I took some defense over to the offense and instead of getting hit, I attacked people and hit *them*."

This was strange talk from a player nicknamed "Sweetness." Payton's toughness went beyond his zest for contact. He was feverish and vomiting from the flu the day he rushed for 275 yards, an NFL record, against the Minnesota Vikings in 1977. Before a game at Minnesota in 1978, Bears trainer Fred Caito told head coach Neill Armstrong that Payton's knee was too swollen with fluid for him to play. Payton insisted on trying the first series and enjoyed yet another 100-yard day.

The Bears were at San Francisco in 1985 to play the 49ers in a matchup of the defending and next Super Bowl champions. The Bears had a slim fourth-quarter lead until Payton ran twelve times on a fourteen-play scoring drive. The 49ers' Ronnie Lott was perhaps the hardest-hitting defensive back in NFL history, and when he and Payton collided, it was the unstoppable force versus the immovable object. The unstoppable force prevailed.

On the fourteenth play of the drive, from the 10-yard line, Payton escaped the grasp of a linebacker, then broke outside and headed for the corner of the end zone. Lott came up to smack him, and both lowered their shoulders to deliver maximum impact. Lott was knocked to his knees, and Payton landed on top of him in the end zone for a touchdown that sent the Bears on their way to a 26–10 victory. That improved their record to 6–0.

"See, the thing about defensive players is that they want to hit you as hard as they can," Payton said. "My coach at Jackson State, Bob Hill, always said that if you are going to die, you should die hard, never easily."

Payton actually once told right guard Revie Sorey to leave the first Minnesota defender unblocked so Payton could hammer him. "I was in front of him going to the corner," Sorey recalled, "and he said, 'Don't hit the first guy; hit the second guy.' And I sprung him for a long run." Sorey then had to explain to a coach during a film review session why he didn't carry out his obvious blocking assignment.

In a 28–27 victory over the Kansas City Chiefs in 1977 at Soldier Field, Sorey blocked for Payton on a sweep, but a defensive back took away the outside. Payton spun inside, cut to the middle, and made a series of dazzling moves. Two defenders barely got a hand on Payton, and he lowered his shoulder and knocked over a few more. Linebacker Whitney Paul, the sixth defender to get his hands on Payton, finally hauled him down from behind. No runner ever worked harder for 18 yards. A week later, a flu-ridden Payton got his 275 yards in a 10–7 victory over the Vikings.

"When I had breakaways," he said, "I probably had to hit four or five people and drag two more with me before I had a 40-yard run." The back called "Sweetness" wouldn't have wanted it any other way.

#58
BEST RECEIVER EVER
RICE'S SIDELINE CATCH BEATS GIANTS
SEPTEMBER 11, 1988

YOU COULD PUT wide receiver Jerry Rice's fifty best catches in a sack, pull one out, and consider it an all-time great play. In fact, that might be easier than selecting one.

Do you pick a catch that helped win a Super Bowl? Or that won a game on the final play? Or that required him to leap above a defender? Or that he made one-handed? Or that he turned into a long gainer with a spectacular run after the catch?

His catch-and-run that beat the New York Giants showcased Rice at his best. It was a marvelous catch, yet Rice, literally and figuratively, took it all in stride. And as usual, just making the catch wasn't good enough for him. Rice burned to turn short passes into first downs and intermediate and long passes into touchdowns.

"When everything's on the line, I would like to have the football," Rice told *NFL Films*. "I like having the weight on my shoulders. If you're gonna be the best receiver ever to play the game, you ought to have to take the pressure of making the big plays. I like being aggressive. When the ball's in the air, I believe the ball belongs to me, and that's the attitude you have to have."

As the San Francisco 49ers entered 1988, they were trying to snap a three-year stretch of one-and-done playoff performances. They won their opening game but a week later trailed the Giants 17–13 and were stuck at their 22-yard line in the final minute. Everybody in the stadium knew Joe Montana had to throw deep and probably for Rice.

Rice sprinted down the right sideline, where free safety Kenny Hill stayed in front of him and appeared to have him blanketed. Once the ball was in the air, cornerback Mark Collins came over to help. Few other receivers would've stood a chance.

Montana's throw led Rice perfectly, though he had to make the catch with his back to the ball. As Rice reached out and grabbed the ball, he switched into another gear and separated from Hill. Collins would've been in time to stop most any other receiver, but not Rice. He was late providing help and ran into Hill, leaving both helpless to do anything but watch Rice score with forty-two seconds left. That gave the 49ers a 20–17 victory.

Rice on that play showcased his speed, concentration, sure hands, ability to beat defenders, and explosion after the catch. Montana routinely threw to him even when he was covered because he knew Rice usually would find a way to come down with the ball. You won't find a better catch in his storied career than the one Rice made against the Giants.

"So many receivers, once they catch the football, they feel like their job's over, and they just fall down," said Rice, whose acceleration and 6-foot-2, 205-pound frame made him tough to catch or tackle. "When I catch the ball, that's when the excitement starts. So, somehow, I'm gonna try to keep my balance and get into the end zone."

Rice's catch against the Giants was one of the big plays that kept the 49ers' slim playoff hopes alive that season. They later tumbled to 6–5 and needed a four-game winning streak just to make the playoffs. Then they romped in both NFC playoff games and gained a 20–16 Super Bowl victory over the Cincinnati Bengals.

That last win was climaxed by a 92-yard touchdown drive in the closing minutes. Rice made three catches on the drive, and two were pivotal. He ran a down-and-out pattern past cornerback Eric Thomas for a 17-yard gain to the Cincinnati 48-yard line. With the drive nearly stalled by a penalty, Rice ran a deep slant inside, splitting defensive backs Lewis Billups, David Fulcher, and Ray Horton. Rice not only made the catch but ran another 14 yards for a 27-yard pickup to the 18.

That gave Rice eleven catches, which tied a Super Bowl record, and 215 receiving yards, which broke one. He made five catches for 109 yards and a touchdown in the fourth quarter alone and was named Most Valuable Player. A year later, he caught three touchdown passes in a 55–10 Super Bowl drubbing of the Denver Broncos.

Rice ended his twenty-year career before the 2005 season when he made the Broncos' roster but learned he wouldn't be among their top three wide receivers. He retired with thirty-eight NFL records, including 208 total touchdowns. Even when past his prime, Rice showed the extraordinary work ethic for which he was famous.

"Not many people that own all the records give that type of commitment," Broncos coach Mike Shanahan said. "That's why, in my opinion, he's the greatest player ever to play the game."

#57
TURNING THE CORNER
JIM BROWN'S CHAMPIONSHIP RUN
DECEMBER 27, 1964

JIM BROWN is widely considered the best running back of all time, yet once seemed destined to lead the list of great runners never to win a championship. That list includes O. J. Simpson, Barry Sanders, Eric Dickerson, Earl Campbell, and Thurman Thomas.

As Brown began the 1964 season with the Cleveland Browns, he'd played in only one NFL championship game, rushing for 69 yards in a 59–14 loss to the Detroit Lions in 1957. A year later, he gained just 8 yards on seven carries in a playoff against the New York Giants for the Eastern Division title. The Giants controlled the ball, keyed on Brown, and won 10–0.

The Browns reached the NFL championship game again in 1964 against the Baltimore Colts, who were heavily favored. Browns quarterback Frank Ryan expected some favorable matchups throwing against the Colts but first needed his punishing fullback to establish a running game. The Colts, like any opponent, focused on smothering Brown. They succeeded for the first half, and the game was scoreless before a crowd of 79,544 at Cleveland's Municipal Stadium.

The Colts in the third quarter were moving into a strong wind, and their first punt died after 25 yards. That set up a 43-yard field goal by Browns kicker Lou Groza for a 3–0 lead. Another punt into the wind started the Browns' next series at their 32-yard line.

On second-and-6, Ryan called for a pitchout to Brown around the left side out of a double-wing formation. Halfback Ernie Green lined up as a flanker on the left side.

"They were playing the corner way off the line," Ryan told Tex Maule of *Sports Illustrated*. "Most clubs play the cornerback up close when we come out in the double wing, figuring he can cross the line and force Jim Brown back and wide on the sweep until help gets there. But they were playing him deep, and when Jim turned the corner, he was home free."

Brown had three linemen and Green in front of him, and as he turned the corner, he cut inside his blockers and toward the middle, against the flow of the defense. Though Brown, a 6-foot-2, 228-pound powerhouse, is best remembered for his sheer strength, this run is a sharp reminder of his ability to change direction and his smooth, fluid stride. He could hit like a sledgehammer, yet juke tacklers as though he were a kick returner. Green, meanwhile, showcased his blocking as Brown ran 46 yards to the Baltimore 18-yard line.

First, Green flattened right end Ordell Braase. Then he got to his feet, ran downfield, and blocked linebacker Bill Pellington. "That play really got us going," Green said. "We finally broke Jim loose, and we knew we were going to be all right."

Ryan now had to decide whether to run Brown again or throw for the end zone while the defense was still reeling from the long run. "I was tempted to call another sweep," Ryan said. "But maybe I would call a sweep into an outside blitz and they would drop Jim for a long loss. Then I thought maybe we can go inside, but if they pinched in and cut off the inside, we wouldn't gain, and the momentum would go from us to them. I know they had been playing Gary Collins for a short pass all afternoon. I decided to call a hook-and-go to Collins, and when he went, he was open."

Ryan hit Collins for 18 yards as the wide receiver crossed the end zone, left to right. The Browns led 10–0, and Collins caught two more touchdown passes in a 27–0 victory, which Maule described as "one of the biggest of all football upsets." The Ryan-

Collins connections, understandably, received more postgame attention than Brown's 114 yards on twenty-seven carries, plus 37 yards on three catches.

Brown led the NFL in rushing in eight of his nine seasons and made four runs longer than 70 yards. He also twice rushed for exactly 237 yards and four touchdowns. Oddly enough, his most important run didn't reach the end zone. But it changed the momentum of the 1964 championship game.

"That was beautiful," Brown said after winning a title. "Just beautiful."

Yet in Terry Pluto's book, *When All the World Was Browns Town*, Brown dwelled mainly on his first-half failures. He couldn't score in three cracks from the 1-yard line on one series and said he also missed a good opportunity to break loose.

"I could have gone for a long gain, maybe all the way," he said. "I had great blocking in front of me. Gene [Hickerson] and John [Wooten] were knocking people on their ass. But I slowed down, and then I cut the wrong way. They caught me from behind. The mistakes I made on those two plays could have been critical. What I remember most from my career is my mistakes, because I agonized over them.

"That was my biggest thrill in football, winning that championship. But I can't help myself. I think about these things."

Brown's opponents wish he'd made more mistakes. The New York Giants boasted one of the NFL's top defenses in 1957 but were in for a shock when they first met the Browns' rookie fullback from Syracuse. "It was early in the third quarter, and here came Jim Brown through a hole, and there I was to meet him," middle linebacker Sam Huff said. "I hit that big sucker head on, and my headgear snapped down and cut my nose, and my teeth hit together so hard the enamel popped off. He broke my nose, broke my teeth, and knocked me cold. I woke up in the training room with an ice pack on my head and my nose bleeding."

Brown made a similar first impression upon defensive tackle Dick Modzelewski, a teammate of Huff's before he joined the Browns in 1964. "He was in the middle of this pack of guys," Modzelewski said. "It was like he was dragging eight of us forward. Really, eight of us had at least one hand on him, and we couldn't bring him down. He just kept moving. I'd never seen a runner like that."

#56
WITHOUT A SHOE
THE BARRY SANDERS SOCK HOP
OCTOBER 2, 1994

IT WAS HUMBLING enough for defenders when Detroit Lions running back Barry Sanders, who stood 5 feet, 8 inches, slammed on the brakes, made a sharp turn, and ran right by them. It was even worse when he embarrassed them, which was often.

"Barry can flat out embarrass anyone," said linebacker Chris Spielman, who played with Sanders in Detroit after coming over from the Buffalo Bills. "I was able to get him a few times because he didn't see me coming. There were a couple of times, though, when he did see me and put me on his highlight film. I tackled nothing but air."

That put Spielman in good company. "I had a front-row seat to some amazing runs," Lions quarterback Scott Mitchell said. "The most amazing thing is that he made really good players look really, really bad. He made them look silly. Think about it—guys like Rod Woodson, Cornelius Bennett . . . the list goes on and on."

Sanders made opponents look silly even when *he* looked silly. He made the longest run of his career with just one shoe, when he went 85 yards in a 24–14 road loss to the Tampa Bay Buccaneers in 1994. From his own 10-yard line, Sanders burst up the middle, then littered the field with fallen would-be tacklers. Because of his quickness, defenders often could grab only his ankles, and his legs were so powerful that he easily broke away. As Sanders darted right, Buccaneers safety Tony Bouie got a hand on his left ankle at the 17-yard line, and as Sanders twisted away, he lost his right shoe.

Sanders with one shoe, however, still was faster than most players with both shoes. He streaked down the right sideline and was almost home free, but cornerback Charles Dimry ran him down at the 5-yard line. Derrick Moore scored on the next play.

The 1994 season was sensational, yet unusual, for Sanders. He kept getting caught from behind, though he rushed for 1,883 yards and helped the Lions reach the playoffs. He broke off six of the league's nine runs that year of more than 60 yards, yet scored on only one of them. In addition to his 85-yard run, he got loose for 84, 69, 63, 62, and 48 yards without scoring. His 237 rushing yards in a 14–9 victory over the Buccaneers were the most ever gained in one game without scoring.

The week before his one-shoe run, in a 23–17 home loss to the New England Patriots, Sanders had another of his most dazzling runs. He went 39 yards for a touchdown by breaking a tackle by cornerback Rod Smith, then turning around strong safety Harlon Barnett three times before he fell as Sanders ran by him. Free safety Myron Guyton grabbed Sanders at the 5-yard line but was dragged into the end zone.

"His legs go in fourteen different directions at one time," Cleveland Browns nose tackle Tim Goad said. "Then he stops, but you usually don't."

Though you can get a lively argument over whether Sanders was the best back of all time, most experts would agree he was the shiftiest. "Our guy has the best vision of anybody I've ever seen," Lions coach Wayne Fontes said. "Our guy has great ability stopping and going . . . great quickness . . . excellent power, and better than that, he's a great person. He's the best runner that's ever touched a football. If anybody thinks he isn't, then they're not watching football."

Or as Green Bay Packers defensive coordinator Fritz Shurmur once said of Sanders: "God only put one pair of feet like that on a human being."

#55
FIRE PITCH
DAN REEVES'S HOT HAND IN THE COLD
DECEMBER 31, 1967

HAD GREEN BAY PACKERS quarterback Bart Starr failed to sneak into the end zone on the final play, "Fire Pitch" would have been the most celebrated play of the 1967 NFL championship game, better known as the "Ice Bowl." That play gave the Dallas Cowboys a 17–14 lead, which stood up right until the Packers' do-or-die run from the 1-yard line.

Cowboys wide receiver Lance Rentzel, who scored on "Fire Pitch," received this wake-up message at his Green Bay hotel the morning of the game: "Good morning, Mister Rentzel. It's 8:00 a.m. It's fifteen below zero, and there's a twenty-mile-per-hour wind coming out of the northwest. Have a nice day."

It wouldn't get much nicer. The temperature at kickoff stood at minus 13 degrees with a wind chill of minus 46. That didn't bode well for either team's passing game, much less a trick pass. The Packers jumped to a 14–0 lead, which was cut to 14–10 by halftime. The third period was scoreless, and the Cowboys opened the fourth quarter with a second-and-5 play at the 50. Running back Dan Reeves, a former quarterback at South Carolina, urged quarterback Don Meredith to call "Fire Pitch," a run-pass option for Reeves.

Meredith agreed, and the play worked perfectly. Reeves began a sweep to the left. Defensive backs Bob Jeter and Willie Wood took the bait and rushed up. Rentzel got wide open behind them and hauled in Reeves's pass for a touchdown. Strong safety Tom Brown could only give futile chase. The 50 yards gained on that play were just 9 shy of Meredith's passing yardage for the day.

That play stunned the Packers and a freezing Lambeau Field crowd. Guard Jerry Kramer, who played on all five championship teams during the Vince Lombardi era, admitted thinking, "Well, maybe this is the year we don't make it, that it all ends." That was, of course, before he and center Ken Bowman threw the block that let Starr score.

The 21–17 loss was especially frustrating for the Cowboys because they were getting tired of being bridesmaids. That marked their second straight loss to the Packers in the NFL championship game. The Cowboys had lost the previous year, 34–27, in Dallas, when Meredith was intercepted in the end zone by Brown near the end.

"It's most disappointing to have that happen twice in a row," Meredith said after the Ice Bowl. "I guess we can do everything but win the big one."

Much was made of the Packers thriving in their frozen tundra. The Packers said they could tell whether the Cowboys were going to run or throw because wide receiver Bob Hayes kept his hands in his pockets on running plays. Reeves, however, never bought that postmortem.

"You hear that stuff about the Packers being able to deal with [the weather] better than we did, and that's a lot of bull," he said. "I think we handled it as well as they did. It's just that they made the play at the end."

Reeves, for sure, handled the ice and cold as well as anybody. Not only did he complete a bomb in the worst possible conditions, but he played much of the game despite a tooth protruding through his lip after his face mask was smashed in a collision.

"My face was so numb, I didn't feel it," Reeves said. "It didn't even start bleeding until they put heat on it."

All of Dallas was bleeding after that game.

#54
A GARRISON FINISH
HEARST BUSTS LOOSE FOR 96 YARDS
SEPTEMBER 6, 1998

SAN FRANCISCO 49ERS coach Steve Mariucci was just hoping to pick up maybe 4 yards when he called Garrison Hearst's number. Instead, Hearst picked up 96 yards and gave the 49ers a 36–30 victory in overtime over the New York Jets.

There wasn't much defense being played by either team. Completions were coming so easily for 49ers quarterback Steve Young, who passed for 363 yards, that he couldn't understand why Mariucci would send in a running play, even if the 49ers were at their 4-yard line after a punt. "Are you kidding?" Young asked his coach.

"When you're backed up like that, the first thing you think about is making a first down," Mariucci said. "Once you get up near the 20, you can get a little more wide open. It was just one play we pulled out of a hat. It was just one of four choices we had. I was hoping to get 4 yards or so."

The play was "90–0," a quick-hitting run to the right. Fullback Marc Edwards threw a lead block, left guard Ray Brown pulled and blocked a linebacker, and the rest of the linemen took care of the other Jets. "It's a smash-mouth play with a backside guard pulling," right guard Kevin Gogan said. "Realistically, it's a 10-yard gain, but Garrison gutted it out for 96."

With Edwards and Brown creating space for him, Hearst turned the corner and saw daylight. "I don't know who it was, but somebody got the D-lineman, and I thought I had a chance," he said.

When Hearst got past the line of scrimmage, only rookie free safety Kevin Williams was in the way. Hearst got rid of him with a stiff-arm. "I'm not much of a stiff-armer," Hearst said. "Maybe I'll have to use it a little more often."

Once Hearst eluded cornerback Otis Smith at the 30-yard line, he was loose, and wide receiver Terrell Owens and left tackle Dave Fiore served as a convoy. They cleared out everybody except linebacker Mo Lewis, who jumped on Hearst's back at the 5-yard line and was carried into the end zone.

"I was running," Fiore said, "and I was thinking, 'All right, we're downfield a lot. All right, keep it going. We're running pretty far downfield, and we don't really do that a lot.'" Owens, meanwhile, was sending bodies flying.

When Hearst reached the New York 20-yard line, he said, "That's when the elephant jumped on me. The last 10 yards, I was pulling everything I had. At the end, I had no wind at all."

That run gave Hearst 187 yards rushing for the game and the 49ers an uplifting opening-day victory at Candlestick Park. Hearst was quickly buried by a pile of teammates in the end zone after breaking off the longest run in franchise history.

"I was just trying to breathe," said Hearst, who was now smothered, as well as exhausted. "They were all on top of me. Finally, Jerry [Rice] came up and said, 'Let him up and let him breathe. I've been there before.'"

There was an old-time jockey named Edward "Snapper" Garrison who rode so aggressively in the stretch that he coined the phrase, "a Garrison finish." A century later, you could chalk one up for Hearst.

#53
TOO MUCH TIME
BENGALS' WYCHE OUTSMARTS HIMSELF
SEPTEMBER 20, 1987

CINCINNATI BENGALS coach Sam Wyche should have known better than anybody that he couldn't afford to leave any time on the clock for Joe Montana and Jerry Rice. Not even two seconds. That's all it took to throw away a certain victory, as well as an entire season. Wyche, an assistant to 49ers coach Bill Walsh in 1979, was Montana's first quarterbacks coach in San Francisco.

Now Wyche was just six seconds away from a sweet victory at home over his mentor and former pupil. The Bengals led 26–20 and faced fourth-and-25 at their 30-yard line. Coaches in this kind of situation always worry about a punt getting blocked and returned for a touchdown. So Wyche considered other ways to drain the clock.

A kneel-down by quarterback Boomer Esiason probably wouldn't burn six seconds. Then the clock would stop on the change of possession, giving the 49ers one last shot. Wyche's best option probably would have been to let a speedy back get to the end zone and take a safety. If that didn't use up six seconds, the Bengals would have had a low-risk kickoff from their 20. Wyche, however, called for running back James Brooks to run a sweep. That was inviting disaster—and disaster accepted.

Brooks took Esiason's pitch and was thrown for a 5-yard loss by tackle Kevin Fagan with two seconds left. Bengals blockers didn't seem to make the effort that would have prolonged the play and ended the game. "Their whole line was only giving it a halfway effort," Fagan said. "They thought they had the game won."

Montana had been in tougher spots than this. He lofted a pass to the right corner of the end zone, where Rice outjumped cornerback Eric Thomas to catch a 25-yard touchdown pass with no time left. Ray Wersching's extra point gave the 49ers a 27–26 victory, and the home crowd booed the Bengals off the field.

The Bengals' season was ruptured by that loss, because it was immediately followed by a players' strike. Some teams were able to recapture their togetherness after the strike ended, but not the Bengals. Esiason, the Bengals' union representative, blasted management for using replacement players, and a rift developed between him and Wyche. A team that finished 10–6 in 1986 fell apart and finished 4–11, including 2–8 after the strike. The gaffe against the 49ers was widely considered the beginning of the end.

"We knew we had talent, but the way that ended put a damper on everything," kicker Jim Breech said.

The striking Bengals organized their own practices. Shortly after the loss to the 49ers, they called over reporters at practice to watch something they'd cooked up. The offense lined up, Esiason handed off to Brooks, and he ran backward to the end zone while teammates counted down: "Six . . . five . . . four . . . three . . . two . . . one . . . zero." Then the players sarcastically cheered, expressing once more their anger over Wyche's decision.

The Bengals shook off their strike hangover in 1988 and reached the Super Bowl but were burned once more by Montana magic. They led 16–13 and had the 49ers pinned at their 8-yard line before Montana orchestrated the most dramatic Super Bowl drive of all time. He beat them with a touchdown pass to John Taylor with thirty-four seconds left.

Wyche couldn't be blamed for having tears in his eyes after that heartbreaker. This time, though, nobody could accuse him of not having done more to prevent it.

#52
THE HELICOPTER
ELWAY LEAPS TO A CONCLUSION
JANUARY 25, 1998

DENVER BRONCOS quarterback John Elway was thirty-seven years old and no longer the dangerous scrambler of yesteryear. He was not even his team's main offensive weapon anymore. That distinction belonged to running back Terrell Davis.

Elway's arm, experience, and leadership guided the Broncos to the Super Bowl in San Diego. They were twelve-point underdogs to the Green Bay Packers, the defending champions. According to the smart money, Elway was headed for his fourth Super Bowl defeat, and the AFC champion was headed for its fourteenth consecutive Super Bowl loss.

The Broncos took command early, however, and the Packers fought back for a 17–17 tie late in the third quarter. The Broncos started at their 8-yard line but marched down the field and faced third-and-6 at the Green Bay 12. Elway, who threw for only 123 yards, dropped back but couldn't spot a receiver and took off down the middle. He weighed 215 and never minded taking a lick for a good cause.

Strong safety LeRoy Butler and linebacker Brian Williams were waiting at the 6-yard line. Butler lowered his head and got ready to drill Elway. But the quarterback, in a move he'd later term his "three-inch vertical leap," went over the top. The collision with the two defenders spun Elway around as if he were a helicopter blade, and he was hit again by safety Mike Prior as he landed. Elway leaped up and pumped his fist, however, because he had a first down at the 4.

"I'll tell you what—I never had so much adrenaline flowing in my life," he recalled upon his Hall of Fame election in 2004. "I mean, it was unbelievable."

Two plays later, Davis scored on a 1-yard run for a 24–17 lead. Though the Packers tied the score again, Elway's leap rejuvenated his teammates. Davis's third touchdown run, with 1:45 left, gave the Broncos a 31–24 victory.

"When Elway, instead of running out of bounds, turned it up and got spun around like a helicopter, it energized us beyond belief," defensive tackle Mike Lodish said.

Added tight end Shannon Sharpe: "When I saw him do that and then got up pumping his fist, I said, 'It's on.' That's when I was sure we were going to win."

Elway completed his sixteen-year career a year later with a 34–19 victory over the Atlanta Falcons in the Super Bowl and finally hoisted the game's MVP trophy. When he retired, there were countless golden Elway moments to recall, but for Broncos coach Mike Shanahan, the helicopter quickly came to mind above the rest.

"Most quarterbacks are going to hit the ground," he said. "Not John. He takes that thing down there. I knew we had won the game. That perseverance, that drive, everything that he stood for, he did it on that play."

Until that play, Elway was regarded by many as a quarterback who couldn't win the big one, though in truth he led three Denver teams with unspectacular supporting casts to AFC championships. The helicopter made it clear that any holes in Elway's résumé were not for lack of determination.

"I was out in LA, having dinner, and Dustin Hoffman is in the restaurant," Elway recalled. "He's walking out, and I'm kind of close to the door. And he kind of makes a V and comes over and pats me on the shoulder while I'm sitting there at the table, and he just says, 'This guy doesn't slide.'"

#51
AN INSPIRED EFFORT
KELLEN WINSLOW BLOCKS A KICK
JANUARY 2, 1982

WE INEVITABLY WONDER where San Diego Chargers tight end Kellen Winslow ever found the energy to leap and block a kick to send one of the NFL's greatest playoff games into overtime. Winslow, like everybody else on the field, was worn out by a fast-paced game with the Miami Dolphins on a humid day in the Orange Bowl.

Winslow made thirteen catches for 166 yards and a touchdown that gave the Chargers a 31–24 lead. His efforts finally left him sick from exhaustion. But when Dolphins kicker Uwe von Schamann lined up for a 43-yard try on the final play of regulation, Winslow still had plenty of work to do. A 6-foot-5 athlete with excellent leaping ability, he was well equipped for blocking kicks.

"I told 'Big Hands' [Gary Johnson] and Louie [Kelcher] to give me some penetration, and I'll get it," Winslow said. "They did, and I think I got one finger on it."

Winslow's block was among a bunch of great plays that made the Chargers' 41–38 victory so memorable. The Dolphins' "Hook and Lateral" touchdown play at the end of the first half was the game's best play, but Winslow's blocked kick proved more decisive. It kept the Chargers alive and also forced a weary bunch of players to see how far they could push themselves.

"Everyone was so beat up and tired that we were going on remote control," Dolphins guard Bob Kuechenberg said.

Winslow was helped off the field twice, for a shoulder injury and for neck and back cramps. "I remember [defensive end] Kim

Bokamper fighting through Don Macek and Ed White to get to [quarterback Dan] Fouts, only I was there to block," he recalled. "After the play, Kim looked up from the ground and said, 'Damn, Kellen, what are you doing back here?' We were both so tired, we just started to laugh."

Nobody was laughing as the tension escalated in overtime. A 35-yard field-goal try by von Schamann was blocked by defensive end Leroy Jones, and the Chargers' Rolf Benirschke missed a kick from 27 yards. Finally, Fouts hit wide receiver Charlie Joiner down the middle for 39 yards to the Miami 10-yard line. This time, Benirschke was on target from 29 yards with 1:08 left in the fifth quarter.

Weary players staggered off the field, and Winslow needed assistance. With a towel over his head, he left on the shoulders of tackle Billy Shields and tight end Eric Sievers. "It was like all the adrenaline rushed out of me, and all the fatigue and soreness rushed in," Winslow said.

Some Dolphins accused Winslow of overplaying his fatigue, but his locker-room behavior suggested it was genuine. He mounted a podium to begin a postgame interview but quickly rushed off as if he were getting sick. Later, he seemed barely conscious as he lay on a bench with only a towel draped over him. Whether he felt the inspiration of legendary figures or was merely delirious, Winslow borrowed phrases from both Martin Luther King Jr. and Muhammad Ali.

"I feel as if I've been to the mountaintop," he said.

Giving new meaning to sudden-death overtime, he added, "I've never felt so close to death before. That's what Muhammad Ali said in Manila [after beating Joe Frazier], and that's how I felt there at the end."

#50
SNOW JOB
BURGLAR STEALS WIN FOR PATRIOTS
DECEMBER 12, 1982

IT WAS THE MOST controversial field goal of all time but not because anybody argued whether it was good. John Smith's 33-yard field goal that beat the Miami Dolphins was made possible by the ultimate stroke of gamesmanship.

The Dolphins and New England Patriots were playing in a blizzard at old Schaefer Stadium in Foxboro, Massachusetts, and neither team could score during the first fifty-five minutes. Each team had tried a field goal, but neither Smith nor Miami's Uwe von Schamann could keep his footing or meet the ball squarely through a layer of snow.

The Patriots drove to the Miami 16-yard line with 4:45 left and called time-out so Smith could try to clear a spot at the 23, where holder Matt Cavanaugh would spot the ball. Normally a routine kick, this one would be hazardous.

During previous time-outs, a John Deere tractor with a broom on the front was clearing yard lines. That gave Patriots first-year coach Ron Meyer a devious idea. "I saw John Smith on his hands and knees trying to get the snow cleared, and all of a sudden it hit me," the coach recalled. "Why not send a snowplow out there?"

Meyer ran down the sideline looking for the tractor driver and finally found him. He was Mark Henderson, 24, who was working on the stadium maintenance crew as part of a work-release program from nearby Norfolk State Prison. He was serving a fifteen-year sentence for burglary.

Henderson was happy to oblige Meyer's request. At first, he ran his tractor along the 20-yard line to make it appear he was

115

simply repeating his game-long routine. Then, following Cavanaugh's directions, Henderson steered to his left and cleared a spot on the artificial turf between the 23- and 25-yard lines, giving Smith a clear kicking surface. As the broom sent snow flying, Cavanaugh blew on his hands to get them warm enough to take the snap and make a good hold.

Once the Dolphins realized what Henderson was up to, they cursed and threatened him and complained to the officials. But their attempts to stop him were futile. "I saw him coming, but what was I supposed to do?" defensive tackle Bob Baumhower asked. "No way I'm going to take on a plow."

Almost twenty-four years later, however, Dolphins coach Don Shula regrets that he hadn't done just that. "In retrospect, I should've gone out and thrown myself in the way of the snowplow," the Hall of Fame coach said after turning seventy-six. "But then I would've gotten a 15-yard penalty for running on the field, and that would've moved them closer to the goal line."

Smith made the kick, and the Patriots won 3–0. The stadium video board didn't show the kick, however. It showed Henderson and his tractor and flashed his name. Many of the 25,716 fans kept chanting his name, and the Patriots gave Henderson the game ball.

Shula, meanwhile, was fuming and claimed the use of the tractor was "completely illegal." But game officials could cite no rule that the Patriots had violated, and Shula received no satisfaction when he filed a complaint with the league office.

"What were they gonna do?" Henderson asked after the game. "Put me in jail?"

Shula's complaint, however, prompted a rules change for 1983 that prohibited any more snow jobs. He also got even a month later when the Dolphins defeated the Patriots 28–13 in the opening round of a sixteen-team playoff tournament in the wake of a strike-shortened season. That game was in Miami, so snow was no factor, and the Dolphins advanced to the Super Bowl. But that did little to diminish Shula's anger.

"That's the most unfair act ever allowed in the history of the NFL," he said. "The score should have been erased and made a scoreless tie. When we got a chance for a field goal, our kicker fell down. When you think of the unfairness . . . he's a hero up there now."

Indeed, Henderson's role in the Snowplow Game has become part of New England sports lore. When the Patriots in 2001 played their final regular-season game in the old stadium, Henderson was invited back to drive his tractor on the field. Long released from prison, he received a standing ovation and performed the coin toss. The opponent? The Dolphins, of course. The Patriots won 20–13 and went on to win their first of three Super Bowls in four years.

Joe Robbie, the Dolphins owner in 1982, was introduced to Smith by league official Don Weiss. "When I introduced John to Robbie," Weiss recalled, "Joe said, 'That's the only game ever stolen from the Dolphins by a convicted felon.'"

#49
CINDERELLA'S THROW
KURT WARNER GOES DEEP ON TITANS
JANUARY 30, 2000

THE 1999 ST. LOUIS RAMS boasted a record-breaking offense known as "The Greatest Show on Turf." They routinely blew away opponents and defeated the Minnesota Vikings 49–37 in a divisional playoff game. But as the games became more important, the Rams faced tougher defenses, and it would take late-minute heroics from Kurt Warner to bring them a championship.

Warner's 30-yard touchdown pass to Ricky Proehl enabled the Rams to eke out an 11–6 victory over the Tampa Bay Buccaneers in the NFC championship game. But the signature throw of Warner's season and career was a 73-yard touchdown pass to Isaac Bruce that scored the winning points of a 23–16 victory over the Tennessee Titans in the Super Bowl at Atlanta.

Warner, whose career represented one of the classic rags-to-riches stories in NFL history, was in a tight spot late in the Super Bowl. The Titans had wiped out a 16–0 deficit and tied the score on Al Del Greco's 43-yard field goal with 2:12 left. Warner hadn't completed a pass since a 9-yard touchdown to Torry Holt midway in the third quarter and started his last possession at the Rams' 27-yard line. He had 2:05 left to find out if he had one more handful of fairy dust to scatter on a magical season.

"We thought, 'We've got two minutes, we've been moving the ball up and down the field all day, and there's no reason we can't kick a field goal and win this thing," Warner said after he threw for 414 yards, a Super Bowl record.

Warner, who threw forty-one touchdown passes in the regular season and six more in two playoff victories, had one more bomb in his arm. Despite absorbing a fierce hit from defensive end Jevon Kearse, Warner lobbed a pass for Bruce, who was streaking down the right sideline past cornerback Denard Walker.

But Bruce noticed the ball was floating, slowed down, and outjumped Walker to make the catch at the Tennessee 40-yard line. Bruce then sprinted around safety Anthony Dorsett into the end zone with 1:56 left. That gave the Rams their first Super Bowl title.

Warner didn't see much after Kearse leveled him. "I missed it," he said. "I kind of got my head opened up. I didn't get a chance to see him catch the ball. I was down on the ground. I did lift my head up and saw that he was running with it."

Rams coach Dick Vermeil revealed that offensive coordinator Mike Martz wanted to try that play on the Rams' previous possession. But the Rams had to punt before they got the chance, and the Titans tied the score. The Rams ran that play earlier in the game, and Bruce was open, but Warner threw to the other side of the field. "I said, 'Let's put the ball in Isaac Bruce's hands,'" Vermeil said.

He got no argument from Martz, whose arrival in St. Louis that season took the Rams' offense to an unprecedented level of scoring 526 points, an NFL record. Martz loved having a quick-strike offense and was frustrated to see the Rams settle for field goals at the end of three long drives in the first half. There was no such frustration on the Rams' final pass.

"It's what we call, 'Twins Right, Ace Right, Nine-Nine-Nine Halfback Balloon,'" Martz said. "We had five seconds left before the two-minute warning. We wanted to take a shot to Isaac over there, and we hadn't gotten it done during the game, for whatever reason. If we got it, great. If not, the two-minute warning would kick off, and he could rest. So we'd go at it again with something else. The two of them just hooked up and made a great play."

That touchdown put the finishing touch on a storybook season. Warner received only a brief look from the Green Bay Packers in 1994 and then stocked shelves in a grocery store in Cedar Falls, Iowa. He resumed his career in the Arena League and NFL Europe before climbing back to the NFL in 1998 as a Rams backup. A year later, starter Trent Green suffered a season-ending knee injury in the next-to-last preseason game, and the Rams appeared doomed. Warner, however, became a star and was named MVP for both the regular season and the Super Bowl.

"It's real life," Vermeil said. "He's an example of what we'd like to be."

Warner had another big season in 2001, but injuries ruined his next two seasons, and he became a journeyman starter and backup for the New York Giants and Arizona Cardinals. Yet what he achieved with the Rams, especially on that game-winning pass to Bruce, underlined the power of unswerving positive thinking.

"Don't ever lose sight of it," Warner said. "Don't let anyone tell you that you can't do something. I believe in the Lord, and I believe in myself. With that, you can accomplish anything."

#48
65 TOSS POWER TRAP
HANK STRAM PUTS ON A SHOW
JANUARY 11, 1970

NOT ONLY DID THIS PLAY score the first touchdown of the Kansas City Chiefs' 23–7 upset of the Minnesota Vikings in the January 1970 Super Bowl, but the play also ushered in an era during which NFL Films would put viewers virtually on the field and sidelines by bringing them the sights, sounds, and passions of pro football.

New York Giants middle linebacker Sam Huff became a national celebrity when he wore a mike during the 1960 preseason for a CBS television documentary. NFL Films founder Ed Sabol convinced the Chiefs' Hank Stram to become the first Super Bowl coach to wear a microphone, though Stram was promised that the footage would be held for a highlights film. Stram, a cocky, wisecracking coach, proved a perfect choice, and his performance in New Orleans would forever change television's presentation of pro football.

The Chiefs led 9–0 in the second quarter and faced a third-down play at the Vikings' 5-yard line. Stram, warming up to his role as narrator, called for a run by halfback Mike Garrett. He announced on the sideline, "We're going to call '65 Toss Power Trap.' Watch this now, boys! Watch this now! This thing just might bust wide open." The play, indeed, busted wide open, and Stram added, "How 'bout that, boys? Huh? How 'bout it?"

Quarterback Len Dawson, recalling Stram's boast that the play could bust wide open, laughed and said, "Or it could have fallen flat on its face." That play wasn't in the Chiefs' game plan, but Stram called it to take advantage of right defensive end Jim Marshall's hard charge.

"I was surprised he sent it in," Dawson said. "We hadn't run it in I don't know how long. You had the left halfback flaring out like it was a pitchout. My job was to turn around and fake the pitchout to him. The left tackle, Jim Tyrer, would be pulling out to influence that defensive end—that was the guy you were trying to trap. Hopefully, he'll chase the tackle out there, thinking it's a pitch, and you run inside him. And the right guard [Mo Moorman] pulls and comes down the line.

"The Vikings chased a lot, so when the tackle pulled out, Jim Marshall went with him. The guard was there to block him but [Marshall] took himself out. So Mo was up there to make a block [on somebody else]. Then Fred Arbanas, the tight end on that side, not only blocked the middle linebacker but the safety as well. Consequently, Mike Garrett was able to run right into the end zone.

"We were trying to trick 'em; that's the whole idea of the thing, and fortunately, it worked. Otherwise, Garrett would've been stuffed on about the 6-yard line."

Now the Chiefs were ahead 16–0, but the Vikings staged a mild comeback and closed the gap to 16–7 early in the third quarter. Then another memorable play, a short pass from Dawson to wide receiver Otis Taylor that turned into a 46-yard touchdown play, put the game on ice. Dawson, a longtime broadcaster in Kansas City, hadn't reviewed that play for several years until Stram phoned and asked him if he recalled the formation. Dawson checked the game tape and was surprised at what he saw.

"They had an all-out blitz on, and that's the only pass I could've gotten off because I took one or two steps back and fired on a hitch pattern," he said. "The safeties were coming, and the linebackers were coming, but I went on a quick count. They were trying to camouflage the blitz, which allowed me to get rid of the football. The job of the tackles was to chop the defensive ends and get their hands down on those quick passes, and they were able to do that. So I had a lane to throw."

Taylor recalled that he and Frank Pitts had no problems catching short passes because the Vikings' secondary played off them. So when Taylor caught another short pass, on the right side, he knew he'd have time to turn and run. Then he made the move that sewed up the Chiefs' 23-7 victory.

"I made my break, turned, and caught the pass," Taylor recalled. "Earlier in the game after catching a short out pass, I had turned to the inside of the field, but this time—purely by instinct—I turned quickly to the outside when the Vikings' [cornerback] Earsell Mackbee hit me. I left him lying on the ground.

"I bolted down the sideline, and Paul Krause, Minnesota's safety, tried to cut me off and run me out of bounds around the 20-yard line. I made a move toward him—it was almost like a shock wave—faking that I was going to come back across the field, but I kept my balance and went straight ahead, staying in bounds. I kept running and pranced like a horse into the end zone. I wasn't showing off. I was just happy to score. That was the biggest single play of my career."

Though Dawson is in the Hall of Fame and was MVP of that Super Bowl, he often points out that the difference between fame and failure so often lies with having the right play for the right situation. "65 Toss Power Trap was the right call at the right time, and it happened to work," he said. "That pass to Otis was the right call at the right time. All these games you watch, they generally come down to a couple of plays. That's what's going to determine the outcome."

#47
GHOST TO THE POST
DAVE CASPER BEATS THE PATRIOTS
DECEMBER 24, 1977

NOT ONLY WAS THIS one of the greatest plays of all time, it also has one of the catchiest nicknames of all time.

Oakland Raiders tight end Dave Casper was nicknamed "The Ghost," after the cartoon character, Casper the Friendly Ghost. And a deep pattern toward the middle of the field is a post. Which is why Casper's famous catch in a 37–31 playoff victory over the Baltimore Colts has ever since been celebrated as "Ghost to the Post."

Casper was among the most complete tight ends of all time. An offensive tackle at Notre Dame, he was a 6-foot-4, 240-pound crunching run blocker, as well as a game-breaking receiver. Only the sixth tight end inducted into the Hall of Fame, Casper's signature play came in a high-scoring first-round playoff game at Baltimore. The Raiders were defending their Super Bowl championship in the 1976 season.

Though Casper had caught two touchdown passes from Ken "Snake" Stabler, the Raiders trailed 31–28 with fewer than three minutes left. "We had time, so it wasn't like we needed a miracle," Raiders coach John Madden recalled. "Snake was so good at using the clock. So we weren't really worried. Well, put it this way, we weren't any more worried than usual."

Stabler passed for a first down. On the next play, he had Casper run a deep post, a changeup from the short patterns he'd been running underneath the Colts' secondary. Casper broke open down the middle and caught the ball in full stride, with his back to Stabler, for a 42-yard pickup at the Colts' 14-yard line.

"The pass was right over my head," Casper said. "Kenny throws such a soft ball that it really was a piece of cake to catch. If it looked tough, it really wasn't. I just ran under it, and it stuck in my hands."

Errol Mann kicked a 22-yard field goal with just twenty-six seconds left, and the game went into sudden-death overtime. "It wasn't real sudden, though," Stabler recalled.

The game turned into the third longest ever played, after a 1971 playoff victory by the Miami Dolphins over the Kansas City Chiefs and the 1962 AFL championship game, won by the Dallas Texans over the Houston Oilers. The Raiders finally prevailed, forty-three seconds into the sixth quarter, when Stabler, on a play fake, hit Casper with a 10-yard touchdown pass. That was the ninth and last lead change of the game.

It was odd that Casper could catch three touchdown passes in a playoff game, yet be best remembered for a play in that game on which he did not score. "It wasn't any big thing," he claimed. "I was more involved in my blocking than pass catching."

It also was odd that a reporter would ask Casper if this grueling game was "fun" to play. Casper, understandably exhausted, replied, "Playing checkers with your daughter is fun. Not this. This was the hardest football game I ever played."

Despite owner Al Davis's famed affection for the deep passing game, the Raiders' attack during Casper's years was built around him and wide receiver Fred Biletnikoff, also a possession receiver. Both were stars of the Raiders' 32–14 Super Bowl victory over the Minnesota Vikings in January 1977.

In a message welcoming Casper to the Hall of Fame in 2002, Raiders Hall of Fame tackle Art Shell said: "I know this: You could adjust to the ball and catch the ball as good as any wide receiver. The 'Ghost to the Post' play was phenomenal, the way you ran that ball down and adjusted to it in flight—that was typical of your great career."

With Cliff Branch providing a deep threat, the Raiders of the late 1970s boasted one of the top receiving threesomes ever. "When a team throws a double zone against us, then Casper goes up the middle," Madden said. "Zingo! Just like that. When you have one or even two great receivers, then defenses can double up. When you have three, it's impossible to stop them. And we have three."

Casper, drafted in 1974, was the NFL's best tight end from 1976 through 1980. "I can't think of anyone I'd rather have," Stabler said. "He's very intelligent and just knows how to get open. He knows how to beat a defensive back one on one, or he can find the open spot in a zone. He's so big and strong, and he overpowers anybody he goes against, blocking or receiving. If other teams try to double up on Fred Biletnikoff or Cliff Branch, Casper can kill them."

#46
PRIME TIME
DEION SANDERS BREAKS ANOTHER ONE
SEPTEMBER 21, 1998

DALLAS COWBOYS cornerback and kick returner Deion Sanders picked a strange time to disavow his nickname, "Prime Time." He said he was doing this for religious reasons and on a night when his team was playing in prime time—a *Monday Night Football* road game against the New York Giants.

"'Prime Time?'" Sanders asked after a 59-yard punt return that helped the Cowboys roll to a 31–7 victory. "I'm trying to bury that. Prime time is God's time now."

Sanders was so respected as a cornerback that coaches routinely instructed their quarterbacks to avoid his side of the field. Passers usually would throw deep only against the cornerback opposite Sanders.

As a kick returner, Sanders was a constant threat to go all the way and break a game open, as he did at Giants Stadium early in the 1998 season. The Cowboys needed all the big plays they could get on defense and special teams because quarterback Troy Aikman, who led them to three Super Bowl wins, was sidelined, and backup Jason Garrett got the start.

In the second quarter, Sanders fielded a low, line-drive punt from Brad Maynard. Despite the kick's brief hang time, the Giants' coverage unit got downfield quickly enough to force Sanders to back up 5 yards. He started to his left, then quickly reversed his field to the right sideline and broke loose for 59 yards. "I'm not like your ordinary punt returner," Sanders explained.

His multiple roles could exhaust him, however, and Sanders sometimes became dehydrated in warm weather. That happened again after his touchdown return, and he left the game. Having received treatment, he returned in the third quarter and picked up where he left off.

Lined up at wide receiver and facing double coverage, Sanders caught a 55-yard pass from Garrett in the third quarter that set up a touchdown. Late in the fourth quarter, he showed why coaches and quarterbacks usually avoided him. He intercepted a Danny Kanell pass and returned it 71 yards to climax a remarkable night. Sanders totaled 226 return and receiving yards, underscoring his reputation as one of the NFL's best cornerbacks and most versatile players ever.

When Sanders retired after the 2005 season, he had scored twenty-two touchdowns—nine on interceptions, six on punt returns, three on kickoff returns, three on receptions, and one on a fumble recovery. His nineteen return touchdowns set an NFL record, and some might argue that his punt return against the Giants wasn't even his most impressive.

For pure drama, you could make a case for his return at the start of 1989, Sanders's rookie season with the Atlanta Falcons. That return covered 68 yards and marked his first NFL touchdown, though the Falcons lost 31–21 to the Los Angeles Rams. The Falcons made Sanders the fifth overall pick of the draft, but he staged a long holdout. That came as no surprise after his draft-day vow that, "I'm gonna ask for so much money, the Falcons are gonna have to put me on layaway."

Sanders finally agreed to a contract in time to join the Falcons for a Friday practice and a Saturday walk-through before he suited up for the season opener. He fielded a first-quarter punt on the dirt baseball infield in old Fulton County Stadium. He fumbled the ball before quickly picking it up and eluding a defender who went flying by. Then, safety Anthony Newman had Sanders in his grasp only to see him wiggle away.

That gave Sanders all the room he needed. He bolted up the middle, cut inside to dodge another defender, then cut to the right sideline and was gone. He broke five tackles, and the last defender chasing him had no chance against Sanders, who'd dazzled NFL scouts at the 1989 scouting combine by running 40 yards in 4.27 seconds on a track considered slow. He'd also played center field for the New York Yankees that year and with that return became the first athlete ever to hit a home run in the major leagues and score a touchdown in professional football in the same week.

Sanders, at age thirty-seven, ended a three-year retirement when he signed with the Baltimore Ravens in 2004. He claimed he no longer felt obliged to live up to his flamboyant reputation, which begged the question whether "Prime Time" was gone.

"When did I stop being Prime Time?" he replied, grinning. "I didn't get that memo."

Actually, he had delivered that very memo after his Monday night punt return six years earlier. Then again, Sanders always was a master at reversing his field.

#45
BIG BEN RIGHT
STEVE BARTKOWSKI THROWS THE BOMB
NOVEMBER 12, 1978

MOST NFL QUARTERBACKS feel fortunate to celebrate one long-shot touchdown heave that pulls out a victory in the final minute. Steve Bartkowski of the Atlanta Falcons threw two of them. That would seem like a lot of luck for one player and franchise, except longtime Falcons fans would tell you they haven't been especially lucky at all.

The Falcons were sad sacks for most of their first dozen seasons after they joined the NFL in 1966. More disappointment arrived early in 1978 as the Falcons dropped to 2–4. They finally caught fire and won four straight games but found their playoff train nearly derailed because they trailed the Saints 17–6 in New Orleans with 2:23 left.

Bartkowski quickly led the Falcons 80 yards to cut the deficit to 17–13 with fifty-nine seconds left. An onside kickoff failed, and the Falcons used their remaining time-outs as the Saints tried to run out the clock. Three straight runs failed to get a first down, so Saints coach Dick Nolan had Chuck Muncie run on fourth down. Defensive tackle Jeff Yeates stopped the big back short of a first down, and the Falcons took over at their 43-yard line.

The Falcons lined up in "Big Ben Right," their "Hail Mary" pass formation, with three wide receivers on the right. Bartkowski had a strong arm and threw for the end zone, where his receivers battled the defenders for the ball. It was tipped by wide receiver Wallace Francis into the hands of teammate Alfred Jackson, whose catch with nineteen seconds left gave the Falcons a 20–17 victory and ultimately their first-ever playoff spot.

"There was no primary receiver," Francis said. "We just batted the ball around and hoped someone would catch it. Seriously, that's what we do."

There wasn't much more the Falcons could plan for a play that desperate. "I just throw it up and hope," Bartkowski said. "I was surprised. I was able to see the whole play, and my first reaction was, 'Praise the Lord.'"

Without Big Ben Right, the Falcons would have had to wait another two years for their maiden playoff voyage. Though they lost three of their last five games in 1978 and were outscored by fifty points for the season, the Falcons squeezed into the playoffs with a 9–7 record. The Falcons mounted yet another big comeback by scoring two touchdowns in the final eight minutes to gain a 14–13 playoff victory at home over the Philadelphia Eagles. Their season ended with a 27–20 loss at Dallas.

Bartkowski's second Big Ben touchdown pass was every bit as spectacular as the first. But it's been largely forgotten amid the rubble of a 7–9 finish in 1983. Five years and eight days after Bartkowski's bomb in New Orleans, the Falcons trailed the San Francisco 49ers 24–21 in Atlanta with two seconds left.

At the San Francisco 48-yard line, Bartkowski sent three wide receivers down the left side—Stacy Bailey, Floyd Hodge, and Billy "White Shoes" Johnson. A mob of defenders was there to greet them and converged on the ball. It was tapped out to the 6-yard line, where Johnson was positioned. He grabbed the ball, but a cluster of defenders stood between him and the end zone.

Johnson was the perfect man for this mission. A celebrated kick returner, he had a knack for eluding would-be tacklers in tight spaces. Sure enough, Johnson flashed some of the moves that made him famous. First, he backpedaled 2 yards to give himself some running room. Then he cut to his right, away from the crowd, as the 49ers defenders chased him frantically.

As Johnson got inside the 5-yard line, it seemed a 50-50 proposition whether he could score. He was tripped up at the 2 and knocked off his feet, yet managed to make a desperate dive for the end zone. He extended his arm and broke the plane of the goal line with the ball for a touchdown and a 28–24 victory. Though videotape suggests Johnson's knee was down before he planted the ball in the end zone, his effort was still magnificent. Few players could have gotten close enough to sell the score.

It's hard to explain how Big Ben could strike twice for Bartkowski, except for one clue. The second time it happened, Bartkowski was throwing under a full moon.

#44

IRON MIKE'S DETERMINATION
THERE WAS NO STOPPING DITKA
NOVEMBER 24, 1963

ASK FOOTBALL FANS to identify the player who redefined the tight end position, and they'll claim it was John Mackey, Dave Casper, Jackie Smith, Kellen Winslow, or Shannon Sharpe. Actually, it was Mike Ditka, who joined the Chicago Bears in 1961 and proved that a tight end could become much more than an extra tackle who occasionally caught a pass.

Ditka's all-around game made him the first tight end inducted into the Hall of Fame. Yet his ferocity evoked the image of linebacker Dick Butkus playing offense.

Ditka was NFL Rookie of the Year and a Pro Bowl choice in 1961 after he caught fifty-six passes for 1,076 yards and twelve touchdowns. This, remember, was during an era when teams played only fourteen games and defenders were allowed to hammer receivers. Ditka, of course, hammered them back. Never were his tenacity, strength, and running ability showcased more than on a 63-yard pass play in a 17–17 tie against the Steelers.

The game was played two days after President John F. Kennedy was assassinated in Dallas. Commissioner Pete Rozelle, in a decision he would come to regret, decided the NFL should go ahead with its Sunday schedule. The Bears, locked in a tight Western Conference race with the Green Bay Packers, were visiting Pittsburgh. Ditka hailed from western Pennsylvania and at the University of Pittsburgh was an All-America tight end, an outfielder, and a basketball forward.

The Bears trailed 17–14 in the fourth quarter and were at their own 22-yard line, facing second-and-36. Quarterback Bill

Wade looked for Ditka, a 6-foot-3, 225-pound receiver who would finish the season with eight touchdown catches.

"I remember I was dead tired," Ditka said. "I came into the huddle, and Wade asked me if I could run a deep pattern, and I said, 'No. Maybe I can hook up 10 yards, see what we can get out of it. But that's it.'"

Wade looked for a deep receiver, but Ditka, about 5 yards past the line of scrimmage, was the only one open. Ditka took the pass and promptly bounced off defensive back Clendon Thomas, then ran over a linebacker. Three defenders converged on Ditka at midfield, but he emerged from the tangle like a truck from a car wash. Thomas kept chasing Ditka and finally tackled him at the Steelers' 15-yard line.

"I lost my legs," Ditka said. "They were completely dead. I just plain ran out of gas. It was just a series of bouncing off people. It wasn't the [great] running, more the lousy tackling. I don't really think it was that special. If it'd been the best play I ever made, I would have scored a touchdown. I would have outrun that last guy."

Ditka's doggedness led to an 18-yard field goal by Roger Leclerc that left the Bears with a tie and their players marveling at Ditka's play. "I was trying to block somebody, but I saw him going down the field, and it was incredible," flanker Johnny Morris said. "He knocked down everybody who touched him. I remember feeling terribly disappointed when the last guy tackled him. If anybody deserved to go all the way, Mike did."

Without Ditka's play, the Bears probably would not have been NFL champions. That tie enabled them to win the Western Conference title with an 11–1–2 record, half a game better than the Packers. A Bears loss to the Steelers would have enabled the Packers to play in the NFL championship game for the fourth straight year.

"It was some fantastic effort," Wade said of Ditka's play. "I mean, inhuman almost."

Ditka made another important catch from Wade in a 14–10 victory over the New York Giants in the NFL championship game on a bitterly cold late-December day in Chicago. Both Bears touchdowns were set up by interceptions, and in the third quarter Wade threw for 12 yards to Ditka in heavy traffic at the 1-yard line. Wade made his second touchdown sneak of the game and wiped out the Giants' 10–7 lead.

That would be the Bears' last league championship for twenty-two seasons, until Ditka was head coach and led them to a 46–10 Super Bowl victory over the New England Patriots. His popularity as a coach might have helped Ditka get elected to the Hall of Fame in 1988, but he went in as the tight end who averaged 13.6 yards for 427 catches. He actually seemed embarrassed by his election and suggested there were other tight ends more deserving of the honor.

Anybody who saw Ditka run through the Steelers would have begged to differ.

#43
RED RIGHT 88
MIKE DAVIS OUTFOXES BROWNS
JANUARY 4, 1981

THIS PLAY IS LESS KINDLY referred to as the "mistake by the lake." When Oakland Raiders safety Mike Davis stepped in front of Cleveland tight end Ozzie Newsome to make an end-zone interception and end the Browns' 1980 season, 77,665 fans in old Municipal Stadium fell silent. For them, the day had just turned as bitterly disappointing as it was bitterly cold.

It was so cold that the day before the game, after the Raiders practiced at the Browns' facility, the home team decided to skip its walk-through. "We thought that was funny," Davis said. "But when we got out there Sunday, we didn't think it was that funny."

This was not the kind of day conducive to throwing, catching, or intercepting passes. The field was frozen, and the temperature at kickoff was one degree, with a minus-37 wind chill. The ball was hard as a rock, and Davis was not exactly sure-handed, even under sunny skies. He had, in fact, notoriously bad hands and was the least likely Raiders defensive back to bring heartbreak to the Browns.

"If you were going to throw the ball to Mike playing catch, he might not get it," Raiders coach Tom Flores said. "Mike had the worst hands of [any of] the guys in our secondary."

The Browns were AFC Central champions and stirred real hopes in Cleveland that they might finally win their first NFL championship since 1964. The Raiders were a wild-card team coming off a first-round victory over the Houston Oilers. Led by quarterback Brian Sipe, the Browns kept winning with heart-stopping finishes and were dubbed the "Kardiac Kids."

Another ulcer-raising finish was in the works as the Browns, trailing 14–12, moved from their 14-yard line to the Oakland 13 with forty-seven seconds left. In decent weather the Browns could have stayed on the ground and kicked a field goal. But in addition to the poor field conditions, the Browns were moving into a wicked wind on the Lake Erie end of the stadium. Kicking toward that end zone had been an adventure all day.

Don Cockroft missed two field-goal tries, saw another messed up by a bad snap and saw an extra-point try blocked by linebacker Ted Hendricks. Cockroft had kicked two field goals in the third quarter, but then the Browns were moving the other way.

On second down from the Oakland 13-yard line, Browns coach Sam Rutigliano called for "Red Right 88," a throw into the end zone primarily for Newsome. Rutigliano told Sipe that if he didn't have a receiver open, he should throw the ball into the stands. Davis claimed he baited Sipe by laying off Newsome until the pass was released, then burst in front of him to intercept the pass with forty-one seconds left. For Sipe, that throw brought a miserable end to a 13-for-40 day, a result of the weather and Raiders defense.

"I made that play with eighty thousand people screaming and cheering like crazy," Davis told the *Alameda Times-Star*, "but when I zipped in front of Ozzie Newsome and intercepted that ball, it happened so quickly that no one knew what had happened. It got so quiet that I could hear [Raiders guard] Gene Upshaw telling [tackle] Art Shell more than 30 yards up the sideline, 'He caught it! He caught it! We're going to San Diego [for the AFC championship game].' It was eerie. There was almost no sound."

The silence was deafening for Rutigliano, too. "When I think back to that game and specifically back to that play," he said, "the first thing that comes to mind is the silence—the unbelievable, utter silence—after it happened."

What happened next became a bit fuzzy to Davis. As he came down with the interception, he slipped, and his helmet struck the frozen turf. "It might have been the hardest hit in my life," he recalled. "When I stood up, I was a little spacey, but I knew what I had done."

That was the biggest play of Davis's career, though his bad hands limited him to just eleven interceptions in eight NFL seasons. That interception paved the way for a Super Bowl visit because the Raiders upset the Chargers 34–27 in the AFC championship game. After the Raiders defeated the Philadelphia Eagles 27–10 in New Orleans, Davis's teammates totaled their postseason booty and dubbed Davis's interception "the eighty-five-thousand-dollar catch."

That play, Davis said, reflected his motto for playing his position, a motto that he said ran through his mind before Sipe's crucial throw. "Hope the play comes your way," Davis said. "When the game is on the line, you want them to throw the ball your way."

#42
STOPPING A FREIGHT TRAIN
CHUCK BEDNARIK WRAPS UP JIM TAYLOR
DECEMBER 26, 1960

ONCE THE GREEN BAY PACKERS got rolling under Vince Lombardi, they usually were unstoppable. But a stubborn Philadelphia Eagles defense, led by middle linebacker Chuck Bednarik, held back the Packer dynasty for a year. With one tenacious, game-saving tackle of fullback Jim Taylor, the Eagles gave Lombardi's Packers their only loss in six NFL championship games and two Super Bowls.

The Packers, two years removed from a 1–10–1 debacle, finished first in the Western Conference in 1960, Lombardi's second season. The Eagles, too, were recovering from hard times when they hired coach Buck Shaw in 1958. His trade for quarterback Norm Van Brocklin helped bring the Eagles an Eastern Conference title in three years.

The NFL championship game was played in Philadelphia and turned into a defensive struggle. A 5-yard run by Ted Dean put the Eagles ahead 17–13 with 5:21 left. The Packers couldn't move the ball on their next possession and didn't get the ball back until a punt stuck them at their 22-yard line with 1:22 left. Quarterback Bart Starr didn't have star halfback Paul Hornung because he'd been knocked out of the game by a vicious hit from linebacker Tommy Brookshier.

Starr patiently led the Packers down the field with short passes, including an 8-yard pass to tight end Gary Knafelc. Bednarik, not missing a trick, sat on Knafelc after the catch, burning a few more seconds. With time left for one last play, Starr threw a short pass to Taylor, a bruising runner, in the left flat.

Taylor cut to the middle and, as Red Smith wrote in the *New York Herald Tribune*, "That wonderful runner ducked his head like a charging bull, bolted like an enraged beer truck into Philadelphia's congested secondary, twisted, staggered, bucked, and wrestled one step at a time."

Taylor was inside the 10 when rookie defensive back Bobby Jackson, who'd just entered the game, made the initial hit and slowed him down. Bednarik wrapped up Taylor and sat on him as time ran out.

"I gave him a big bear-hug tackle up high and wrestled him to the ground at the 9-yard line," Bednarik said. "I was on top of him, and I stayed there. You're darn right I was watching the clock.

"I made up my mind I was going to lay on him until it was over. I jumped up—not like these freaks do today after any old tackle—because I was jubilant that I had won a title. The game was over, we were champions, and it was time to celebrate."

It was only happenstance that Bednarik was at middle line-backer. He'd been a two-way starter for the Eagles for much of his career but started the 1960 season at center, the position at which he entered the Hall of Fame. But an early-season injury to Bob Pellegrini left Shaw short at linebacker.

He and Bednarik drove to the stadium together each day, and on the way the coach asked his center if he'd return to double duty. Bednarik agreed and made a huge impact at linebacker. He played more than fifty minutes in three games that season.

"Mind over matter," Bednarik said. "I was in good condition, and if you're winning, you never get tired, and you don't want to get out of the game. It's when you get the hell kicked out of you that you're mentally and physically fatigued. It was part of my job. I never tried to do that figuring I'm going to do something ex-traordinary, something nobody else can do. As long as we were winning, I was happy."

Bednarik played fifty-eight minutes against the Packers and was entitled to be weary. So was Taylor, who remained sprawled on the field well after the final gun. Bednarik finally told him, "Get up, this goddamn game is over!"

Then Bednarik lifted his fists above his head triumphantly, not unlike his famous pose over a fallen Frank Gifford earlier that year. As Taylor rose, Hornung came from the bench to compliment him for a great effort. Bednarik stepped between the Packer stars, hugged them both, and told them they'd be back in the championship game the next year. The three future Hall of Fame players walked off the field, arm in arm and limping.

Lombardi, too, told his players they'd be back in the championship game. "Perhaps you didn't realize that you could have won this game," he said. "But I think there's no doubt in your minds now. And that's why you will win it all next year. This will never happen again. You will never lose another championship."

The Packers proved their coach a prophet. They would never have lost even one championship game had not the Eagles been able to drag down Taylor.

#41
A GIFT FOR RANDALL
ERIC ALLEN'S THOUGHTFUL INTERCEPTION
OCTOBER 3, 1993

CORNERBACK ERIC ALLEN made an unforgettable interception return in an unforgettable comeback for the Philadelphia Eagles. He completed the play by showing unforgettable compassion for injured quarterback Randall Cunningham.

Cunningham limped off the Giants Stadium field with a season-ending injury as the Eagles trailed the New York Jets 21–0. The Eagles mounted a furious rally and closed the gap to 30–28 in the fourth quarter, but the Jets were driving in Eagles' territory and threatening to wrap up the victory.

Quarterback Boomer Esiason spotted wide receiver Ryan Yarborough open at the 6-yard line, near his left sideline, but threw behind him. Allen made the interception. "Esiason loves to take chances with his arm," Allen said, "so when he put the ball up, I broke on it, and it all seemed like slow motion."

Esiason slapped his helmet with both hands in frustration. Allen at first didn't plan on going anywhere because he was hemmed in near the sideline. But he spun away from two would-be tacklers and saw a big hole down the middle of the field.

"As soon as I caught the ball," he recalled, "I thought to myself, 'I should get out of bounds because something crazy's going to happen.' But then I wanted to get the offense some breathing room. I looked upfield and see two Jets players walking off the field, like, 'This guy's going out of bounds,' and I said, 'Wait a minute, I'm going to make as many yards as I can.'

"So I decided to reverse field and picked up 10 yards. I saw the hole and said, 'If I can make it through the hole, I can make something happen.' Then, after making two guys miss, I saw a lot of green, so I kept running. Then I hear [defensive back] Ben Smith yelling, 'Pitch the ball,' at midfield. And I yelled, 'Are you crazy, after making it this far? I'm taking this one myself.' It was clear sailing at the end."

Allen finally cut to the left sideline and into the end zone to give the Eagles a 35–30 victory. Jets tight end Johnny Mitchell, the last player with an angle on Allen, was blocked inside the Jets' 10-yard line. All his running and weaving left Allen weary, and he recalled, "They say it was 94 yards, but it seemed like 200."

But once he was in the end zone, Allen wasn't too tired to notice Cunningham seated on a folding chair at the entrance of the runway to the locker room. As teammates rushed over to congratulate Allen, he decided also to share the moment with Cunningham, whose ninth season with the Eagles was over.

"I look straight ahead and see Randall there with crutches," Allen said. "I gave him the ball because he was the leader of our team and said, 'We're all with you, and come back as soon as you can.' I told him, we survived this game without him, but we will need a lot more great plays to survive the season without him."

Even with Allen returning four interceptions for touchdowns, the Eagles didn't make enough great plays to reach the playoffs in 1993. Their win over the Jets boosted the Eagles to 4–0, but they lost their next six games with Ken O'Brien and Bubby Brister at quarterback. They finally snapped their skid behind Brister and won four of their last six games to finish 8–8. They actually remained in contention for a wild-card playoff spot until the final week of the season.

Allen was voted to six Pro Bowls, five with the Eagles and one with the New Orleans Saints. He became the first NFL player ever to return three or more interceptions for touchdowns in two different seasons. With the Oakland Raiders in 2001, Allen, at age thirty-six, went out in style by grabbing seven interceptions and returning three of them for touchdowns.

When he joined the Raiders in 1998, coach Jon Gruden described Allen as "a great veteran player, a guy that's backed it up for a decade." His last victory, appropriately, came in a playoff game against the Jets. His career ended a week later in the Raiders' 16–13 overtime loss at New England.

During a fourteen-year career, Allen made fifty-four interceptions and returned nine of them for touchdowns. He showed no mercy to quarterbacks, except for his own.

#40
BLAST FROM CANNON
MR. HEISMAN FINALLY COMES THROUGH
JANUARY 15, 1961

CONSIDERING THAT the American Football League was famous for shootouts and that two high-scoring teams were facing off in the first championship game, it was surprising to see the Houston Oilers clinging to a 17–16 lead over the Los Angeles Chargers early in the fourth quarter. Fans expected more points than that in the first quarter alone.

The Chargers were coached by Sid Gillman, who loved quick-strike passing attacks. Behind quarterback Jack Kemp and half-back Paul Lowe, they scored 184 points over their last four regular-season games. The Oilers' offense was led by George Blanda and wide receivers Bill Groman and Charlie Hennigan. Heisman Trophy winner Billy Cannon from LSU was expected to be a difference maker for the Oilers but ran for just 644 yards as a rookie. He did his best work that year as a receiver and return specialist. His 42-yard kickoff return set up a touchdown that gave the Oilers a 17–9 lead over the Chargers at Houston's Jeppesen Stadium.

The Oilers were ahead by just one point and backed up to their 12-yard line when Blanda exploited safety Jim Sears's tendency to keep cheating closer to the line of scrimmage to stop the run. Blanda told Cannon and Hennigan to run slants to the same side, where Sears would have to cover one of them. The other receiver then would cut upfield to the area where Sears would've sat had he been playing deep.

Sears followed Hennigan, and Cannon broke open as instructed. Blanda was right on target with his throw as Cannon beat cornerback Charlie McNeil, broke a tackle, and completed an 88-yard scoring play to give the Oilers a 24–16 victory. The Chargers had one last chance to tie the score but came up short on fourth down inside the Oilers' 20.

Blanda passed for 301 yards, but Cannon, with 259 yards of total offense, was the game's MVP. He was the AFL's most valuable player that day, too, because a league playing its first championship game needed all the star power it could muster. Signing the Heisman Trophy winner was a major coup for the Oilers and the AFL, though the league first had to defend itself in federal court.

Because of fierce competition for college stars, both leagues held their annual drafts around Thanksgiving and sometimes cut shady deals. Cannon had been selected by the Oilers and the NFL's Los Angeles Rams and signed with Rams general manager Pete Rozelle before he ended his college career in a 21–0 loss to Mississippi in the Sugar Bowl. But Cannon changed his mind when Oilers owner Bud Adams offered him a much better deal, which was guaranteed even if the league folded. Cannon returned the Rams' uncashed checks for $10,500 before the Sugar Bowl and immediately after the game signed with the Oilers under a goal post.

Rozelle, now the new NFL Commissioner, claimed the AFL had violated a deal between the leagues not to tamper with players under contract. The Rams filed suit to enforce Cannon's contract but lost their case because they'd signed him before his college eligibility expired. A federal judge ruled that Cannon was a naïve country boy who'd been misled about the document he'd signed.

Cannon was a welcome addition for Blanda, who'd played in the NFL. Blanda's former boss, Chicago Bears coach and owner George Halas, belittled the AFL as "a Mickey Mouse league." He added, "How can it be anything else? Isn't George Blanda a first-string quarterback over there?"

Blanda led the Oilers to two straight AFL championships and later joined the Oakland Raiders, with whom he finished a twenty-six-year, 340-game professional career that would land him in the Hall of Fame. Though most experts would suggest AFL teams in the early years were a cut or two below those in the NFL, Blanda insisted the leagues were on a par as far back as the day he made that big throw to Cannon.

"That first year, the Oilers or Chargers could have beaten the NFL in a Super Bowl," he claimed. "I think the AFL was capable of beating the NFL in a Super Bowl game as far back as 1960 or '61. I just regret we didn't get the chance to prove it."

#39
HURTS SO GOOD
DARRELL GREEN'S PAINFUL PUNT RETURN
JANUARY 10, 1988

WASHINGTON REDSKINS coach Joe Gibbs didn't want Darrell Green to return punts except in emergencies. Green, the NFL's fastest player and a premier cornerback, could have been one of the top punt returners in NFL history. But he stood just 5 feet, 9 inches, and Gibbs was leery to let his best pass defender risk injury on special teams.

But Gibbs faced an emergency when the Redskins fell behind 14–0 in a playoff game against the Chicago Bears at Soldier Field. The Redskins rallied for a 14–14 halftime tie, and the Bears had to punt from their end zone early in the third quarter. It was time for Green to give a command performance, despite a wind-chill factor of minus 21 degrees.

Green fielded Tom Barnhardt's punt at the Redskins 48-yard line, near the right sideline. When a defender took a shot at him, Green avoided him with a breathtaking hurdle. He then cut across the field and had clear sailing to the end zone with 11:40 left in the quarter. That proved the decisive play of the Redskins' 21–17 victory that propelled them to their third of four Super Bowl appearances in the first Gibbs era.

The lore of Green's return was enhanced when it was learned that he suffered sprained rib cartilage while making his famous hurdle. Green held his left hand over his ribs for the last 30 yards to ease the pain. The hurdle, he explained, was a spur-of-the-moment move and definitely not premeditated.

"Oh, no, that's a reactionary kind of thing," Green said. "When it was pulled, I put direct pressure on it and was able to put [the ball] into the end zone."

Green returned for one play at cornerback but was in obvious pain and sat out the rest of the game. He'd already broken the Bears' backs. They still had the brilliant talent of their 1985 team that dominated the league during their Super Bowl run, but for the next few years they kept getting tripped up in the playoffs.

Green, amazingly, played twenty seasons for the Redskins without slowing down much. When he came into the NFL in 1983, he had world-class speed, having run 100 meters in 10.08 seconds at Texas A&I. Green had claimed to be the league's fastest player and got the chance to prove it with the inauguration of the NFL's Fastest Man competition in 1986.

Eight players competed in a 40-yard dash, and Green won the annual event the first three times he entered. Among his defeated rivals were U.S. Olympic runners Ron Brown of the Los Angeles Rams, Sam Graddy of the Oakland Raiders, Willie Gault of the Chicago Bears, and world-class hurdler Rod Woodson of the Pittsburgh Steelers. Green's toughest race came in 1986 against Green Bay Packers wide receiver Phillip Epps, whom Green defeated in a photo finish.

"I am the fastest man in the NFL," Green declared. "I can outrun all the defensive linemen, I can outrun all the linebackers, I can outrun all the quarterbacks, I can outrun all the running backs, I can outrun all the coaches, I can outrun all the trainers, I can outrun all the ladies working upstairs in the offices. I can outrun all the general managers, I can outrun all the owners. I've said it before, but no one believed me. Now I have the proof."

He proved it again that frigid day at Soldier Field in a game that also marked an inglorious end to running back Walter Payton's Hall of Fame career. The Bears still had a chance to win until the Redskins stopped Payton inches short of a first down.

Green returned to play against the Minnesota Vikings a week later in the NFC championship game at Washington. Despite needing a pain-killing injection for his rib injury, Green did a decent job covering star wide receiver Anthony Carter. Green was in so much pain that he left the game for five plays but returned late in the fourth quarter after the Redskins scored the touchdown that put them ahead 17–10.

The Vikings faced fourth down at the Washington 6-yard line with just over a minute left. Wade Wilson threw what appeared a likely touchdown pass to running back Darrin Nelson at the 1-yard line. But the receiver was blasted by Green, sore ribs and all, and the pass fell incomplete. "The ball hit my hands, and then it was knocked away," Nelson said. "Any time the ball hits your hands, you should catch it."

The Redskins ran out the clock and were headed for a Super Bowl victory over the Denver Broncos. Green, who weighed 184 pounds, wasn't just the fastest man in the NFL. Pound for pound, he could be one of the toughest, too.

New England cornerback Ty Law reads the pattern of St. Louis Rams wide receiver Isaac Bruce perfectly, then moves into position for an interception. Law returned the ball 47 yards for a touchdown to put the Patriots ahead 7–3 in the February 2002 Super Bowl. That play sparked a 20–17 Patriots win, one of the biggest Super Bowl upsets ever. *Tony Gutierrez/AP Photo*

Indianapolis quarterback Peyton Manning raises his fist triumphantly because he's just thrown his forty-ninth touchdown pass of 2004, breaking Dan Marino's twenty-year-old record. Manning still had work to do, though, because the Colts still trailed the San Diego Chargers 31–29. They got the two-point conversion and won in overtime. *Darron Cummings/AP Photo*

Packers cornerback Al Harris begins to celebrate his game-winning interception as he heads for the end zone ahead of Seattle Seahawks wide receiver Alex Bannister in overtime of a wild-card playoff game in January 2004. Harris and fans at Lambeau Field kept the celebration going at the end of a 33–27 victory. *Mike Roemer/AP Photo*

Tennessee wide receiver Kevin Dyson desperately reaches for the goal line on the final play of the January 2000 Super Bowl, but St. Louis linebacker Mike Jones holds on to Dyson just as desperately. Jones brought him down just short of the goal line to preserve the Rams' 23–16 victory over the Titans. *Mark Humphrey/AP Photo*

Denver quarterback John Elway goes airborne to make the play of the game in the January 1998 Super Bowl against the Green Bay Packers. Linebacker Brian Williams (51) and LeRoy Butler (36) flipped Elway and safety Mike Prior (39) hit him as he landed. Elway gained a first down that set up the Broncos' go-ahead touchdown in their 31–24 upset victory. *Elaine Thompson / AP Photo*

Deion Sanders, never one to pass up the chance to celebrate, plays to the crowd after returning a punt 59 yards for a touchdown in the Dallas Cowboys' 31–7 victory over the Giants in 1998. Sanders played three positions, scored twice, and totaled 226 yards in the Monday night game at Giants Stadium. *John Greilick / AP Photo*

For freezing Cleveland fans, Raiders safety Mike Davis made the most coldhearted play of all. Davis tried to make it appear to Browns quarterback Brian Sipe that tight end Ozzie Newsome was open. Then he cut in front of him to make an interception that clinched Oakland's 14–12 win in a January 1981 playoff game. *AP Photo*

Steelers wide receiver Antwaan Randle El shows the Seattle Seahawks why he played quarterback in college. He throws a 43-yard touchdown pass to Hines Ward on the key play of Pittsburgh's 21–10 Super Bowl victory in February 2006. Tight end Jerame Tuman blocks for Randle El. *David J. Phillip/AP Photo*

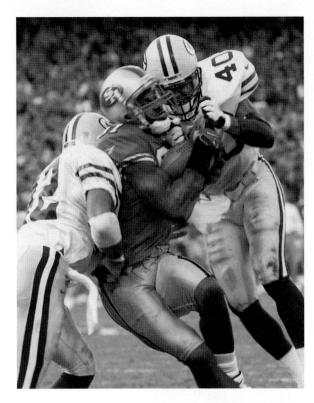

Packers defensive backs Pat Terrell, right, and Darren Sharper combine for a crunching hit on San Francisco wide receiver Terrell Owens. Unfortunately for them, Owens is in the end zone with a 25-yard touchdown pass from Steve Young with three seconds left that gives the 49ers a 30–27 playoff victory in January 1999. *Susan Ragan/ AP Photo*

New England kicker Adam Vinatieri makes the biggest field goal in Super Bowl history, a 48-yarder on the final play to complete the Patriots' 20–17 upset of the Rams in February 2002. Vinatieri gets a good hold from Ken Walter and the Rams' Jerametrius Butler can't get through in time to block the kick. *David J. Phillip/ AP Photo*

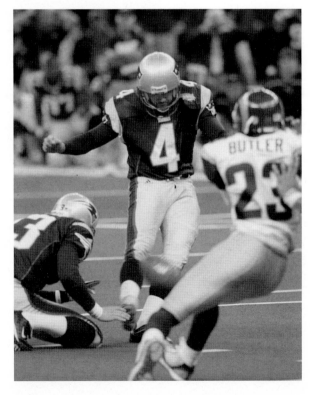

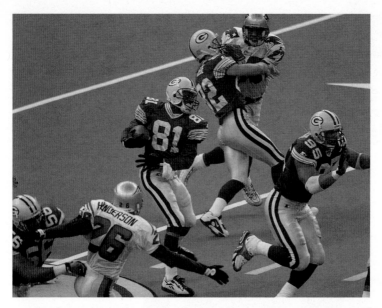

Green Bay's Desmond Howard has a wall of blockers for his 99-yard kickoff return against New England in the January 1997 Super Bowl. Keith McKenzie (95) is out in front while Lamont Hollinquest (56), bottom, keeps Jerome Henderson out of the play and Don Beebe (82) blocks another Patriot. *Mark Duncan/AP Photo*

Washington Redskins defensive end Dexter Manley (72) frantically tries to run down Los Angeles running back Marcus Allen before he busts loose. Nobody could catch Allen as he went 74 yards on a dazzling run that wrapped up the Raiders' 38–9 victory in the January 1984 Super Bowl. *AP Photo*

The Titans' Kevin Dyson streaks 75 yards down the sideline to pull off the Music City Miracle, the trick kickoff return that defeated the Buffalo Bills 22–16 in a January 2000 playoff game. Quarterback Steve McNair (9) watches in shocked disbelief from the Tennessee bench while the crowd in Nashville goes berserk. *Wade Payne/AP Photo*

Pittsburgh Steelers wide receiver Lynn Swann completes one of his three spectacular catches in a 21–17 victory over the Dallas Cowboys in the January 1976 Super Bowl. Though cornerback Mark Washington had him covered, Swann leaped for the ball, bobbled it in the air, and hauled it in while falling on his back. *AP Photo*

Baltimore fullback Alan "The Horse" Ameche plows through a huge hole for the touchdown that climaxed a 23–17 overtime victory over the New York Giants in the 1958 NFL championship game. Colts halfback Lenny Moore, left, takes safety Emlen Tunnell out of the play and safety Jim Patton (20) can't reach the hole in time. *AP Photo*

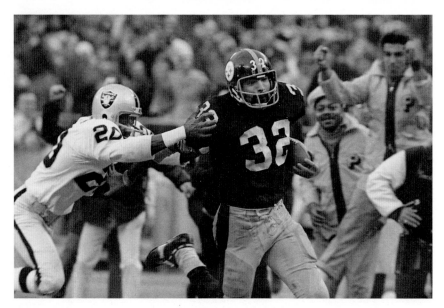

Pittsburgh running back Franco Harris heads for the end zone to complete The Immaculate Reception, the greatest play in pro football history. Harris made a shoestring catch of a deflected pass and turned a near-certain Steeler defeat into a 13–7 victory over the Oakland Raiders in the 1972 playoffs. Defensive back Jimmy Warren, above, was the last Raider to get a hand on Harris. *Harry Cabluck/AP Photo*

#38

SUPER GADGET
ANTWAAN RANDLE EL FLAUNTS HIS ARM
FEBRUARY 5, 2006

SUPER BOWLS are not famous for trick plays because few coaches care to get cute in the biggest game of their lives. And nobody ever accused Pittsburgh Steelers coach Bill Cowher of being cute, especially not when a scowl formed above that famous chin. Cowher has a weakness for gadget plays, though, and one of them proved a key play in the Steelers' 21–10 Super Bowl victory over the Seattle Seahawks.

With the Steelers ahead 14–10 and at the Seahawks 43-yard line in the fourth quarter, offensive coordinator Ken Whisenhunt called for "Fake 39 Toss X-Reverse Pass." This meant that quarterback Ben Roethlisberger would toss the ball to running back Willie Parker (number 39), who would head around left end. Parker would then pitch the ball to wide receiver Antwaan Randle El, who would pretend to run a reverse to his right but throw deep to wide receiver Hines Ward. Roethlisberger, noted for his enthusiastic physical play, would block.

"I saw the free safety blitz and blocked him," Roethlisberger recalled. "I saw Antwaan throw it and Hines catch it. It was an amazing feeling."

Randle El, the first wide receiver ever to throw a touchdown pass in a Super Bowl game, was the perfect guy for this play. He was a star quarterback at Indiana, and his throw for Ward, who was running toward the right corner of the end zone, was right on the money. Ward was wide open and caught the ball in stride at the 2-yard line before scoring with 6:56 left.

"As soon as I let it go," Randle El said, "I was like, 'Oooh, catch it!' And Hines did. That's something we've been doing for a long time. We hit that one earlier in the season for a touchdown, and we had it set up for this game. It's one thing to throw a touchdown in the regular season, but the Super Bowl? Wow! When he called it, my eyes lit up, and I had to try not to give it away. What went through my mind was hope.

"I felt somebody coming from the backside from the other end and hoped Ben got him on the cutdown. I knew Hines was going to cut free, but if Hines didn't get free, I had Willie Parker on the sideline."

That play broke the Seahawks' backs and gave the Steelers their long-sought "one for the thumb," a fifth Super Bowl victory to go with the four Lombardi trophies they won in the 1970s. It also enabled Ward to finish with five catches for 123 yards and earn MVP honors.

Randle El and Ward used the same play to hook up for a 51-yard touchdown pass in a 34–21 victory over the Cleveland Browns in mid-November. The Steelers decided to reach into their bag of tricks again, partly because two of the Seahawks' starting defensive backs were injured during the Super Bowl and the play had been set up by a wide receiver reverse. "We've been working on that play for seven weeks," tackle Max Starks said. "We knew they were overpursuing our toss play."

Though tough defense and a bruising running game have been hallmarks of Cowher's teams, he's notorious for pestering his offensive coordinators with ideas for trick plays. Being able to employ the versatility of Randle El and Ward, also a quarterback in high school, only increased Cowher's appetite for gadgets.

"The guys get tired of practicing those plays because you don't call them," Whisenhunt said. "They were in the right defense, and I felt like it was the right time."

Ward's touchdown catch helped soothe the disappointment of dropping a pass in the end zone late in the second quarter when the Steelers trailed 3–0. Three plays later, though, when the drive was losing steam, Ward caught a 37-yard pass at the 3-yard line and set up the Steelers' first touchdown.

"I dropped the first touchdown because I was worried about my feet," he said. "I usually don't get caught up in drops, I just work to redeem myself. The great ones don't miss balls in the Super Bowl. You can't do that and be considered great."

While every misstep is magnified in a Super Bowl, so is every success. Randle El was handed a contract for $40,000 to cross the street after the game and tape a brief segment for the *Jimmy Kimmel Show*. The Super Bowl payoff was just starting for him because after the game Randle El became a free agent. A month later, he signed a seven-year contract with the Washington Redskins potentially worth $31 million.

That was a pretty neat trick for a number-two wide receiver. But then again, so was his pass that clinched a Super Bowl win.

#37
THE LONGEST KICK
TOM DEMPSEY STUNS THE LIONS
NOVEMBER 8, 1970

THE MOST IMPROBABLE part of Tom Dempsey's record-breaking, 63-yard field goal wasn't that he made it. It's that he was kicking at all.

Dempsey was born with no toes on his right foot, his kicking foot, and no right hand. Yet in 1969 he became the New Orleans Saints placekicker, thanks to a special shoe with a plate on the front. The Saints came into the NFL in 1967 and didn't win often during their first two decades. But one early victory remains unforgettable.

The Saints, on their way to a 2–11–1 finish, were facing the playoff-bound Detroit Lions at Tulane Stadium. The Saints appeared out of luck again when Errol Mann kicked an 18-yard field goal to give the Lions a 17–16 lead with eleven seconds left. Saints offensive coordinator Don Heinrich called down to the sideline and told the coaches to get Dempsey ready. Heinrich planned to have the kickoff returner quickly get out of bounds, try to complete one sideline pass and give Dempsey a shot at a long field goal.

"I don't think anybody had a 63-yarder in mind, but I knew all along we were going to try for a long one," Dempsey told *Football Digest*. "We lined it up, and I didn't even look up to see how far away we were. I didn't want to know. I just wanted to put my head down and kick it as hard as I could. A lot of people probably didn't think we could do it. The Lions probably didn't think we could do it."

A bizarre series of events conspired to allow this historic kick. On the Lions' go-ahead drive, which started with 6:42 left, an official mistakenly let them have an extra down deep in their territory. They should have been forced to punt with about four minutes left. But the Saints caught a break when Lions quarterback Greg Landry called time-out right after a running play that set up the go-ahead field goal. He could have let the clock run down to a few seconds and made sure that Mann's kick ended the game.

The Saints got more help when officials ruled a 17-yard pass from Billy Kilmer to Al Dodd, which set up Dempsey's kick, was legal. Films showed that Dodd didn't have both feet in bounds when he made the catch at the Saints' 45-yard line, which gave Dempsey a chance because the goal posts were still on the goal lines then. The field goal unit came out with two seconds left.

"By now, the stadium was half empty," Dempsey said. "A lot of people had left, thinking we had lost. But I think 300,000 people have claimed to have been at that game."

Dempsey's main worry was that swirling winds might push his kick wide, as they often could in that stadium. He told his holder, Joe Scarpati, to line up eight yards deep, instead of the usual seven, and asked his linemen to hold their blocks longer than usual. "I tried to do it like I do on a kickoff," Dempsey explained. "I started my left foot six inches back of where it is on a regular kick to get more leg swing."

The Lions didn't put on a heavy rush because they didn't want to jump offside and move Dempsey 5 yards closer. Also, they didn't seriously expect Dempsey to make the kick, which was seven yards longer than the NFL record. That was set by Bert Rechichar of the Baltimore Colts in 1953.

"I was confident I could make this kick, even though there wasn't much breeze and the balls hadn't been carrying much that day," Dempsey said. "But I had made field goals from way past that point in practice many times."

He had been struggling on game days, however. Partly because of a pulled hip muscle, Dempsey had made only five of fifteen kicks in 1970 before that game. But against the Lions, he'd already kicked field goals from 29, 27, and 8 yards. A former junior college defensive end, Dempsey put all of his 275 pounds behind the kick.

"I got a perfect snap, I got a perfect hold, and I got a lot of protection," he recalled. "I thought I kicked it pretty well—thought it had a chance. I was hoping the winds wouldn't swirl and drive the ball off course. It seemed like it took forever to get there. I just kept watching it, wondering if it had enough distance. Finally, the referees raised their hands that it was good."

Dempsey's teammates mobbed him, and fans spilled out onto the field. He couldn't reach the locker room for fifteen minutes. The Lions, meanwhile, were still reeling.

"You'll never see it again," coach Joe Schmidt said. "It's like winning the Masters with a 390-yard hole-in-one on the last shot."

Mann was impressed, too. "He could stand there and kick it two hundred times and not hit it that sweet again," he said. "Boy, did he ever hit it sweet."

Added Lions linebacker Wayne Walker: "Dempsey didn't kick that football. God did."

Just about the only person in the league not praising Dempsey was Dallas Cowboys general manager Tex Schramm. He complained that Dempsey's unusually large kicking surface gave him an unfair advantage. Schramm was harshly criticized for his remarks and backed off. But in 1977 the NFL passed a rule that stated, "A shoe on an artificial limb must have a kicking surface that conforms to that of a normal kicking shoe." This was nicknamed the "Tom Dempsey Rule" and applied to him, even though his right foot was not artificial.

The biggest tribute to Dempsey's achievement is that, despite an increase in domed stadiums and uniform playing surfaces, his record wasn't even tied until Jason Elam of the Denver Broncos kicked a 63-yarder in 1998. Dempsey sent him a letter of congratulations, and Elam replied with a phone call.

"I wanted to congratulate Jason because when I set the record Bert Rechichar was very gracious to me," Dempsey said. "I told Jason that if someone breaks our record, it would be up to him to do the same thing. He just laughed."

#36

T. O. STEPS OUT
TERRELL OWENS'S CAREER-CHANGING CATCH
JANUARY 3, 1999

IT'S HARD TO BELIEVE that once upon a time, Terrell Owens did not command center stage in every production in which he performed. Before he became T. O., the NFL's most volatile and controversial player, Owens was an up-and-coming San Francisco 49ers wide receiver trying to make a name for himself.

Owens remained relatively unnoticed until he caught a game-winning touchdown pass from Steve Young in a first-round playoff game against the Green Bay Packers at Candlestick Park. That catch, for better or worse, began his transformation into T. O.

"That game changed my career," Owens wrote in his autobiography. "That one play turned me into a hero set on a path toward stardom. One play can really mean that much. This game is very unforgiving, and all it takes is one play to haunt a player for the remainder of his career. At the same time, one catch can make a player into a hero forever."

Despite leading the 49ers in touchdowns for two straight years and posting his first 1,000-yard receiving season in 1998, Owens was still playing second fiddle to teammate Jerry Rice. For most of the playoff game against the Packers, Owens wasn't even part of the band. He dropped four passes, including one in the end zone. When he finally made a catch, he fumbled it away.

When a Wade Richey field goal broke a 20–20 tie with 4:19 left, it seemed that the 49ers would be able to survive Owens's miscues. However, Brett Favre led the Packers on an 89-yard scoring drive, climaxed by a 15-yard touchdown pass to wide receiver Antonio Freeman with 1:56 left.

This game had already had four lead changes and three ties when the 49ers started their final drive at their 24-yard line with 1:50 left. Young, throwing mostly short passes, guided the 49ers downfield. They caught a break when Rice was ruled down at the Green Bay 41 after a 6-yard catch, though he'd clearly fumbled. Still, the 49ers were running out of chances when they faced third-and-3 at the 25 with only eight seconds left and no time-outs remaining.

On their decisive play, the 49ers called the "All Go Double Comeback," which, Owens recalled, "was designed for two receivers on the outside to run straight into the end zone by the sidelines and for two other receivers to slant inside toward the middle of the end zone."

Owens ran an inside route, and safeties Pat Terrell and Darren Sharper converged on him. Young, meanwhile, was having trouble merely getting rid of the ball. He stumbled after taking the snap and had to regain his footing. Then he fired a bullet into the end zone to Owens, right between the defenders. Owens held on to the ball, despite getting hammered and knocked to the ground. That catch, with three seconds left, gave the 49ers a 30–27 victory and snapped a five-game losing streak against the Packers, the two-time defending NFC champions.

"I wanted that ball like I never wanted anything in my life," Owens wrote. "As I jumped for it, I could see nothing but the ball, while the two defenders were coming to take my head off from both sides. They could have been armed with baseball bats, and I was still going to get that ball. I made the catch! I scored! We won! Game over!"

Owens remained highly emotional in the locker room and thanked his teammates, especially Young, and coaches for sticking with him despite the drops. Such displays of humility from the receiver have been rare ever since. As Young and other veterans who'd been anchors for Owens retired, his behavior became increasingly outrageous. When he caught a touchdown pass at Seattle in 2002 and pulled a Sharpie out of his sock to autograph the ball for a friend in the stands, Owens began a pattern of show-stopping celebrations that made him a lightning rod for attention and criticism.

He feuded with 49ers quarterback Jeff Garcia and went to the Philadelphia Eagles in 2004, finishing the season with a brilliant Super Bowl performance. The next year, however, he demanded a new contract, was briefly kicked out of training camp, and feuded with quarterback Donovan McNabb.

Owens moved on to the Dallas Cowboys in 2006 and early in the season was hospitalized for what was described as an accidental overdose of painkiller tablets. His season was filled with controversies, including a $35,000 fine for spitting in the face of Atlanta Falcons cornerback DeAngelo Hall.

Nobody has fully explained how a humble young player turned into troublesome T. O. But it's easy to identify when Owens was first recognized as a premier receiver—when he made as big and as tough a catch as anybody could make in a playoff game.

"I gained a tremendous amount of confidence in myself," Owens wrote, "and knew deep down now that I was a winner."

#35
CHARLIE HITCH
DOUG WILLIAMS STARTS A RAMPAGE
JANUARY 31, 1988

WASHINGTON REDSKINS quarterback Doug Williams didn't seem in the best of shape to throw one of the most important passes in any Super Bowl.

The day before the biggest game of his career, Williams needed an emergency root-canal procedure. A twisted knee forced him out of the game for one play late in the first quarter, and the Denver Broncos led 10–0. John Elway, considered the marquee quarterback of this Super Bowl, already had completed a long touchdown pass.

But from the opening play of the second quarter, it was Williams who owned the stage. He was at his own 20-yard line and was supposed to throw "Charlie Hitch," a 7-yard pass to wide receiver Ricky Sanders. But cornerback Mark Haynes bumped Sanders at the line of scrimmage, and he adjusted by running deep. Sanders beat Haynes, caught a perfect pass from Williams at the 50, and sprinted into the end zone. That 80-yard pass tied for the longest ever in a Super Bowl.

"The turning point," was how Redskins coach Joe Gibbs described that play. "You could feel the sidelines come alive. We caught fire."

The Redskins erupted for a thirty-five-point second quarter as Williams played like the player so many expected him to become when he was the first overall pick of the 1978 draft. His bomb to Sanders was the first of four touchdown passes that sent the Redskins on their way to a 42–10 victory. Wide receiver Gary Clark, running the same pattern as Sanders, beat Steve Wilson for a 27-yard touchdown catch. On a play fake, Williams hit Sanders with a 50-yard touchdown pass. Williams finished his scoring binge with an 8-yard pass to tight end Clint Didier. The Redskins' other second-quarter touchdown came on a 58-yard run by Charlie Smith, who finished the game with 204 yards.

"Doug was hitting everybody, no matter what you did," Clark said. "If it didn't work, it was the receiver's fault."

Williams was named MVP, which was nothing out of the ordinary for the winning quarterback in the Super Bowl. Williams, however, was the first black quarterback ever to start in a Super Bowl, and that was during an era when black quarterbacks still struggled for equal opportunities. Only a decade earlier, it was considered a major breakthrough for black quarterbacks when Williams, a big, strong, pro-style passer from Grambling, was drafted so high by the Tampa Bay Buccaneers.

"I'm no Jackie Robinson," he insisted, trying to downplay the historic significance of his Super Bowl performance.

Yet Williams's performance helped shatter the stereotype that blacks lacked the smarts, leadership, and passing skills for the game's most important position. His saga, like that of Jim Plunkett and Kurt Warner, also underlined that merely being in the right place at the right time can separate a championship quarterback from a journeyman.

Williams's rocky climb to the top prompted President Ronald Reagan, upon greeting the Redskins at the White House, to credit him with having had "one of the most inspiring performances displayed by any quarterback in football history."

Williams often struggled with accuracy, and even in the 1979 season, when the Buccaneers reached the NFC championship game, he completed just 41.8 percent of his passes. His passer rating topped 70 only once in his first five years, so it wasn't surprising that the Buccaneers balked at giving him a new contract after the 1982 season.

Soon after that, Williams's wife died because of a brain tumor, and he was left with an infant daughter to raise. He went to the United States Football League and dropped off the NFL's radar. When the USFL folded in 1985, Williams was out of football until Gibbs, his position coach at Tampa Bay, asked him to back up Jay Schroeder in 1986.

Williams threw just one pass in 1986 but became the Redskins' starter when Schroeder was injured in the 1987 opener. Williams wasn't steady enough to claim the job for keeps until the last regular-season game. He leaned on his defense during the playoffs until he turned into an offensive force in the Super Bowl.

"The Redskins didn't bring me here to become the first black quarterback in the Super Bowl," Williams said. "They brought me here to be the quarterback of a Super Bowl team."

#34
A GIANT HIT
LEONARD MARSHALL RUINS 49ERS CHANCES
JANUARY 20, 1991

DEFENSIVE END LEONARD MARSHALL'S bone-rattling tackle shattered Joe Montana's invincibility and broke his right hand. That was the kind of ferocity to expect when the New York Giants and San Francisco 49ers met for the NFC championship.

Montana had led the 49ers to four Super Bowl victories, but against the Giants this championship quarterback was facing a championship defense. The 49ers had defeated the Giants 7–3 the previous month on the same Candlestick Park field, so it came as no surprise when another low-scoring dogfight developed.

The 49ers led 13–9 early in the fourth quarter when Marshall blasted Montana and forced him out of the game with a bruised sternum and fractured pinky finger on his passing hand. Rushing from his right side, Marshall was blocked by fullback Tom Rathman, and both went down in a tangle. Marshall got on his hands and knees, scrambled to his feet, and had a clear path to Montana's blind side.

The injury blow was especially devastating for the 49ers because they didn't have a running game to take over in Montana's absence. Though they'd lost only twice that season, the 49ers had no back who'd rushed for even 500 yards. Montana's 61-yard touchdown pass to wide receiver John Taylor in the third quarter provided the only touchdown against the Giants.

The Giants exploited the 49ers' one-dimensional offense with frequent blitzes. In their December matchup, the Giants forced Montana to throw with rare inaccuracy. In the rematch, he completed eighteen of twenty-six passes for 190 yards but was sacked three times and repeatedly pressured. His running game produced just 39 yards on eleven carries.

"We weren't worried about the run; we knew we had to stop Montana," said Giants linebacker Pepper Johnson. "We got after him early and often. I don't care who you are—even the greatest quarterback—you won't be successful with pressure in your face. That was the key to this game—we got to Joe Montana."

Montana would recover from his injuries but never started again for the 49ers because of an elbow ailment. He said Marshall's hit was the hardest he'd ever taken.

"It was a good, clean hit, just a football hit, but I knew it hurt him bad," Marshall said. "I knew he wasn't going to be back. I could hear him moaning."

Montana remained in pain after the game. "I still don't know what happened," he said. "I'm still having a tough time breathing deeply."

The Giants threatened retaliation shortly before Montana's injury when their quarterback, Jeff Hostetler, was laid out for several minutes after taking a helmet on the knee from tackle Jim Burt, a former Giant. Hostetler, who took over at quarterback after Phil Simms was injured late in the season, left the game for one series.

"I yelled at Burt," Giants linebacker Lawrence Taylor said. "I hollered, 'If that's the way you want to play, that's how we'll play.' But someone else was going to lose a quarterback."

Marshall said he initially considered Burt's hit as a cheap shot but after reviewing the play suggested it was a good hustle play. "Hitting Montana was the same thing for me," he said. "I just wanted to make a play to help my team win. I was hoping to hit him, cause a fumble, and have L. T. grab the ball out of the air and run it in, and have a glamorous touchdown. That's what was going through my mind."

Marshall's play was big enough as it was. The 49ers had to punt, and their defense held the Giants—until linebacker Gary

Reasons ran 30 yards on a fake punt, setting up a 38-yard field goal by Matt Bahr that made the score 13–12 with 5:47 left.

Steve Young replaced Montana and completed a 24-yard pass to tight end Brent Jones. Otherwise, Young just handed off as the 49ers tried to run out the clock. But nose tackle Erik Howard forced Roger Craig to fumble on a first-down run up the middle, and Taylor recovered at the Giants 43-yard line with 2:36 left. Hostetler led the Giants into position for Bahr's fifth field goal, a 42-yard kick on the final play for a 15–13 victory. Marshall threw himself to the turf and gleefully banged his helmet on the ground.

Though some may consider Howard's play bigger than Marshall's, it's hard to overestimate the impact of Montana's loss. The 49ers seldom made critical mistakes with him in charge, as evidenced by their victories in four of five previous NFC championship games. NFL Films, accordingly, ranked Marshall's hit as the defensive gem of that game.

Marshall totaled four tackles, two sacks, and two forced fumbles against the 49ers. A week later he had the Giants' only sack of a 20–19 Super Bowl victory over the Buffalo Bills. He had made two Super Bowl sacks of Denver's John Elway four years earlier.

"When you have an opportunity to play and showcase your talents to the world, you should do so," Marshall said. "One thing [coach Bill] Parcells would say to me all the time was, 'Leonard, you show up big-time in big games. Big-time athletes show up in big-time games.' And if you go back and look at the history of any game that we've ever had of that caliber, I've always outplayed guys at my position."

#33
KEY TO THE COMEBACK
FRANK REICH CLICKS WITH ANDRE REED
JANUARY 3, 1993

LOOK AT ANY FANTASTIC COMEBACK, and you'll find at least one point where it almost died. The greatest comeback in NFL history almost stalled when the Bills faced fourth-and-5 at the Houston 18 late in the third quarter of a wild-card playoff game at Buffalo.

The Bills narrowed a 35–3 deficit to 35–24 during the third quarter, and the high-percentage decision on fourth down would've been to try a field goal. Coach Marv Levy, however, saw a miracle within his grasp and didn't want to let it slip away. He decided to go for the first down—and got much more than that.

Quarterback Frank Reich hit wide receiver Andre Reed for a touchdown pass with 2:00 left in the third period and closed the gap to 35–31. That was the Bills' fourth touchdown in fewer than seven minutes, and without it their 41–38 win over the Oilers instead would have been remembered as just a gallant effort that came up short.

"I told the other coaches, if we hit a fourth down, we're going for it if it's anywhere near reasonable distance for the first down," Levy recalled. "I didn't know that we'd get a touchdown on the play, but the reasoning was that if we made a field goal, we were still down by eight. The quarter was nearly over, and we'd be going into the wind, and you'd have to get very close to try a field goal in the fourth quarter."

Levy called time-out and asked Reich and offensive coordinator Jim Shofner to select a play likely to pick up a first down. When other coaches disagreed, Levy reassured Reich and Shofner, "If that's the play you want, that's the play we're using."

Reed and tight end Keith McKeller ran routes down the middle. Reed broke wide open and scored as the Oilers' secondary continued to come unglued. "We only have so much time that we have to make a gutsy call," Reed said. "We gotta call this play."

As the comeback gathered steam, fans who had walked out in disgust came speeding back to Rich Stadium. When ticket attendants wouldn't let them back through the gates, they climbed the fences.

The Bills' historic comeback was happening despite the absence of three stars of their Super Bowl era. Quarterback Jim Kelly and linebacker Cornelius Bennett were out with injuries, and running back Thurman Thomas had been knocked out of the game.

At least Reich was experienced in seemingly lost causes. He'd led the biggest comeback in major college football history. Against the Oilers, Reich had a hot hand again and threw four touchdown passes in the second half. His third, and most crucial one, was set up when cornerback Henry Jones intercepted a Warren Moon pass and returned it to the Houston 23-yard line. Four plays later, he hit pay dirt with Reed.

The Oilers drove to the Buffalo 14-yard line in the fourth quarter but botched a field-goal try with a bobbled snap. Kenneth Davis, replacing Thomas, broke loose for 35 yards on a drive that Reich ended with a 17-yard touchdown pass to Reed with 3:08 left. The Bills finally led, 38–35, but Al Del Greco's 26-yard field goal with twelve seconds left sent the game into overtime.

The Oilers got the ball first in overtime, but an interception by cornerback Nate Odomes set up a 32-yard field goal by Steve Christie. That win propelled the Bills to two more playoff victories and their third of four straight Super Bowl appearances.

"Here we were, AFC champions, being humiliated at home in the playoffs," Levy said, referring to a 28–3 halftime deficit. "There was no great pep talk like you'd see in the movies. Halftime is only twelve minutes long. I really had only three minutes to make adjustments. The only thing I recall saying to our players was, 'You are two-time defending AFC champions. When you walk off the field thirty minutes from now, don't let anybody say that you quit or gave up.'

"Whether it meant anything or not, I don't know, but on our first possession of the second half, the ball went off [McKeller's] hands, and the Oilers ran it back for a touchdown to make it 35–3. On the kickoff, the kicker flubbed it, and it somehow hit one of our front five players, and they nearly recovered the ball. We got it, though, and we scored on the next play. Then we recovered an onside kick, scored quickly, and got back in the game.

"It was beautiful—a remarkable event. You have to coach for forty-seven years to have a few moments like that occur, and it's one that I very much treasure."

Reich enjoyed two such moments in one decade. With Maryland trailing 31–0 at Miami in 1984, he relieved Stan Gelbaugh and rallied the Terrapins to a 42–40 win. Yet he had to pinch himself to believe he'd pulled off a similar stunt in an NFL playoff game.

"I guess there have been a couple of times when my wife and I would look at each other and say, 'Did that really happen?'" Reich said. "We just kinda shake our heads in awe of the game. We had to shut them down on every count. I don't look at it like a choke [by the Oilers]. I look at it as a miracle from God."

#32
A FINISHING TOUCH
MONTANA CLOSES A DEAL IN DENVER
OCTOBER 17, 1994

GREAT QUARTERBACKS finish what they started. The difference between the great Joe and the average Joes has never been more evident than at crunch time. The average Joes lead a team inside the red zone in the final minutes only to come up short.

Joe Montana, more often than not, closed the deal. Except for "The Catch" and his Super Bowl–winning pass to John Taylor, none of Montana's last-minute throws captures that knack better than a 5-yard touchdown pass to Willie Davis.

"Lord, you can take me now, I've seen it all," ABC announcer Dan Dierdorf exclaimed after Montana's throw gave the Kansas City Chiefs a 31–28 victory on a Monday night in Denver.

This was one of Montana's greatest touchdown passes partly because it came at a stage of his career when he was running out of magic. He was traded to the Chiefs in 1993 after losing his starting job in San Francisco. And this touchdown's drama was magnified because it trumped one by the Broncos' John Elway, whose ability to finish off last-minute touchdown drives in big games also helped define his greatness.

"Those kind of battles you get in are the fun games for a quarterback," Montana said. "You're going against the guy that you know, if you let him back on the field, he'll do the same thing back to you."

Elway's 4-yard run from the shotgun formation gave the Broncos a 28–24 lead with just 1:29 left. That was plenty of time for Montana, at thirty-eight, to generate yet another comeback and end the Chiefs' eleven-game losing streak at Mile High Stadium.

Montana took over at his own 25-yard line and guided the Chiefs down the field. They got a first down at the Broncos' 5-yard line and called time-out with thirteen seconds left. On the next play, Davis, a wide receiver, went down the right side and outmaneuvered cornerback Ben Smith. Montana drilled a pass to Davis just in front of the goal line, and Davis made one more move to get in the end zone with eight seconds left.

"They played off me in a zone," Davis said. "I was the third receiver on the play. The man was inside of me. Joe threw it to where it had to be, on the outside."

Montana not only spotted Davis but also Joe's wife, Jennifer, and one of their daughters. "He makes a great catch, squeezes it in the end zone, and it was right in front of my wife and daughter, who happened to be on the field," Montana recalled. "She was working for one of the TV stations there, and I kind of knew in the back of my mind that it was closing in on the end of my career, and to be able to do that and have them there was pretty special."

On the Chiefs' last drive, the Broncos played a soft prevent defense. "We felt we had a pretty good chance," Montana said. "We knew they'd concede a certain part of the field to us, so we could throw underneath. We did that and kept moving."

On the winning drive, Montana completed seven of eight passes for 65 yards. Running back Marcus Allen made amends for a costly fumble by making an 8-yard catch and a 10-yard run and getting out of bounds to stop the clock after both plays. Montana kept stinging the Broncos with short passes, then threw to little-used tight end Tracy Greene for 19 yards to the 5-yard line. The Broncos finally tightened their defense, but it was too late.

"Guys laugh about playing the prevent defense, that all it does is prevent you from winning," Montana said after throwing for 393 yards and three touchdowns. "We figured they would give us some room. Most teams try to stop you, but when you've got a long way to go, they don't put a lot of pressure on you until you get around midfield. They'll concede a certain amount of yards, figuring that will eat up a lot of the clock."

Considering that Montana was the master of the ball-control passing attack, the Broncos were playing right into his hands. "We had to be willing to throw the ball underneath," Chiefs coach Marty Schottenheimer said. "He did a masterful job of it. The key element in the whole thing was pass protection. He stood, and he looked, and he looked, and he looked, and that gave us a chance to make those plays."

Defensive coordinators who confront a two-minute drill consider the prevent defense as unbeatable as a blackjack dealer. The odds are in the house's favor, and most quarterbacks will lose. Montana, though, made the Hall of Fame by beating the dealer.

"All we had to do was tackle them in bounds," Broncos coach Wade Phillips said with exasperation. "We played it so soft that when they caught the ball in the flat we didn't have anyone there to keep them in bounds."

Montana already had guided three touchdown drives, and it didn't seem that a fourth would be necessary. A fumble by Broncos tight end Shannon Sharpe gave the Chiefs the ball with a 24–21 lead and 2:45 left. But on the next play, nose tackle Ted Washington stripped the ball from Allen and linebacker Karl Mecklenburg recovered the fumble. Elway was back in business at the Kansas City 39-yard line and needed about a minute to put the Broncos back ahead.

Montana not only regained the lead but left just eight seconds for Elway, who threw incomplete, then was sacked on the final play. Elway threw for 263 yards and two touchdowns, and Montana knew better than to give him too many more chances.

"That's how everybody feels with John," Montana said. "You can't afford to give a player that relishes being in that time of the game any time on the clock. And the best thing you can see is when it says "zero," because then you know, even if he's got the ball in his hand, he can't do anything with it."

#31
THE GREAT ESCAPE
DAVE KRIEG TURNS A SACK INTO A SCORE
NOVEMBER 11, 1990

ONE MOMENT, DAVE KRIEG was about to be sacked for the tenth time in one game. The next moment, he made a breathtaking escape and gave the Seattle Seahawks one of the most remarkable game-winning plays in NFL history.

The Kansas City Chiefs sacked Krieg nine times, including seven times by Derrick Thomas, a second-year linebacker. Thomas broke the league's single-game record of six sacks, and his third forced a Krieg fumble that was recovered in the end zone by tackle Dan Saleaumua. That gave the Chiefs a 16–10 lead, which they held right up to the game's final play.

Thomas had been eating Seahawk blockers for lunch all day and was stepping in for dessert on the last play. Instead, he got a taste of bitter defeat.

The Seahawks were at the Kansas City 25-yard line, and Thomas once again got his arms on Krieg. Thomas merely had to reel him in for his eighth sack. Krieg, however, managed to wiggle off the hook and throw a strike to wide receiver Paul Skansi in the middle of the end zone. Norm Johnson's extra point gave the Seahawks a 17–16 victory.

The Arrowhead Stadium crowd, which had been raucous as usual all day, fell stone quiet. "That was one of the greatest victories in the history of the franchise," Seahawks guard Bryan Millard said. "This team has a never-say-die attitude, and you have to give a lot of credit to Dave Krieg. In order to be a championship team, you have to have a championship-type quarterback. And Dave can be that."

Krieg never did lead a team to a championship, which explains why, despite his 38,147 yards and 261 touchdown passes, many less-productive quarterbacks are better remembered. His legacy also suffers because of his propensity for fumbling. Because of his small hands and porous lines, Krieg totaled 153 fumbles, including six in a 20–10 home loss to the Chiefs in 1989.

Krieg, however, also played in twelve postseason games and was selected to three Pro Bowls. Until the Seahawks reached the Super Bowl in the 2005 season, he was the only quarterback to lead them to a conference championship game. Krieg's trademark was a flair for leading improbable comebacks, as the Chiefs learned the hard way.

"The key is that Dave puts us in position to win games," Millard said. "I'm not sure what happens in the first fifty-nine-and-a-half minutes, but with Dave, we know we can win in those last thirty seconds."

Thomas was stunned by what happened in the waning seconds that day at Arrowhead Stadium. "I would've felt a lot better had we won the game," said Thomas, who broke the single-game sacks record set by the San Francisco 49ers' Fred Dean in 1983. "Maybe ten or twenty years down the road, I'll look at it as a major accomplishment. But right now, it lingers in my mind as a loss."

Thomas finished the season with twenty sacks, at that time the fifth-highest total in NFL history. A year later, he and Krieg became teammates in Kansas City. The Seahawks let Krieg go because they wanted to take a good look at Dan McGwire, a 6-foot-8 raw talent and brother of eventual major league home-run king Mark McGwire. The Seahawks quickly decided he wasn't the answer.

Krieg paid the Chiefs back for breaking their hearts by topping 3,000 yards passing as their starter in 1992 and leading them into the playoffs. He only stayed there one more year, however, because in 1993 he lost his starting job to a better-known comeback quarterback—Joe Montana.

Just like the guy who'd been sacked nine times in one game, Krieg kept popping up and making comebacks. He went on to the Detroit Lions, the Arizona Cardinals, the Chicago Bears, and finally the Houston Oilers in 1997 and 1998. Krieg wanted to play in 1999, which would have been his twentieth NFL season, but couldn't find a team that was interested in him. Only then did he finally run out of comebacks.

#30
TOUCHDOWN TONY
DORSETT'S SHORT-HANDED RECORD RUN
JANUARY 3, 1983

FORMER DALLAS COWBOYS running back Tony Dorsett doesn't have to worry about anybody breaking his most famous record. His 99-yard run against the Minnesota Vikings was the longest in NFL history and might be tied but not broken, unless the NFL lengthens the playing field. And it's an excellent bet that Dorsett's 99-yard run will always remain the only one ever achieved with just ten offensive players on the field.

Golden memories are scarce from the 1982 season. A fifty-seven-day players' strike resulted in a nine-weekend season, which came to an unlamented end when the Cowboys lost 31–27 to the Vikings at Minnesota on a Monday night. Few remember or care much about that game, except for what Dorsett did when he got the ball at his 1-yard line.

"The ball was as close to the goal line as any ball could get," he recalled.

The Cowboys, looking for some room to operate, called for a handoff to fullback Ron Springs. However, Springs misunderstood the call and stayed on the sideline, leaving the Cowboys a man short. Dorsett instead took the handoff from quarterback Danny White in the end zone and hit the middle against a bunched-up defense.

Just as it appeared he had nowhere to go, Dorsett found a big hole off tackle. He cut to the right sideline, picked up a key block from wide receiver Drew Pearson, and used his balance to avoid getting knocked out of bounds at the Minnesota 25-yard line.

"He hit [the hole] flying," Vikings defensive end Doug Martin said. "Before anyone realized anything, he was down the field fifty yards. There was nothing we could possibly do."

Dorsett had the same impression. "I just saw a lot of green," he recalled. "When I came to the sideline, [player personnel director] Gil Brandt said, 'I think that was an NFL record.' And the first thing that came to mind was, I should've kept the ball."

A Heisman Trophy winner at the University of Pittsburgh, Dorsett was an instinctive runner with a knack for turning broken plays into big runs. But when he joined the Cowboys in 1977, coach Tom Landry wanted Dorsett to trust the playbook more than his instincts.

During his rookie season, Dorsett's runs often bore little resemblance to how they were drawn up. His style resulted in a 77-yard touchdown run early in the season but also led to blowups with offensive assistant coach Dan Reeves.

"You drafted me as a runner; let me run!" Dorsett yelled at Reeves when the back was chewed out during a game. "I'm tired of being a robot."

Landry, much to his team's amazement, agreed that Dorsett had a point. The day after the blowup with Reeves, he announced in a team meeting that he was giving Dorsett the freedom to pick his holes. "Guys, usually the back has to adjust to our offense, but we're going to adjust to Dorsett and run to daylight," running back Robert Newhouse recalled Landry saying.

"I couldn't believe it. He changed the whole scheme and philosophy for one guy—Tony Dorsett—and it worked out perfectly. I realized Tony had special ability, and if we carried out our assignments, things would work out."

As the 99-yard run proved, sometimes Dorsett could make things work out even when assignments were missed. The old record for the longest run from scrimmage, 97 yards, had stood since Bob Gage of the Pittsburgh Steelers tied it in 1949. The original record was set ten years earlier by Andy Uram of the Chicago Cardinals.

Dorsett was in his seventh professional season when he broke the record and got the last laugh on those who doubted that a slim 5-foot-11 running back could survive a pounding in the NFL. Not only did Dorsett survive, he enjoyed a Hall of Fame career that was long for any running back.

"Coming out of college, someone said I would be too small to play professional football at 188 pounds," Dorsett said. "To be honest with you, I figured maybe I could play four or five years, and that would be it. I never dreamed I would play twelve seasons."

Dorsett's 99-yard run wasn't his only unprecedented feat. He also became the first player ever to play for the collegiate national champion one year and the Super Bowl winner the next.

He also inspired the first predraft blockbuster trade. The Seattle Seahawks owned the second overall pick in 1976 but traded it to the Dallas Cowboys for the fourteenth, thirtieth, and thirty-first picks. After the Tampa Bay Buccaneers took running back Ricky Bell from Southern California, the Cowboys grabbed Dorsett.

As a rookie he ran for 1,007 yards and twelve touchdowns, including one that covered 84 yards. "When his career is over, there probably won't be many NFL records that won't have his name on them," Buffalo Bills running back O. J. Simpson said.

Dorsett, actually, was second on the all-time rushing list, behind Walter Payton, when he retired. But it's always just a matter of time before the career rushing record gets broken, anyway. Not so with Dorsett's record run.

#29
PACKING A WALLOP
KEN NORTON SCORES A KNOCKDOWN
JANUARY 31, 1993

THE SURPRISING FREQUENCY of Super Bowl blowouts raises the question: how can matchups between outstanding teams become so lopsided? Perhaps both teams have so much emotion invested that one big play can prove unusually uplifting to one team and unusually deflating to the other.

The goal-line stop by Dallas Cowboys linebacker Ken Norton Jr. against the Buffalo Bills was that kind of play. A cursory review of the Cowboys' 52–17 runaway makes it easy to forget that the Bills remained very much in the game until Norton's second-quarter stop of running back Kenneth Davis.

The Bills, despite turnovers that led to two Dallas touchdowns in fifteen seconds, trailed only 14–7 when they got a first down at the Dallas 4-yard line early in the second quarter. As losers of the previous two Super Bowls, the Bills seemed especially hungry to win this one. Fullback Carwell Gardner went up the middle for 3 yards, then on second down Thurman Thomas was stopped for no gain and limped off the field.

Davis replaced Thomas on third down and got the call. He saw a huge hole up the middle after Gardner moved out line-backer Dixon Edwards. But before Davis could cross the goal line, Norton charged out of the end zone and hit him high. Norton was pushing Davis back before a swarm of Cowboys helped bring him down.

"I've made some big hits in goal-line stands before, but not like this one," said Norton, son of former heavyweight champion Ken Norton. "Seven points would have really hurt us at that point. I came across and met him straight in the hole. We were both driving our legs as hard as we could, and I was just the stronger man on the play."

Norton's stop paid extra dividends for the Cowboys because it led to a costly fourth-down mistake by the Bills. Coach Marv Levy called for a rollout pass by Jim Kelly against the Cowboys' goal-line defense. However, Cowboys defensive coordinator Dave Wannstedt substituted two players and went back to his base defense, which had no trouble with Kelly's rollout. Bills players said they expected time-out would be called to change the play.

Kelly looked for Thomas, but his route was blocked. Kelly instead lobbed deep in the end zone for tight end Pete Metzelaars, but safety Thomas Everett cut in front of him and made the interception. That was Kelly's third turnover and would be his last chance to get the Bills back in the game.

"I was surprised, and I know a lot of players were," Thomas said of the decision to stay with the rollout. "You can't question the coach's call. You just try to execute it. But we should have known at the time when they brought in their regular defense that we should have gone with a different play."

Levy, a Hall of Fame coach, agreed in hindsight. "I should have called time-out," he said. "We had a [good] play called but not for that defense."

The Bills' situation became even bleaker on their next series. Norton was blitzing Kelly on a pass and was blocked into his right knee. That collision aggravated sprained ligaments that knocked Kelly out of the Bills' first two playoff games before he returned to help win the AFC championship game in Miami.

Kelly was relieved by Frank Reich, hero of the Bills' historic comeback from a thirty-two-point deficit against the Houston Oilers in a first-round playoff game. Reich briefly gave the Bills hope for another comeback when he led them to a Steve Christie field goal that made the score 14–10. But then the Bills were buried under a flurry of Troy Aikman touchdown passes.

The Cowboys led 45–17 when Reich, backed up near his goal line, fumbled a high snap. Norton scooped up the ball and returned it for 9 yards and a touchdown, putting the finish on his extraordinary defensive performance. Teammate Leon Lett was on his way to an even more dramatic fumble return until Bills wide receiver Don Beebe made the most famous Super Bowl play ever by a member of a hopelessly beaten team.

Reich was sacked and fumbled, leaving Lett, a quick defensive lineman, with 64 yards of clear sailing to the goal line. He began celebrating prematurely, though, and held the ball out just before he reached the goal line. Beebe, who'd given Lett a 31-yard head start in a seemingly futile pursuit, caught him just as he exposed the ball and batted it through the end zone for a touchback. "I learned not to celebrate too soon," Lett said.

Though Beebe's play meant little on the scoreboard, it was hardly meaningless to those who admired his refusal to surrender. "We were getting blown out," Kelly recalled, "and for him to do that . . . it sends chills down my body every time I see it because Don Beebe reflected the Buffalo Bills, the whole attitude of our team, in just one play."

Norton, however, reflected the Cowboys' superiority in just one play.

#28
AN UNCLUTTERED MIND
CLINT LONGLEY'S SHOT IN THE DARK
NOVEMBER 28, 1974

WE USUALLY EXPECT a great play to be made by a great player. Every once in a while, though, a shooting star flies out of nowhere and shows unmistakable brilliance, only to vanish as suddenly as it appeared. That's the story of Dallas Cowboys quarterback Clint Longley, who climaxed a remarkable comeback against the Washington Redskins with a 50-yard touchdown pass to wide receiver Drew Pearson.

After their 24–23 victory in Dallas on Thanksgiving, Cowboys guard Blaine Nye described Longley's bomb as "the triumph of an uncluttered mind."

Roger Staubach and Troy Aikman are icons among Dallas quarterbacks because each led the Cowboys to multiple Super Bowls. Yet, for one day, Longley was as memorable as either. He stepped into the thick of one of the NFL's fiercest rivalries and left his footprint on one of its most entertaining games.

Tom Landry's Cowboys were nicknamed "America's Team," for their popularity and star power. George Allen's Redskins were the "Over-the-Hill Gang," because of Allen's knack for squeezing good years from long-in-the-tooth veterans. In 1974 the Redskins were still a regular playoff visitor while the Cowboys were going through their only nonplayoff season between 1967 and 1983.

The Redskins took a 16–3 lead with ten minutes left in the third period. The Cowboys seemed finished when Staubach scrambled and was knocked out of the game by linebacker Dave Robinson.

"If you can knock Staubach out, you've got that rookie facing you," defensive tackle Diron Talbert said before the game. "That's one of our goals. If we can do that, it's great."

Perhaps Talbert never heard the old warning about being careful what you ask for. "I wasn't nervous, but I sure was excited," Longley said after his big win. "I had heard about that Talbert quote earlier in the week, and it kind of hurt me."

The Cowboys were thin at quarterback because they had traded backup and one-time starter Craig Morton to the New York Giants the previous month. Landry saw a lot of raw talent in Longley, though. He sent a fifth-round pick to the Cincinnati Bengals for the rights to Longley, a supplemental draft choice from Abilene Christian. He hadn't taken a regular-season snap when Staubach went down.

"He's too young to read the defenses correctly, but he has a special football sense," Landry said. "He's going to be a good one."

For one day and especially one play, Longley was a great one. A *Dallas Morning News* retrospective related that before taking the field, Longley had to address an equipment problem. "They told me to grab my helmet and get in there," he said. "I had to find my helmet first."

Five plays later, Longley threw a 35-yard touchdown pass to tight end Billy Joe DuPree, and the Cowboys were back in the game. They took the lead on their next drive, which covered 70 yards and reached the 1-yard line on a pass interference call. Walt Garrison scored, and the extra point made the score 17–16.

A touchdown run by former Cowboy Duane Thomas put the Redskins ahead 23–17 early in the fourth quarter. Longley guided the Cowboys back into scoring position, but wide receiver Drew Pearson fumbled at the 25-yard line. That turnover seemed fatal for the Cowboys when Mark Moseley lined up for a 24-yard field-goal attempt that could have put the game out of reach. But the kick was blocked by Ed "Too Tall" Jones.

The Cowboys started their final drive at their 40-yard line with 1:45 left. On fourth-and-6, Longley passed to Bob Hayes, who barely got the first down at midfield. Two plays later, Pearson more than made up for his fumble. Despite the Redskins' prevent defense, he got open at the 15-yard line, caught Longley's pass, and scored with twenty-eight seconds left.

"Longley just threw a perfect strike, that's all," safety Brig Owens said. "He was hot. He really came in and did a job. We really let Dallas off the hook."

The rookie seemed primed to play a big part in the Cowboys' future. Instead, he was a one-game wonder. He never started a game for the Cowboys and soon became better known for his eccentricities than talent. Cowboys safety Charlie Waters recalled that he agreed to let Longley keep a pony on his property, and the quarterback drove up in a 1957 Cadillac with the animal sticking out of both back windows.

Longley's most bizarre stunt came during training camp of 1976. He sucker-punched Staubach, probably the best-loved Cowboy of all time. Longley was promptly traded to the San Diego Chargers and soon washed out of the league. Oddly enough, a hit on Staubach both started and ended the Longley saga in Dallas.

#27
CLUTCH KICKER
ADAM VINATIERI DELIVERS
FEBRUARY 3, 2002

ADAM VINATIERI was quietly becoming one of the NFL's top kickers during his first five years with the New England Patriots. He'd made eight game-winning field goals and as a rookie kicked in a Super Bowl loss to the Green Bay Packers.

But it's hard for a kicker to get noticed unless he makes kicks that win big games. Vinatieri soon made a habit of that.

No one in Super Bowl history had made a more dramatic kick than Vinatieri's 48-yard field goal that snapped a 17–17 tie against the St. Louis Rams on the final play in New Orleans. That was the first of three Vinatieri field goals that gave the Patriots the margin of victory in a Super Bowl.

The Rams were fourteen-point favorites, but Vinatieri's 37-yard field goal in the third quarter provided a 17–3 lead. Then quarterback Kurt Warner led the Rams to two touchdowns that tied the score 17–17 with 1:30 left.

With his offense in poor field position, Patriots coach Bill Belichick could have run out the clock and taken his chances in overtime. Or he could have told Tom Brady to try to get the Patriots into field-goal range. With Vinatieri available, the second option made a lot more sense. "If you want a guy making the play at the end of the game, Adam Vinatieri is the one," Belichick said after the Patriots won their first Super Bowl.

Brady attacked the Rams' zone defense by completing three short passes to running back J. R. Redmond. Then he got the big pickup he needed—a 23-yard pass to wide receiver Troy Brown at the St. Louis 36-yard line. Brady passed for 6 more yards to tight end Jermaine Wiggins and spiked the ball with six seconds left, to give Vinatieri a 48-yard attempt. The kick was long but makeable, given the artificial turf and absence of wind in the Louisiana Superdome. But the pressure of trying to win a Super Bowl had to be as daunting as the distance. A kicker doesn't usually put his foot into the ball with thousands of flash cameras exploding.

As soon as the ball left Vinatieri's foot, however, the suspense was over. The kick was nearly perfect, and he thrust his arms triumphantly in the air. This was the final surprise of a season of surprises for a team that had finished 5–11 the year before.

"Once I kicked it, I knew it was good," Vinatieri said. "I wasn't nervous. I was more nervous in the snow."

He was referring to a 45-yard field goal with thirty-two seconds left that had tied a playoff game against the Oakland Raiders at Foxboro, Massachusetts, two weeks earlier. The Patriots trailed 13–10 in heavy snow and appeared doomed when the Raiders stripped the ball from Brady late in the game. But referee Walt Coleman, citing the "tuck" rule, said Brady had thrown an incomplete pass because he hadn't brought the ball back to his body and therefore was still in his throwing motion.

Vinatieri's 23-yard field goal in overtime ended that game. That was the third time that season his kicks won games in overtime. After he made so many clutch kicks, Vinatieri's teammates had no doubt that he would come through against the Rams. Well, maybe a small doubt.

"We were all down praying," cornerback Ty Law recalled. "I think he was already a clutch kicker from the snow game, but when you do that at the Super Bowl, that's the only game in town. Everyone's watching, in all these different countries, and then you can see the significance of that game."

It would be a once-in-a-lifetime thrill for most kickers to decide a Super Bowl. Vinatieri achieved that three times in four seasons. His 41-yard field goal with four seconds left gave the Patriots a 32–29 victory over the Carolina Panthers in February 2004 at Houston. A year later, he made a 22-yard field goal midway through the fourth quarter to give the Patriots a 24–14 lead over the Philadelphia Eagles. The Patriots held on to win 24–21 in Jacksonville.

In ten seasons with the Patriots, Vinatieri kicked eighteen field goals that won games, playoffs included, in the last minute of regulation or in overtime. He was a highly sought free agent in 2006 and signed with the Indianapolis Colts, then kicked three field goals in their 29-17 Super Bowl victory over the Chicago Bears.

Jan Stenerud, who kicked for three teams during nineteen seasons, in 1991 became the first pure kicker elected to the Hall of Fame. That 48-yard kick against the Rams should have put Vinatieri next in line.

#26
A BACKBREAKING RETURN
DESMOND HOWARD BURIES THE PATRIOTS
JANUARY 26, 1997

DESMOND HOWARD was a forgotten Heisman Trophy winner until he jarred a lot of memories with an electrifying 99-yard kickoff return that changed the momentum of a Super Bowl.

A game-breaking wide receiver from Michigan who was drafted by the Washington Redskins with the fourth overall pick of the 1992 draft, Howard found his niche as a record-breaking kick returner for the Green Bay Packers. Yet, as the Packers prepared for the Super Bowl, Howard still couldn't get much respect. He steamed as the Patriots announced they wouldn't hesitate to kick to Howard in the Super Bowl. That was a strategy they soon would regret.

Howard returned his first punt 32 yards and gave the Packers good field position for their first touchdown. A second-quarter punt return for 34 yards set up a field goal. Still, the Patriots were trash-talking and telling Howard, "Nothing for you today, baby. We're going to shut you down."

With the Packers ahead 27–14 at halftime, Howard went to quarterback Brett Favre in the Louisiana Superdome locker room and said, "I'm going to take one of these kicks back. It's only a matter of time."

That time arrived late in the third quarter. The momentum shifted to the Patriots when Curtis Martin burst 18 yards up the middle for a touchdown that made the score 27–21. Then, just as quickly, the momentum shifted back to the Packers, this time for good.

The Packers during the season used twin kickoff returners, Howard on the left side and Don Beebe on the right. But the Packers switched them for the Super Bowl because they noticed the Patriots tended to kick off to an opponent's right. Howard was astonished the Patriots were kicking off to him and recalled thinking, "I can't believe [Patriots coach Bill Parcells] is rolling the dice and kicking me the ball."

Howard fielded the kickoff at his own 1-yard line and burst through his wedge of blockers. His blazing speed left everybody in his wake except Patriots kicker Adam Vinatieri. With one move, Howard was past him, too, and scored the longest touchdown in Super Bowl history. It was the biggest play of a 35–21 victory.

"We were feeling good before that, and then Desmond broke our backs," Patriots safety Willie Clay said.

Now it was time for Howard to get even. He began yelling at the Patriots, giving them a taste of the medicine he'd had to swallow all day. "I have never, ever talked so much in a game," he said, hoarsely. "I knew that sooner or later I was going to scorch 'em."

Howard totaled 244 return yards against the Patriots and became the first special-teams player ever named Super Bowl MVP. "It's really one of those honors that, when it's bestowed upon you, there's really no words that explain it," he said. "There are probably a handful of experiences in life that can fall under that same category. That's just one of those *crème de la crème* [moments]. It doesn't get any better than that."

Howard wanted to make sure, though, that his Super Bowl heroics were remembered as the climax of a successful season, not just as bolts out of the blue. His 875 punt-return yards in the regular season blew away the previous NFL record. Two of his returns helped give the Packers a 14–0 lead in a 35–14 playoff victory over the San Francisco 49ers. That's why Howard suggests he did nothing new in the Super Bowl.

"I don't think it was an extraordinary performance for me or our special teams," he said. "We broke records throughout the season. Then against San Francisco we lit it up again. I had two punt returns, one for a [71-yard] touchdown and one I took down to the 7-yard line. I led the league in every category possible as a punt returner."

Howard credited Reggie White, the Packers defensive end and team leader, for giving the return units a wake-up call late in the season. White was distressed to watch game films that showed Howard taking a beating in a mid-November loss to the Cowboys, the Packers' last defeat of the season.

"I pretty much got pummeled by their best special-teams coverage person," Howard said. "I remember Reggie stood up at the meeting, and he was like, 'Listen, I don't want to see little Desmond getting hit like that back there again. If you got an assignment, you've got to get your man because we've got a guy who at any point, at any time, can go the distance. And if not go the distance, at least put us in excellent field position. So I don't want to see this happen again.'"

White surely didn't see that happen in the Super Bowl.

#25
STALLWORTH'S TURN
STEELER RECEIVER FINALLY GETS HIS DUE
JANUARY 20, 1980

THE PITTSBURGH STEELERS' second Super Bowl victory belonged to Lynn Swann. Their fourth belonged to John Stallworth. Without his 73-yard touchdown catch, there may have been no fourth Super Bowl victory for coach Chuck Noll's Steelers.

The Los Angeles Rams, coming off a 9–7 regular season, were supposed to serve as fall guys for another celebration of the dynasty that ruled the NFL in the 1970s. Then the Rams shocked the Steelers by leading 13–10 at halftime and fighting the good fight right into the fourth quarter.

Before beating the Steelers, though, an opponent had to neutralize an amazing array of weapons on both offense and defense. The Steelers' two starting wide receivers, Swann and Stallworth, were headed for the Hall of Fame. Swann leaped three feet to catch a 47-yard touchdown pass against the Rams in the third quarter.

Swann and Stallworth were terrific complements. Swann, 5 feet, 11 inches and 180, had the spring and body control of a ballet dancer. Stallworth, 6 feet, 2 inches and 191, was strong enough to run over defenders, as well as by them. Both were sure-handed and fast. Swann, however, had been the higher-profile athlete since the 1974 draft, when the Steelers drafted him in the first round and Stallworth in the fourth.

Both spent their first four seasons playing under rules that enabled defensive backs to virtually mug receivers. The Oakland Raiders used such tactics to give Swann a concussion in the 1975 season. When the NFL restricted defensive contact with receivers in 1978, Swann and Stallworth could run free. Stallworth in 1979 enjoyed the best receiving season in Steeler history, yet still remained in Swann's shadow. It was time in the Super Bowl for Stallworth to receive equal billing.

The Steelers were jolted again early in the fourth quarter when a halfback pass from Lawrence McCutcheon to Rod Smith put the Rams ahead 19–17, the fifth lead change of the game. On the Steelers' next possession, they faced third-and-8 at their 27-yard line. Noll sent in, "60 Prevent, Slot, Hook and Go."

The Rams had six defensive backs in a prevent defense for an obvious passing situation. Stallworth lined up in the slot and was supposed to fake a 15-yard hook pattern, then break deep. The play worked perfectly because two defensive backs covered the hook before Stallworth blew by them.

"Usually, on that play, the receiver hooks and slides," explained quarterback Terry Bradshaw. "And that's the way the Rams defensed it."

Bradshaw was off his game in the first half but didn't miss this opportunity. He threw a perfect pass near the right hash mark, and it was just high enough to get over cornerback Rod Perry's outstretched hands. He got caught in single coverage and fell after making a futile leap for the ball. Stallworth made the catch at the Rams 34-yard line and scored easily, giving the Steelers a 24–19 lead with 12:04 left.

"I saw Rod Perry's hand over me just as I was about to catch the ball," Stallworth said. "He came very close to making a damn good play."

Perry, five inches shorter than Stallworth, said, "Bradshaw put just enough arc on the ball to get it over my hands." Perry should have had deep help from strong safety Eddie Brown, but Brown mistakenly covered an outside receiver.

Oddly enough, the Steelers had practiced that touchdown play eight times the week of the game, and it didn't work once.

When Noll sent in that play earlier in the game, Bradshaw ignored him. Before the touchdown, however, Stallworth convinced his quarterback to give the play a try.

"It's hard to have confidence in a play that never works," Stallworth said. "But I think it didn't work because the [practice] field was soggy. Terry was throwing the ball long, and I couldn't get it."

After the touchdown, Bradshaw suddenly couldn't get enough of that play. Linebacker Jack Lambert's interception of Vince Ferragamo gave the Steelers the ball back at their 30-yard line. On third-and-7, Bradshaw was pleasantly surprised to see the same defense he saw on the bomb. He called the same play and got a similar result. Stallworth caught a 45-yard pass, setting up the final touchdown of a 31–19 victory that marked the climax of the Noll era. Stallworth finished with three catches for 121 yards.

"I felt all along I could deliver the big play," Stallworth said. "I feel that I can go deep on anybody in the NFL." Nobody watching that game would argue otherwise.

#24

BO'S MAGIC CARPET RIDE
JACKSON BEATS A PATH FOR TACOMA
NOVEMBER 30, 1987

OAKLAND RAIDERS running back Bo Jackson was arguably the greatest all-around athlete ever to play in the NFL. He combined pro football and Major League Baseball careers, and anybody who watched him one night in Seattle might wonder why he ever bothered with baseball.

In a 37–14 victory over the Seahawks, Jackson showed his game-breaking speed on a 91-yard touchdown burst, the greatest run of his career. He displayed his enormous strength by bowling over linebacker Brian Bosworth on a 2-yard touchdown run.

As the NFL's commercial era began to flower, this Monday night game featured two of the most heavily publicized and advertised rookies ever. Jackson, a Kansas City Royals outfielder and Heisman Trophy winner at Auburn, caused a national uproar when he announced during the 1987 baseball season that he would join the Raiders as a "hobby." Bosworth, nicknamed "The Boz," caused an uproar with his Mohawk hairstyle, earrings, and cockiness. His performances as a linebacker seldom lived up to his hype.

Jackson had the rare ability to rise to the occasion when the spotlight was brightest. His biggest game ever came not only in prime time but on his twenty-fifth birthday. The game was in the Seattle Kingdome, known as the Temple of Doom to Oakland fans because the Raiders had lost six straight games there. But the Kingdome carpet was an autobahn for Jackson.

He fumbled on the opening possession, and the Seahawks responded with a 64-yard touchdown drive for a 7–0 lead. The

Raiders tied the score, and Jackson gave them a 14–7 lead when he caught a 14-yard touchdown pass from Marc Wilson. Jackson was wide open because safety Kenny Easley fell after they collided.

On the Raiders' next possession, Jackson broke the game open on a third-down play from his own 9-yard line. He took a handoff from Wilson and sprinted around left end, picking up speed. Only one Seahawk, safety Eugene Robinson, had a chance to stop Jackson. When the 6-foot-1, 225-pound back reached the corner, Robinson dived at him and missed.

Jackson had clear sailing down the left sideline, and the ever-widening gap between him and his pursuers accentuated his blinding speed. He built up such a full head of steam that he had to run through the end zone and down the runway to the locker rooms before he could apply the brakes. "He may not stop 'til Tacoma," ABC analyst Dan Dierdorf said, laughing, as Jackson disappeared from the field.

A moment of suspense ensued, as if the crowd was wondering if Jackson would come back. When he finally emerged from the runway, he tossed the football in the air and swung an imaginary baseball bat. The 91-yard run was the longest in Raider history, and it didn't seem possible Jackson could come up with an encore performance that night. But he did.

The Raiders led 27–7 at halftime, and Bosworth was barely noticeable—until Jackson steamrolled him on the Raiders' first drive of the third quarter. "If my mother put on a helmet and shoulder pads and a uniform that wasn't the same as the one I was wearing, I'd run her over if she was in my way," Jackson said. "And I love my mother."

Bosworth usually relished his role as the NFL's antihero. Not on this night. He was embarrassed. "It was my own fault," he explained. "He came up inside, and I didn't know if he was going to cut it back and try to run it inside or go outside. So I hesitated for a second, and that's all it took. I wasn't set, and he knocked my [butt] over. I'm sure they ran that one back a few times in the ABC booth."

Jackson finished the night with 221 yards rushing, and it was apparent he'd be Hall of Fame material if he concentrated on football and gave his body the luxury of an off-season. He had a 92-yard run in 1989 in a 28–7 victory over the Cincinnati Bengals. But in a playoff victory over the Bengals the next season, Jackson's NFL career ended. On a routine tackle by safety David Fulcher, he suffered a left hip injury. X-rays revealed that Jackson was afflicted with avascular necrosis, an incurable deterioration of cartilage and bone.

Who could have guessed this extraordinary athlete, who averaged an amazing 5.4 yards per carry for his career, could be so vulnerable? No back ever looked more invincible than Jackson when he took off on his 91-yard magic carpet ride.

#23
BEST SCRAMBLE EVER
STEVE YOUNG OUTRUNS THE VIKINGS
OCTOBER 30, 1988

BECAUSE STEVE YOUNG came into the NFL as a much more dangerous runner than passer, he was dismissed by many talent evaluators as a legitimate quarterback prospect. That was before his arm and legs helped him win a Super Bowl and a spot in the Hall of Fame.

Young spent his first four seasons with the San Francisco 49ers backing up Joe Montana. Young picked up two Super Bowl rings during that stretch, yet was best known for—what else?— an amazing scramble that beat the Minnesota Vikings 24–21.

"It has to go down as one of the greatest runs ever by a quarterback," said Lynn Stiles, Bill Walsh's special-teams coach.

It should go down as the greatest run by anybody, insisted Paul Zimmerman of *Sports Illustrated* in 2000. "Every time I think of Steve Young," he wrote, "I see that dodging, twisting, stop-start, tackle-breaking run, which ended in collapse."

Young, who joined the 49ers in 1987, had to move mountains to win over the Montana faithful. He was even getting booed at home before his famous run because he was replacing Montana, who was injured, and the 49ers trailed 21–17 in the final minutes. Young faced third-and-2 at the Vikings 49-yard line and dropped back to pass. But he couldn't find an open receiver and thus began a scramble for the ages.

"He went to his right, then back to his left," Stiles recalled. "He couldn't find anybody and took off down the field. And I didn't see anybody blocking for him. It was just a sheer effort on his part and one of those things that showed what he was made out of. Seven or eight guys had shots at him. There's no way you'll ever duplicate that. I mean, he ran through them all. They were all there. It was on a short field. It's not like he took off from the 10-yard line and everybody was strung out. The field was condensed to a certain degree. He wasn't going to be denied. It was just one of those great plays."

Young bobbed and weaved and broke or avoided seven tackles with safety Brad Edwards the last defender giving chase. As Young stumbled into the end zone with 1:58 left, he bore the agonized expression of a dying man reaching out with his final gasp. Teammates, showing their admiration and concern, kept coming up to Young on the bench. They patted his head and shoulder and wanted to make sure he was all right.

"I can't think of another play with a quarterback making a run that influenced a game more," Stiles said. "That was big time. Then he stumbled into the end zone—a dive, really. So he originated the dive into the end zone. It was just a great athletic play."

Yet it was also a play that reinforced Young's reputation as nothing more than a scrambler. But why should he have avoided the chance to showcase his formidable running gifts? "He was always bugging me about returning punts," Stiles recalled, "and sometimes he'd go out and practice, and I had him as the backup [return] guy. But I said, 'You know what you're going to do if you return one? Signal for a fair catch!'"

That wasn't just the 49ers' most dazzling play of the year. It was also their most important. Had the 49ers lost that game, they would not have reached the playoffs in Walsh's final season. Instead, they won their third Super Bowl title. "Talk about your all-time significant runs!" Zimmerman wrote. "I've never seen a bigger one."

Most NFL scouts and coaches forgot about Young when, after a brilliant career at Brigham Young, he signed with the Los Angeles

Express of the United States Football League. Young became the first professional player ever to pass for 300 yards and rush for 100 yards in one game. He even became a running back when injuries reduced the Express offense to eleven players and there was no money left to sign replacements. When the USFL folded in the summer of 1985, Young joined the Tampa Bay Buccaneers and started a year later for a 2–14 team. Few in the NFL thought much of Young's talent except Walsh. He gave the Buccaneers two draft choices and $1 million to acquire him.

"He's the best athlete to have ever played the quarterback position," Walsh said years later. Who would argue with him after Young's run against the Vikings? But Young was determined to become a complete quarterback, and that would require more than stunning touchdown runs.

He finally took over the 49ers' starting job when Montana developed elbow problems during training camp in 1991. Young went on to win two league MVP awards and six passing titles. He set a Super Bowl record by throwing six touchdown passes in a 49–26 victory over the San Diego Chargers in the January 1995 Super Bowl.

"My whole career," Young said, "I wanted to make a statement: 'Yes, you could be a scrambler, but you could also be a really top, efficient pocket passer.'"

It took him years to prove that point. How many people, for instance, do you suppose remember that Young also threw a 73-yard touchdown pass to wide receiver John Taylor earlier in that game against the Vikings?

"The scrambler always gets people's eyes, like fireworks," Young said. "You tend to look up. If you're not careful, you lose appreciation for everything that's happening in the pocket. People tended to remember the touchdown runs more than they remembered the throws."

#22
KING FOR THE DAY
JOHN RIGGINS'S RUN WINS A SUPER BOWL
JANUARY 30, 1983

JOHN RIGGINS peaked at just the right time—in the Super Bowl.

He retired for a year and was rusty when he returned to the Washington Redskins in 1981. For two regular seasons, he hardly resembled the 1,000-yard rusher he'd been before he retreated to his Kansas farm in the summer of 1980 because of a contract dispute.

But after the strike-shortened 1982 regular season, Riggins rushed for 100 yards in each of the three NFC playoff games that put the Redskins in the Super Bowl against the Miami Dolphins. When someone asked Riggins about his leap from retirement to the Super Bowl, he replied, "Yes, it is a little amazing. Then I was camping out in my car some place in Kansas. If you had told me that now I would be in the Super Bowl, I wouldn't have believed it."

And maybe he wouldn't have believed that he would make the decisive run in a 27–17 victory that gave coach Joe Gibbs his first of three Super Bowl victories.

The Redskins trailed 17–13 early in the fourth quarter but took possession at their 48-yard line. Three plays later, they faced fourth-and-inches at the Miami 43. Instead of trying a 60-yard field goal or punting, Gibbs called "70-Chip" out of the I-formation. That was a Riggins run off left tackle with tight end Clint Didier blocking the cornerback. Gibbs had decided to try this play on fourth down if the third-down run came up short.

"We knew if we didn't make it then, it would be a risky field goal," Gibbs said. "We decided to take our best play and go at them.

We didn't want to lose a Super Bowl by not being tough enough. I think they thought we were slanting one way and got caught when we went the other way."

Didier went in motion from left to right, and cornerback Don McNeal followed him. The tight end then quickly turned back to his original position, which caused McNeal to slip. He didn't quite recover in time to stop Riggins from bolting through the spot where McNeal initially lined up. McNeal was the only defender to get a hand on Riggins as he ran 43 yards for a touchdown with 10:01 remaining and put the Redskins ahead, 20–17, their first lead of the game. They remained in control the rest of the way.

"It's something we've used all season," Riggins said. "We must have run it seven or eight times against Dallas [in the NFC championship game]."

That play dramatized how dangerous Riggins could be at the top of his game. Though generally considered an old-time power fullback, Riggins was a state high school sprint champion in Centralia, Kansas. He was tough to catch when he put his 6-foot-2, 240-pound frame into high gear.

His reputation as a battering ram was well deserved, too. Against the Dolphins, he carried thirty-eight times for 166 yards, a Super Bowl record. For the four postseason games, he carried 136 times for 610 yards. Riggins hadn't been especially busy in the regular season and told Gibbs before the playoffs that he wanted to start hammering at defenses.

"Gimme the ball twenty to twenty-five times a game, and we'll do it," he promised. Riggins rushed for 185 yards on thirty-seven carries against the Minnesota Vikings in a second-round game. He claimed that he needed that many carries to get a feel for how a defense was adjusting from one play to the next. He told his offensive linemen that he needed their help to carry another big load in the Super Bowl.

"He came to the offensive line the night before," tackle Joe Jacoby said. "He told us he'd been in trouble with the coaches and could we open some holes for him? Not big holes, he added. Just ones that would let him get four or five yards. He didn't want anything where—fifteen or so yards down the field—he might run out of gas."

If Riggins was running out of gas in the Super Bowl, he never showed it. He carried thirteen times in the fourth quarter. Once the Dolphins were forced to become conscious of Riggins on every down, Gibbs used him as a decoy to set up trick plays. The Redskins started cutting into Miami's 17–10 halftime lead when wide receiver Alvin Garrett took a handoff from Riggins and ran a reverse that picked up 44 yards and set up a Mark Moseley field goal.

On the Washington possession prior to Riggins's game-breaking run, he took a handoff from quarterback Joe Theismann, then lateraled back to him on a play that would one day end Theismann's career. The Dolphins weren't fooled, though, and a pass for wide receiver Charlie Brown was intercepted at the 1-yard line.

Riggins was the obvious pick as Super Bowl MVP, which moved him to say, "Ronnie [Reagan] may be president, but I'm king for the day."

#21
MAKING A STAND
49ERS DENY THE BENGALS
JANUARY 24, 1982

A GOAL-LINE STAND poses football's stiffest challenge. Trying to prevent an offense from moving just 1 yard into the end zone seems an improbable feat. That's especially true when the offense has as many weapons as the Cincinnati Bengals mounted against the San Francisco 49ers in the Super Bowl. The 49ers' stand, which included three stops at the 1-yard line, was so gallant that the entire sequence deserves special mention.

The Bengals featured 250-pound fullback Pete Johnson, a 1,000-yard rusher who was terrific in short-yardage situations, and Charles Alexander, a halfback who was also a dangerous receiver. Johnson showed his power by bulling his way 2 yards to give the Bengals a first down at the San Francisco 3-yard line.

The Bengals, down 20–0 at halftime in the Pontiac Silverdome, had closed the gap to 20–7 and needed to cash in on this great opportunity late in the third quarter. But they were stopped on four consecutive plays. Each was a great defensive play in its own right, but the stop on third down from the 1 stands out.

Quarterback Ken Anderson threw to the right flat for Alexander, who was so close to the goal line that all he had to do to score was plant his feet. But linebacker Dan Bunz closed in a flash, grabbed Alexander around the waist, and threw him back just as he stood inches from a touchdown.

"The man made one great play on me," Alexander said. "I never saw him coming. He arrived as soon as the ball arrived. I had no chance to get my feet down for some second effort. I don't even know who hit me, to tell you the truth. I just know we didn't get in, and it would have changed the game around."

On first down, Johnson picked up 2 yards to the 1. On second down, he tried left guard but was stopped for no gain. After Alexander was stopped on third down, Bengals coach Forrest Gregg decided against a field-goal try.

Johnson tried ramming into the end zone one more time but was stopped by middle linebacker Jack "Hacksaw" Reynolds. Gregg said that was the first time all season Johnson was stopped on that play. Bunz played a big role on that stop, too. He neutralized Alexander's lead block and denied Johnson a second effort.

"Because as big as he is, once he gets past the line of scrimmage, he's tough to stop," Reynolds said. "I think I hit him with my head mostly, but Dan Bunz had stacked him up."

San Francisco coach Bill Walsh described the fourth-down stop as "the play that won the game for us." Defensive coordinator Chuck Studley, though, considered Bunz's stop on Alexander more difficult.

"Dan had to make a perfect tackle in the open," Studley said. "Here's a guy who weighs 220 pounds and can run, and he has only a yard to go for the end zone. Bunz had to hit him perfectly to stop him. The Bengals tried to shield Danny off and make him run around, but he hit Alexander quick in the flat. We worked like hell on that play."

Though the 49ers' goal-line defense included several starters, it also had such backups as linebackers Craig Puki and Bunz and tackle John Choma, who was otherwise an offensive lineman. "I don't get four or five good pops a game, and I wasn't going to miss my chance," Bunz said.

Choma stopped Johnson on second down as the Bengals double-teamed nose tackle Archie Reese. They didn't block Choma because they expected him to overrun the play. "What they didn't know," Studley said, "was that we worked our tails off all week on that play, too."

For all their practice, the 49ers' defense committed a gaffe that could have been more costly. When they sent in their goal-line defense on the Bengals' fourth-and-1 play from the 5, linebacker Keena Turner didn't hear Studley's instructions, and the 49ers had only ten men on the field. But that was the last mistake the 49ers' defense would make on that drive.

"We just didn't move anybody off the ball," Bengals left guard Dave Lapham said. "Their defense would shift as late as possible before the snap of the ball, and we often didn't know who or where a guy would come into the gap. They forced us to change quite a bit on every play."

Gregg didn't second-guess his decision to pass up a field goal and implied that too big a deal was made of the goal-line stand. After all, he pointed out, the 49ers were still pinned and had to punt, giving the Bengals the good field position they used to drive for a touchdown, anyway. Anderson's 4-yard pass to tight end Dan Ross early in the fourth quarter closed the gap to 20–14. But two Ray Wersching field goals wrapped up the win.

The Bengals scored in the final minute, and their comeback ended with a failed onside kick. As far as the 49ers were concerned, it ended with their goal-line stand.

#20
SQUADRON RIGHT
BUD GRANT FINALLY GETS SOME LUCK
DECEMBER 14, 1980

WHILE FANS have no business expecting miracles, Minnesota Vikings fans could be excused if they figured they were owed this one.

They were on the wrong end of the original "Hail Mary" pass five years earlier when Roger Staubach threw to Drew Pearson in the NFC title game. Now they enjoyed that same kind of last-play thunderbolt when Tommy Kramer threw a 46-yard bomb to wide receiver Ahmad Rashad to clinch the NFC Central title for the Vikings.

The 1980 Vikings stood 8–6 and could clinch the title with a home victory over the Cleveland Browns, whose late-game heroics that year earned them the nickname "Kardiac Kids." The Vikings trailed 23–22 after a Don Cockroft field goal nearly pulled out yet another close victory for the Browns. The ensuing kickoff left the Vikings at their 20-yard line with just twelve seconds left. They had time for one or two plays.

"One thing all coaches possess—[the attitude that] the game's not over until it's over," said Vikings Hall of Fame coach Bud Grant. "If you've been in the game long enough, [strange] things happen. We've all been recipients both ways. We lost a berth in the Super Bowl when Pearson makes that play [for the Dallas Cowboys]. You know something like that can happen for you and against you, so you don't live and die with each play."

Grant first called for "Handoff Pass." Kramer threw 12 yards down the middle to tight end Joe Senser, who lateraled to trailing running back Ted Brown. There was plenty of daylight down the left side, but Brown kept an eye on the game clock, above the end zone he was facing. He alertly stepped out of bounds at the Cleveland 46-yard line with one second left.

"It's a situation where the linebackers drop off," Grant said. "It's harder to run nowadays because people are more aware. I remember running that when I played [in the 1950s]. It's been around a long time. Here was a player who ran as fast as he could, as far as he could, and got out of bounds. He had the presence of mind to give us another shot. Not all players do."

Because the Vikings were still out of field-goal range, Grant only had one play to call now. His "Hail Mary" formation was called "Squadron Right." Wide receivers Ahmad Rashad, Sammy White, and Terry LeCount lined up on the right side. Senser and Brown stayed in to protect Kramer. The Browns rushed four linemen and used everybody else to defend against the inevitable long throw. Rashad lined up outside, with LeCount and White inside him. They were hoping to knock the ball around, and maybe one of them would be lucky enough to grab it. That's exactly what happened to give the Vikings a 28–23 victory at old Metropolitan Stadium.

"It's a luck play," Grant said. "You don't know a guy can get up that high in the air and get it. We practiced it every week. We'd run it two or three times and always cross our fingers and hope that nobody gets hurt."

Kramer took a deep drop and threw a high pass that came down at the 5-yard line, where six defenders converged. The wide receivers were a split-second late reaching the ball, but LeCount knifed through the pack and leaped high for the ball. The Browns leaped, too, and safety Thom Darden tipped the ball—right to Rashad, who was by himself near the sideline. He reached out, grabbed the ball with one hand, and pulled it in as he backed into the end zone. That play is remembered in Vikings country as the "Miracle Catch."

Rashad held up the ball triumphantly and was swarmed by LeCount and White, with the rest of the Vikings soon arriving from their bench to join the celebration. Many in the crowd of 42,202 had given up hope and left, but, according to some accounts, those who remained literally caused the old stadium to shake.

"That stadium only held forty-seven thousand people," Grant recalled, "and I've already talked to a hundred-fifty thousand who were there that day."

The Browns had led 20–9 with 7:15 left. Kramer brought the Vikings back with three touchdowns, including two in the last 1:35. A missed extra-point attempt, however, left the Vikings behind when Cockroft made his late field goal. Kramer's final pass gave him 456 yards, the most ever in one game against the Browns.

Rashad's catch gave the Vikings their eleventh playoff berth in thirteen years, and without that win they would have lost the division race to the Detroit Lions. The Vikings lost their playoff opener on the road to the Philadelphia Eagles, eventual NFC champions. But folks around the Twin Cities will always remember the magic that pushed the 1980 Vikings into the playoffs more than how they fared once they got there.

"It was a memorable one," Grant agreed. "But being a coach for so many games, you don't sit around the fireplace and replay it."

#19

EARL OF HOUSTON
CAMPBELL'S MONDAY NIGHT MASTERPIECE
NOVEMBER 20, 1978

EARL CAMPBELL had to be exhausted. We always hear that the great running backs wear down defenses in the fourth quarter, but try telling that to a back who's already carried twenty-seven times and scored three touchdowns.

Campbell had carried on nine of the Houston Oilers' thirteen previous plays, including a 12-yard touchdown run, when coach Bum Phillips called on him to run out the clock in a Monday night game against the Miami Dolphins. Linebacker Steve Kiner intercepted a pass by Dolphins quarterback Bob Griese at the Houston 19-yard line with fewer than ninety seconds left and the Oilers leading 28–23. The Oilers needed just one first down to run out the clock and end a game that had whipped the Astrodome crowd into a frenzy.

Everybody in that crowd knew that Campbell was going to get the ball. Though he was worn down and sitting in the sights of every Dolphin defender, Campbell just needed to get one first down, and the Oilers would be able to run out the clock.

The Oilers, as expected, called on Campbell, the sensational rookie running back from the University of Texas. He gave them a lot more than a first down. He gave them the most famous run in the history of the Oilers and *Monday Night Football*.

The Oilers called a pitch right to Campbell, who stumbled briefly as one defender dived through the block of fullback Tim Wilson. Campbell recovered quickly and, with a block on the corner from tight end Mike Barber, headed for the sideline. Defensive end Vern Den Herder, safety Charlie Babb, and cornerback

Norris Thomas seemed to have Campbell hemmed in against the sideline, yet he sprinted by them all. Linebacker Kim Bokamper kept chasing Campbell and got a hand on him, but he quickly pulled away. Cornerback Curtis Johnson finally made a desperate dive at Campbell before he finished his 81-yard touchdown run and sewed up a 35–30 victory.

Campbell, 5 feet, 11 inches and 233, was built like a fullback, and it was astounding to see him run away from a defense on his twenty-eighth carry of the night. Because it wrapped up a big game in prime time and climaxed Campbell's NFL coming-out party, that run stands as the most memorable of his Hall of Fame career.

"About five people had an angle on him," Phillips recalled, "and two of them were cornerbacks, and they couldn't catch him. Earl never could get caught once he got out into the open. I really believe he's the best running back to ever put on the pads, especially in the fourth quarter. From his twentieth carry to his fortieth carry, he was great. He had more stamina than anybody in the world."

Campbell's last touchdown, with 1:11 left, gave him 199 yards for the night. That performance would endure as the highlight of a career that included four 200-yard rushing games and 1,934 rushing yards in 1980. Recalling his 81-yard dash, Campbell said, "I think that put Earl Campbell on the map, even after winning the Heisman Trophy. That run created a whole new atmosphere, a whole other life for me."

Monday Night Football was still a big deal in 1978, especially for Houston fans, who hadn't been able to support a playoff team since 1967. The atmosphere in the Astrodome was electric, as a full house roared and waved light blue pompoms. The pandemonium peaked during Campbell's long run, which moved announcer Howard Cosell to say, "It synthesized and yet epitomized the fact that professional football remains the golden sport in this country."

Campbell finished his rookie season with 1,450 rushing yards. He earned the NFL's rushing title, the MVP award, and the Rookie of the Year award. "I don't know if Earl's in a class by himself," Phillips said. "But it sure don't take long to call roll."

Campbell remained a workhorse, and his heavy load would limit his career to six strong seasons and eight overall. The Oilers stood 28–11 when he ran for at least 100 yards, and more often than not, Campbell eventually wore down a defense. The Dolphins could attest to that.

Campbell's performance against the Dolphins stole the thunder from a 349-yard passing night by Griese. He threw an 11-yard touchdown pass on the game's final play.

"Griese had an unbelievable day, and our offense put up a lot of points," Dolphins coach Don Shula recalled. "But we couldn't stop Earl Campbell. He had to be a remarkable athlete. He made the big play when he had to."

Campbell scored on a 1-yard run, bowling over Babb, to tie the score at 7–7. His 6-yard run in the third quarter put the Oilers ahead 21–14. The Dolphins tied the score after three quarters and went ahead 23–21 in the fourth. With under five minutes left, Campbell's third touchdown put the Oilers ahead to stay. Who in the Astrodome could have guessed that Campbell's biggest run was yet to come?

#18
SUPER BOWL HANGOVER
MAX MCGEE'S BIG NIGHT, BIG DAY
JANUARY 15, 1967

THERE ARE THREE GOOD REASONS why Max McGee's 37-yard touchdown catch from Bart Starr ranks among the greatest catches of all time. It marked the first touchdown in Super Bowl history. The pass was thrown slightly behind McGee, who adjusted by making a spectacular one-handed grab. And he'd been up all night before the Green Bay Packers' 35–10 victory over the Kansas City Chiefs in the Los Angeles Coliseum.

McGee never expected to make an impact in the first game between the NFL and AFL champions. He never, in fact, expected to play at all. So his conscience never bothered him when he snuck out of the team's hotel near downtown Los Angeles to join a few flight attendants for a night on the town.

McGee went out alone because his roommate and running mate, Paul Hornung, was going to be married three days later. Coach Vince Lombardi had announced curfew breakers would be fined $5,000. McGee was under the covers for the 11:30 p.m. bed check but was fully dressed. When assistant coach Dave Hanner let on that he wouldn't check the room again, McGee was gone.

"I waddled in about 7:30 in the morning, and I could barely stand up for the kickoff," McGee said. "On the bench, Paul kept needling me, 'What would you do if you had to play?' And I said, 'No way, there's no way I could make it.'"

Starr was in the hotel lobby when McGee dragged himself in. "He was extremely talented—'clutch' is what he was," Starr said. "He and Hornung didn't like curfews, but nobody worked harder in practice."

McGee, a reserve who'd caught just four passes all season, and Hornung, who was out with a neck injury that would end his career, were mere spectators for the start of what eventually would be called the first Super Bowl. At kickoff, they were on the bench, discussing Hornung's wedding rehearsal the next night in Los Angeles. Then, before the third play, McGee heard Lombardi scream for him. His first reaction was fear that the explosive coach had learned of his night out. It was much more serious than that. Lombardi was sending McGee into the game.

Starting flanker Boyd Dowler was still hurting from a shoulder injury suffered in the NFL championship game against the Dallas Cowboys. McGee's touchdown catch provided the margin of victory in that game. Against the Chiefs, however, McGee was so unprepared that he hadn't bothered to find his helmet. So he grabbed one that belonged to a lineman. Fortunately for McGee, he had studied film of the Kansas City secondary and napped an hour when he got back to the hotel Sunday morning.

After running a few routes, McGee told Starr that the Chiefs secondary was ignoring him. Starr then threw to McGee, who was able to pull the ball to his chest before cornerback Willie Mitchell could make a play. Then cornerback Fred "The Hammer" Williamson gave chase as McGee romped into the end zone.

"You pay a quarterback a hundred thousand a year, you expect him to throw it a little better to a twenty-five-thousand dollar end," McGee joked. "I thought the ball was going to be intercepted. I was trying to knock it down . . . and it stuck to my hand."

McGee, thirty-four and in his eleventh season, finished the game with seven catches for 138 yards and two touchdowns. He should have been a strong candidate to receive the new Corvette that *Sport* magazine was giving to the game's most valuable player. When McGee came back to the bench after his first score, he told Hornung, "Hey, if Bart throws me the ball, I know I can win the damned car."

McGee's second touchdown catch, for 13 yards, gave the Packers a 28–10 lead in the third quarter. A hard hit caused McGee to juggle the ball. Asked if he was trying to make that catch appear as tough as the first one, McGee laughed and replied, "Make it look tough? I'd just got my bell rung. Lucky I held on to it."

Though McGee is the most celebrated player from that game, Starr was the MVP. "They should've given two, my man," Hornung told his pal.

Lombardi told McGee to make sure he got Hornung to the church on time. He also congratulated him for his great catches.

"Most any end could've done the same thing," McGee replied.

"You're right," agreed Lombardi.

"I looked at him," McGee recalled, "and said, 'Well, you sure took the edge off that, you s.o.b.'"

#17
HOLY ROLLER
RAIDERS WIN BY HOOK OR BY CROOK
SEPTEMBER 10, 1978

IN OAKLAND the play is known as the "Holy Roller." In San Diego it's known as the "Immaculate Deception." The Raiders pulled a fast one to beat the Chargers 21–20 with a play that you'll never see again. That's because NFL rules makers outlawed the play before the next season.

The Raiders had a well-deserved reputation for bending the rules, but at San Diego early in 1978 they outdid themselves. Even a Raider hater would have to give quarterback Ken "The Snake" Stabler credit for thinking on his feet. The "Holy Roller" is as famous for its creativity as for its audacity.

The Raiders trailed 20–14 and were stuck at their 19-yard line with only 1:07 left. Stabler proceeded to show why he was one of the top comeback quarterbacks of his era and completed five passes, including one for 27 yards to tight end Raymond Chester. Stabler moved the Raiders to a first down at the San Diego 14 but had no time-outs remaining. He threw incomplete on first down and tried another throw with just ten seconds left.

His protection broke down, however, and he was hit at the 24-yard line by linebacker Woodrow Lowe. As he fell, Stabler deliberately fumbled the ball forward. It bounced to the 8-yard line, where running back Pete Banaszak pretended to grope for the ball while batting and kicking it to the goal line. Tight end Dave Casper finally kicked the ball into the end zone and fell on it, tying the score. Errol Mann kicked the extra point with no time left, and the heist was complete.

"I was about to get my hands on Kenny," Lowe recalled. "Kenny was backing away, and I thought Kenny had tried to throw the ball underhanded. I thought it was an incomplete pass. I thought I was the hero of the game, to be honest."

Chargers coach Tommy Prothro understandably was livid. "There's no way the officials can justify the call," he said. "It was an illegal play. The rules will back it up that it was an illegal play." The rule to which he referred stated: "It is considered intentional grounding of a forward pass when the ball strikes the ground after the passer throws, tosses or lobs the ball to prevent a loss of yards by his team."

But the rule didn't cover an unintentional fumble, and referee Jerry Markbreit allowed the touchdown because he couldn't prove Stabler fumbled on purpose. Once the victory was in the bag, however, Stabler made a full confession. "I tried to fumble," he admitted. "If I get sacked, the game is over."

Banaszak's stumbling and fumbling was also an act. "Sure, I batted it," he said. "I could see a San Diego guy right along side me. If I picked it up, he would have tackled me, and the game would have been over."

Casper chimed in, "Sure, I helped the ball along into the end zone."

Raiders guard Gene Upshaw explained, "The play is in our playbook. It's called 'win at any cost.'"

The Chargers-Raiders rivalry was nasty long before Stabler's underhanded ploy. Both teams were AFL charter members, and their rivalry heated up once Al Davis became Raiders coach in 1963. One of the most famous moments in the rivalry came in the early 1970s when Chargers coach Harland Svare suspected Davis had bugged the visitors' locker room in Oakland. Svare warily looked at a light fixture and said, "I know you're up there, Al Davis."

Davis, happy to confirm that far-fetched suspicion, said, "I'll tell you this: the thing wasn't in the light fixture."

Outraged San Diego fans wouldn't soon forget the "Holy Roller." They made up T-shirts that showed a blindfolded referee signaling a touchdown, with the caption, "Immaculate Deception." That was, of course, a pun on the "Immaculate Reception," the Pittsburgh Steelers' touchdown play that shocked the Raiders in the 1972 AFC playoffs.

Because of the "Holy Roller," NFL rules makers voted to relieve the referee of having to judge the intent of a forward fumble. According to the new rule, which remains in place today, if a player fumbles in the last two minutes of a half, only he is allowed to advance the ball. The same goes for any fumble on a fourth-down play from scrimmage any time in a game. Any defensive player, however, can advance a fumble.

John Madden, the TV analyst and video-game icon who was then coaching the Raiders, tried to rationalize the "Holy Roller" in classic Madden-ese.

"It was one of those things," he said, "that maybe you can't do that, but the rules say you can do that, so you can do that, and if you don't want to do that, then go change the rule. And that's exactly what they did. Now you can't do it anymore."

#16
THE DRIVE
THE START OF JOHN ELWAY'S LEGEND
JANUARY 11, 1987

JOHN ELWAY'S pass for wide receiver Mark Jackson in the end zone was hard and low, where no defender could knock it away. Jackson, sliding on his knees, cradled the ball for a 5-yard touchdown catch that ended "The Drive," and started a legend.

That play meant for Elway what "The Catch" meant for Joe Montana. The Denver Broncos quarterback began the transition from most publicized NFL rookie ever to Hall of Fame quarterback. Elway, the first overall pick of the 1983 draft, would total forty-seven comebacks that won games in the fourth quarter or in overtime. But there's no dispute over which comeback belongs at the top of the list.

Jackson's catch, with thirty-seven seconds left in regulation, opened the door to a 23–20 overtime victory against the Cleveland Browns in the AFC championship game. The Browns received the kickoff at the start of overtime but were forced to punt. Elway quickly moved the Broncos into position for Rich Karlis's 33-yard field goal.

"The Drive was something that put me on the map," Elway said upon his Hall of Fame election in 2004. "I think that coming in as a first pick, and then not playing really well my first year and getting benched, and going through some tough times. . . . Then when we went to Cleveland and had The Drive, that was something that kind of put me on the map and legitimized me as a good pro football player and good pro quarterback.

"That was a huge confidence booster for me, the fact that it's an AFC championship game and you do it on the road. That, to me, is the single biggest moment that I can remember that really kind of said, 'All right, you're not bad. You're really pretty good. You're gonna make it in the NFL.'"

The Broncos trailed the Browns 20–13 and were backed up at their 2-yard line with 5:43 left. The famous drive included fifteen plays and survived a near fiasco on third-and-18. Elway lined up in the shotgun as wide receiver Steve Watson went in motion. But the snap from center grazed Watson, and the ball fell to the ground. Elway scooped it up and threw a 20-yard pass to Jackson for a first down at the Cleveland 28-yard line.

Elway passed to running back Steve Sewell for a first down at the 14-yard line with fifty-seven seconds left. Elway threw incomplete, then ran 9 yards to the 5. The Broncos called a pass, with running back Gerald Willhite the primary receiver in the flat. But he was covered, and Jackson put a move on rookie cornerback Mark Harper that left him alone in the middle of the end zone. Jackson recalled that Elway's eyes widened when he spotted the open receiver. Elway described that pass as the hardest of his career.

"What happens in life is, sometimes we get thrown into situations we don't expect," Jackson said. "Some of us go forward, but many of us kind of see the dangers and retreat to our comfort zone. John was the type who, once he was out of his comfort zone, he seemed to enjoy it. It's a funny thing about him. Each time he hit that area, it became a new common ground for him. That's when he played his best."

As Elway's backup and later his quarterbacks coach, Gary Kubiak watched most of Elway's escape acts. "You knew if it was a close game, we were going to win because we had John," said Kubiak, who became the Houston Texans' head coach in 2006. "There was nothing like him when the game was on the line."

Any opponent who saw Elway's throw to Jackson had to remain nervous in the fourth quarter as long as Elway had the ball. Each stunning comeback gave Elway and his teammates the confidence that they could pull off the next one. Elway once complained that he faced so many comeback situations early in his career because Dan Reeves, his first coach in Denver, wouldn't turn Elway loose until the situation became desperate. Elway later made peace with Reeves, however, and credited the coach with instilling in his players the attitude that they were never out of a game until the final gun.

"There are several ways you can look at those comebacks," Elway said. "One way is to say, 'Well, you had a lot of comebacks because you were always behind, and why were you always behind?'

"When Dan was there, that was something where the games were always close, and Dan's competitiveness kind of went through the whole football team, so we were always in football games. We had, as an organization and as a team, a mindset that once we started to come back late in the game, until the clock was zero-zero-zero, we really felt we had a chance to win."

Marty Schottenheimer, who faced Elway as coach of the Browns and the Kansas City Chiefs, was on the wrong end of more Elway comebacks, including "The Drive," than he would care to remember. "He ultimately may be the greatest to have ever played this game at that position," Schottenheimer said. "The guy is the greatest competitor I have ever witnessed in sport."

#15

MARCUS MAKES THEM MISS
ALLEN RUNS CIRCLES AROUND REDSKINS
JANUARY 22, 1984

MARCUS ALLEN wasn't the greatest running back who ever lived. But he may have been the most versatile—he was the first NFL player to total 10,000 rushing yards and 5,000 receiving yards. He wasn't the fastest back who ever lived, either. But few other backs could match Allen's knack for making the first would-be tackler miss. That knack enabled him to be one of the best short-yardage runners of his era.

Allen could make the game-breaking play, too. He proved that with a 74-yard touchdown run in the Los Angeles Raiders' 38–9 victory over the Washington Redskins in the Super Bowl. The Raiders already led 28–9 when Allen broke loose, so his run must have been spectacular to stand out in such a lopsided game.

Allen's third-quarter run in Tampa Stadium was the longest in Super Bowl history and came against the NFL's top regular-season rushing defense. That run, for his second touchdown of the game, earned MVP honors for Allen and sealed the victory. "The last touchdown by Marcus Allen took the air out," Redskins running back Joe Washington acknowledged.

The Redskins put themselves in a 21–3 halftime hole when they tried a high-risk, low-reward play near their goal line. Joe Theismann's screen pass for Washington was easy pickings for linebacker Jack Squirek, who returned the interception 5 yards for a touchdown just before the half.

The Redskins closed the gap to 21–9 early in the third quarter, but Allen began closing the door by scoring on a 5-yard run. Washington's last decent chance to get back in the game ended when fullback John Riggins was stopped by linebacker Rod Martin and safety Mike Davis on fourth down at the Raiders 26-yard line. "I came up and 'Pow!'" Davis said. "We stopped him 8 inches short."

On the next play, Allen took a handoff and started left but had nowhere to go. Running like a schoolyard player, he reversed his field and found room up the middle. He shot through the hole before any defender could get a good shot at him, and all this happened because Allen didn't follow a block from his right guard.

"I really screwed up that play," he said. "The play is called '17 Bob Trail.' The tight end and tackle double-team the linebacker, and the guard pulls. Mickey Marvin did a good job on the block, and I should have gone inside him. But somebody grabbed me from behind. I put on the brakes and made a quick U-turn. I pulled away, and there was an alley."

Most Redskins defenders by now were out of position. Wide receiver Cliff Branch made one downfield block, and Allen was gone. "My first thought was not to get caught, and then I hoped there was no penalty," he said. "It was the best run I have ever had on this level. I didn't think of what to do on the run. I just let instinct take over.

"I knew long before I made it to the end zone that I was going to score. I felt as if I was the fastest thing on the field. I felt as if I had wings while everyone and everything around me moved in superslow motion. As I ran, I did something I'd never done before, sneaking a glance into the stands."

Allen realized he was achieving something special and wanted to frame the crowd's reaction for posterity. But he didn't have to look hard to capture his teammates' reaction. Because that play ended the third quarter, the rest of the Raiders could come off the bench to mob Allen and not invite a penalty.

"As my teammates ran from the bench to join me in the end zone, you could feel the Raiders' confidence soar," he recalled.

"With a 35–9 lead and only fifteen minutes left to play, we were not only in control of the game. We were dominating."

Allen finished with twenty carries for 191 yards and two catches for 18 yards. That gave him an average gain of 9.5 yards each time his touched the ball. His MVP trophy gave him a book-end for the Heisman he'd won at Southern California.

President Ronald Reagan made the traditional congratula-tory phone call to the Super Bowl champion. Using Cold War ter-minology, he compared Allen to a secret weapon and the Raiders to a nuclear missile. Allen, in just his second NFL season, had not even reached his peak.

He showcased his versatility in 1985 with 1,759 rushing and 555 receiving yards. He was held under 100 total yards from scrimmage just once that season and finished with ten consecu-tive 100-yard rushing games, including one in the playoffs.

By the time he retired from the Kansas City Chiefs after the 1997 season, Allen had played sixteen seasons. You wouldn't ex-pect that just one run would stand out from such a long and dis-tinguished Hall of Fame career. Yet one does and always will.

#14

ISN'T THAT JOHN CANDY?
JOE MONTANA'S PASS WINS SUPER BOWL
JANUARY 22, 1989

QUARTERBACK JOE MONTANA was nicknamed "Joe Cool" because he seemed to thrive on pressure. He also possessed a quick wit. He displayed both characteristics in the waning minutes of a Super Bowl to complete one of the most dramatic drives and touchdown passes in the NFL's championship-game history.

Montana already owned two Super Bowl rings before the San Francisco 49ers met the Cincinnati Bengals in a rematch of the January 1982 Super Bowl. Montana's big-game invincibility was put to a stern test by the Bengals when they took a 16–13 lead in Miami with 3:20 left. The 49ers started their final drive at their 8-yard line, and Montana at first just wanted to move into field-goal position and force overtime. He went into a hurry-up offense and called the plays. Joe was cool, but some teammates were not.

"Some of the guys seemed more than normally tense, especially Harris Barton, a great offensive tackle who has a tendency to get nervous," Montana recalled. "As usual, I was just focusing on the situation, how far we had to go, how much time we had left, and just then I spotted John Candy, the late actor, sitting in the stands. He just happened to be in my line of vision. 'Look,' I said in the huddle. 'Isn't that John Candy?'

"It wasn't exactly what my teammates expected to hear with three minutes left in the Super Bowl. Everybody kind of smiled, and even Harris relaxed, and then we could all concentrate on the job we had to do."

Perhaps the 49ers didn't concentrate hard enough, because the winning play, "20 Halfback Curl X-Up," wasn't executed as it was drawn up. On second down from the Cincinnati 10-yard line, Montana planned to go to halfback Roger Craig over the middle.

"We had noticed that near the goal line, the Bengals like to bracket their coverage, doubling the outside receivers," Montana said. "We wanted to use our wide receivers to spread it out and open the middle."

Craig and fullback Tom Rathman, however, lined up on the wrong sides. Because Craig had just caught an 8-yard pass down the middle, the Bengals were keeping a close eye on him now.

"When we broke the huddle, I saw Tom line up on the left," Craig said, "and that wasn't the time to argue, so I just lined up on the right. The fact that I was on the wrong side didn't even affect Joe. He is so smooth, it's incredible. He looked at me first, just as he's supposed to, despite the fact I was on the wrong side. I was double-covered, so he went to the next guy."

Montana still had two standout wide receivers running routes. Jerry Rice, the game's MVP after making eleven catches for 215 yards, was a decoy for the Bengals' zone coverage. So Montana's next read was John Taylor, who was single-covered by nickelback Ray Horton. Taylor made a head fake to the outside, then cut inside, and Horton was late covering him deep in the end zone. Montana hit Taylor in full stride with thirty-four seconds left, and the 49ers won 20–16.

"All I could think was, 'Catch the ball,'" Taylor said. "I was just trying to draw a defensive back, but when I turned around, no one was inside."

Montana completed eight of nine passes on that eleven-play drive, yet it nearly stalled twice. Montana hyperventilated and nearly passed out in the Miami heat. He also had to overcome a second-and-20 situation at the Cincinnati 45-yard line. Montana found Rice in the midst of three defenders, and Rice ran to the 18. That's when, Montana said, he began to look for more than just a field goal. Center Randy Cross cracked, "Even if we had to pick up Joe en masse and carry him over the goal line, we were going to get a touchdown."

No previous Super Bowl had been decided so late. Montana would not have to provide such dramatics a year later, when he led the 49ers to their fourth Super Bowl victory, a 55–10 blowout of the Denver Broncos. No wonder former 49ers owner Eddie DeBartolo introduced Montana at his Hall of Fame induction by saying, "Joe Montana, simply stated, was the greatest quarterback to ever play the game, and I don't think we'll see the likes of him again."

When Montana retired, he and Terry Bradshaw of the Pittsburgh Steelers were the only quarterbacks with four Super Bowl rings. Montana in Super Bowls completed 83 of 122 passes for 1,142 yards and eleven touchdowns with no interceptions. His Super Bowl passer rating was 127.8, and he won three MVP awards. Yet nobody remembers those numbers like they remember the pass he threw to Taylor.

#13
HOOK AND LATERAL
DOLPHINS FOOL THE CHARGERS
JANUARY 2, 1982

DON SHULA wants to set the record straight about this razzle-dazzle touchdown play by his Miami Dolphins. It's not the "Hook and Ladder," as it's often been called over the years. "It's the hook and *lateral*," the Hall of Fame coach explained.

But no matter what you call it, Don Strock's pass to Duriel Harris, who lateraled to Tony Nathan, remains an unforgettable play from an unforgettable AFC playoff game. The Dolphins were getting embarrassed at home as the San Diego Chargers took a 24–0 first-quarter lead. Then Shula replaced second-year quarterback David Woodley with Strock, and the Dolphins began chipping away at the Chargers' lead.

"We weren't going to the desperation stuff," Strock said. "It was only the second quarter, and the short stuff was open. We'd start airing it out if it was late, but even though we were down 24, we still had enough time to do something about it."

The Dolphins were behind 24–10 and at the San Diego 40 when Strock called time-out six seconds before halftime. He went to the sideline to check with Shula, who told him to run "87 Circle Curl Lateral." Shula explained, "I just thought that was the time to use it. It's one of those plays where you have to keep the ball alive because you know that's the only way you're going to get into the end zone.

"Before the end of the half or late in a game or in sudden death, you want to have a chance to turn a play into a big play. Usually, the defense is playing a loose prevent, so that gives you time to do it. You want them to converge on the hook and hope to have the lateral break free."

Strock threw a bullet pass to Harris, who was lined up wide right and caught the ball at the San Diego 25-yard line. Harris then curled inside, and as defensive backs Willie Buchanon and Allen Ellis converged on him, he pitched the ball to Nathan, who was trailing on the right sideline. Nathan was all by himself and held the ball over his head when he reached the 20, then sprinted into the end zone.

The Miami crowd had been like a bear emerging from hibernation. The 24-point deficit had left fans lifeless, but murmurs of hope were audible once the Dolphins finally got on the board. Then as the fans saw the trickery unfolding before them, they jumped to their feet and screamed and turned the Orange Bowl into a volcano of sound. Even after the Dolphins went to their locker room trailing 24–17, the crowd's excitement and noise became an electric current that wouldn't be turned off.

"All of a sudden, Nathan's hauling into the end zone, and they're back in the game," recalled Chargers linebacker Linden King.

Considering that the Chargers boasted one of the NFL's most explosive offenses of all time, it came as a surprise that the day's flashiest play would be made by the Dolphins. "That was a great call by Shula," recalled Chargers wide receiver Charlie Joiner. "It didn't kill us, but we went in and knew we were going to be in for a dogfight. We were dejected, but we knew we had the talent to win the game."

The crowd of 73,735 at the Orange Bowl cheered as loudly as it ever did during the Shula era. "I remember how quiet it was in the Orange Bowl when we went ahead 24–0," Chargers tight end Kellen Winslow recalled. "And then I remember how loud it got when the Dolphins came back and scored just before the half. It was so noisy at halftime under those rickety stands, we couldn't hear the coaches in the locker room."

Many a great play has been forgotten because it came in a losing effort. Not this one. Though the Dolphins lost 41–38 in overtime, the Hook and Lateral remains the best-remembered play in a game filled with great plays.

"That was one of the best plays of all time," Shula recalled. "I'll never forget it. I'm told our fans were so excited, they never sat down. I came into the locker room, and I thought the worst thing I could do was try to motivate our players. After the Hook and Lateral, they were so fired up, they couldn't wait to get back on the field."

The Dolphins took their first lead, 38–31, when Nathan scored on a 12-yard sweep on the first play of the fourth quarter. The Chargers tied the score in the final minute on a 9-yard pass from Dan Fouts to running back James Brooks.

Then the game turned into an agonizing series of botched kicks. The Dolphins' Uwe von Schamann saw two kicks blocked—a 43-yard field-goal attempt on the last play of regulation and a 35-yard try late in overtime. Rolf Benirschke missed a 27-yard attempt six minutes into overtime, and by the time he made a 29-yard kick after 13:52, both teams totaled 1,036 yards. It marked the first time in NFL history that both quarterbacks passed for more than 400 yards in a game.

Super Bowl–winning quarterback Bob Griese had retired the year before, and Shula masterfully platooned his quarterbacks until Dan Marino came along in 1983. Woodley was starting for the second straight year, but when Shula saw his season slipping away, he called on Strock, a veteran backup with a cool head and strong arm.

"You could sense the difference," King said. "Strock had a real presence out there, and you could tell the rest of the Dolphins were responding to him."

Over the years Shula has been able to appreciate that he called a great play in a memorable game. In the immediate aftermath, however, the loss just hurt.

"It had to be a great game, maybe one of the greatest ever," he said. "But it's really tough for me to talk about something being great, realizing we didn't win."

#12
SNAKE EYES FOR DOLPHINS
KEN STABLER'S GREATEST THROW
DECEMBER 21, 1974

IT WAS ONE OF THE MOST improbable touchdown passes ever thrown, in one of the most dramatic playoff games ever played, and it captured the grit and slipperiness of the quarterback known as "Snake." Though Ken Stabler would lead the Raiders to a Super Bowl victory two years later, he never threw another pass as memorable as the one that beat the Miami Dolphins in the 1974 playoffs at Oakland.

The Dolphins led 26–21 when Stabler led a 68-yard drive, climaxed by an 8-yard touchdown pass to halfback Clarence Davis with twenty-six seconds left. Defensive end Vern Den Herder had both arms around the back of Stabler's legs and was bringing him down. Stabler fell forward grudgingly, like an actor dying an exaggerated death in an old cowboy movie. Though his knees stayed well off the ground, Stabler had lost his footing and couldn't put any zip on the ball.

Any coach would want his quarterback to throw the ball away or even take the sack. Stabler, though, was a risk taker and went for broke. He resembled a shot-putter as he lobbed a wobbly pass. Davis was covered in the end zone by three defenders but outwrestled them to grab Stabler's fourth touchdown pass of the day and a 28–26 victory.

Stabler had good protection on the winning play, but his wide receivers and tight end, all on the right side, were covered. "I moved to the left to avoid pressure," he recalled. "Just as I felt someone hit me from behind at the ankles, I saw Clarence Davis run into the end zone. He wasn't exactly wide open.

There were an awful lot of people around him. I never should have thrown the ball. It was a great catch, but a dumb play. If it would have been intercepted, I'd be kicking myself for not throwing it away."

Raiders coach John Madden might have been kicking him first. "That last pass wasn't really what the hell I had in mind," he recalled. "When I saw Davis under that pile with the ball and the official's arms in the air, well, it was just a tremendous feeling."

For the Dolphins, that was a heartbreaking way to end a streak of three straight AFC championships and back-to-back Super Bowl victories. They took the lead when rookie Benny Malone broke two tackles on a 23-yard run with 2:08 left.

"I just wish Benny had fallen down at about the 3-yard line," Dolphins quarterback Bob Griese said. "Benny made a beautiful run, but if he'd stopped just short of the goal, we could have eaten up another minute and probably scored with less than a minute to go."

Instead, Stabler was left with enough time to guide the Raiders down the field. "We can do it, we can do it," guard Gene Upshaw said in the Raiders' huddle. That became the Raiders' chant after every play, and their drive was fueled by 18- and 20-yard passes to wide receiver Fred Biletnikoff.

Davis ran off tackle for 6 yards for a first down at the Miami 8-yard line, but only thirty-five seconds remained, and the Raiders were out of time-outs. Had Stabler taken a sack on his pass to Davis, he probably would have been left with just one last desperate throw.

"Den Herder had him and was pulling him down," recalled Dolphins coach Don Shula. "He shot puts the ball, it went end over end, and Clarence Davis made the catch. It was a great play on Stabler's part and on Davis's part."

The Raiders were accustomed to seeing Stabler make great plays out of nothing. Were it not for the "Immaculate Reception," his 30-yard touchdown run against the Pittsburgh Steelers would have been the defining moment of a 1972 playoff game. When he improvised, Stabler put pressure on defenses, which often led to breakdowns. On Stabler's pass to Davis, safety Charlie Babb and linebackers Mike Kolen and Larry Ball were all behind Davis. Had Ball stepped in front of Davis, as he should have, Stabler's pass wouldn't have been completed. But the sands of NFL history turn on what-ifs.

The Raiders advanced to the AFC title game that year and the next, only to lose both times to the Pittsburgh Steelers. Finally, in the 1976 season, they won their first Super Bowl with a 32–14 victory over the Minnesota Vikings.

The Dolphins, meanwhile, went into a three-year playoff drought. Running backs Larry Csonka and Jim Kiick and wide receiver Paul Warfield signed big contracts to play in the World Football League in 1975. Those three gave the Dolphins dynasty much of its heart and soul, and had they stayed, the team might have made another Super Bowl run.

"This was the toughest loss I've ever suffered in coaching," said Shula, who'd been a head coach since 1963. "When you lose them like that, you know it wasn't meant to be. The season was meant to end here in Oakland, and it did."

#11
HAIL MARY
ROGER STAUBACH COINS A PHRASE
DECEMBER 28, 1975

THIS WAS THE ORIGINAL "HAIL MARY" pass, the mother of every last-minute desperation heave since then. With the Vikings leading 14–10 in a first-round NFC playoff game at Minnesota, Dallas Cowboys quarterback Roger Staubach fired a 50-yard touchdown pass to wide receiver Drew Pearson with twenty-four seconds left.

Even for the leader known as "Captain Comeback," this pass was something special. "I closed my eyes and said a Hail Mary," Staubach revealed after a 17–14 victory that dethroned the NFC champions of the previous two seasons.

The game was played on a cold, gray day in old Metropolitan Stadium and, as expected, turned into a defensive struggle. The Vikings' defense was nicknamed "The Purple People Eaters," and featured a famous front four of Jim Marshall, Alan Page, Carl Eller, and Gary Larsen. The Cowboys' counterpart was the "Doomsday Defense," which featured end Ed "Too Tall" Jones, middle linebacker Lee Roy Jordan, and cornerback Mel Renfro. The Dallas defense remained in charge until the Vikings took a 14–10 lead with 1:51 left.

The Cowboys began their final drive at their 15-yard line. Staubach had to shake off not just the Vikings' vaunted pass rush but sore ribs that were aggravated by the cold. After nine plays, the Cowboys were only at midfield. Fewer than thirty seconds remained, and the Cowboys had no time-outs left.

Staubach lined up in the shotgun formation, pump-faked to his left, and then turned to his right and threw deep for Pearson.

He was covered by cornerback Nate Wright, and both turned toward the sideline to await the ball. Wright slipped but recovered in time to regain position. The pass was underthrown, and Pearson and Wright bumped. Wright fell as Pearson caught the ball on his hip at the 5-yard line, scored, and raised the ball above his head in celebration.

"When the ball hit my hands, I thought I had dropped it," Pearson said. "I said, 'Oh, no, I blew it!' But I was bending over, and the ball just stuck between my elbow and my hip.

"I was looking for the ball out and away, and I felt I had one more gear to get past Nate, but then I saw the ball was underthrown. Nate was running at an angle a little in front of me to cut me off if the ball went deep. But I came back with my arm in a swim move, reaching over Nate's shoulder for the ball. I was as surprised as anyone in that stadium that I caught that ball."

Pearson was mobbed by the entire Cowboys' team. The Vikings, though, were livid because they were convinced Wright had been pushed down. As the cornerback lay on the ground, safety Paul Krause leaped over him and yelled at field judge Armen Terzian that pass interference should have been called. A whiskey bottle thrown from the stands cut Terzian's head. Page also came over to dispute the call and argued so vehemently that the Vikings were penalized 15 yards on the ensuing kickoff for unsportsmanlike conduct.

"They won on a push-off," Vikings coach Bud Grant still insists.

Staubach didn't see the play because he was knocked down just as he released the pass. Wright, who saw more of the play than he would have liked, explained, "I really thought I could intercept it because I was in good position. Suddenly, my mind became confused. Next thing I knew, I was on the ground, and I saw Drew catch the ball on his hip and run into the end zone. I was in shock."

That wasn't the first or last time Staubach would leave an opponent in shock in the waning moments. He nearly threw another Hail Mary touchdown pass in a 21–17 Super Bowl loss that season when the ball eluded the fingertips of rookie Percy Howard. Staubach closed out his career in 1983 with two touchdown passes in the last 2:20 for a 35–34 victory over the Washington Redskins. During an eleven-year career, Staubach led twenty-three fourth-quarter comebacks in the regular season and playoffs, including fourteen in the last two minutes or in overtime. But the original "Hail Mary" is the comeback pass for which he's best remembered.

"You learn to be competitive, but I think that's something inside you," Staubach said, explaining his comeback knack. "My father once mentioned to me, 'You're the only one I've seen who wanted to be at bat in the ninth inning with two out and two runners on and who wanted to be at the free-throw line [in a close game].'

"I remember once I was at the free-throw line, shooting a one-on-one, and I missed the first shot. I never forgot that, and it challenged me that if I ever was in a tight situation again, I would do the very best I could and be grateful for the opportunity.

"I relished the opportunity to pull out a game. It didn't always happen that way, but if you have the confidence it can get done and transfer the confidence to your teammates, a lot of good things can happen. A good quarterback can't let anybody think it can't happen."

Gil Brandt was the Cowboys' player personnel director who helped draft Staubach and watched him stage comeback after comeback. "He never lost a game," Brandt said. "Time just ran out on him." Not on a cold, desperate day at Minnesota.

#10
BLOODY SUNDAY
A GORED JOHN UNITAS BEATS THE BEARS
NOVEMBER 13, 1960

THOUGH JIM PARKER was one of the best offensive linemen of all time, he knew that every time the Baltimore Colts faced the Chicago Bears, he was one missed block away from having a bloodied quarterback. Parker went one-on-one with 6-foot-8, 275-pound defensive end Doug Atkins, who was as mean as he was huge. And if Parker was bested, quarterback John Unitas could expect a beating.

"If Doug was playing, you were in trouble and in for a long day," Unitas said. "One of his favorite tricks was to throw a blocker at the quarterback."

But giving Unitas a beating wasn't the same as beating Unitas. Far from it. Despite blood gushing from his nose, Unitas threw one of the most courageous game-winning touchdown passes in pro football history.

The Colts trailed the Bears 20–17 in the final minute when Atkins gained the upper hand on Parker. He smashed Unitas's nose and turned it into a bloody mess. Parker's embarrassment was matched only by his queasiness.

"Blood squirted all over the place, and [right guard] Alex Sandusky scooped up some mud and stuffed it up John's nose to stop the bleeding," Parker recalled. "But the blood kept coming. When I came into the huddle, I almost got sick at how he looked. I couldn't look at him, but he looked me in the eye and said, 'It's okay, baby. We'll get him next time.'"

Trainers tried treating the laceration, which Parker said later required some twenty stitches. "The ref stuck his head in the huddle and said, 'Take all the time you need,'" recalled Colts center Buzz Nutter. "You know what John said to him? He said, 'Get the hell out of here so I can call the play.'"

Injured or not, Unitas would never back down. Whether it was Atkins or Godzilla coming at him, he was not going to get rid of the ball until a receiver broke open.

"He was just extremely accurate, and what he did better than any other quarterback I've ever seen was to stay in the pocket to release the ball," said Don Shula, who played with and coached Unitas. "That gave receivers that extra step to get open, and he had the toughness and courage to take the punishment that would come with the hit."

Though Atkins tore up Unitas's nose, his golden arm was working fine, and he had Hall of Fame receivers in Raymond Berry and Lenny Moore. Unitas dropped back from the Bears' 40-yard line with time running short and saw Moore beat cornerback J. C. Caroline down the right sideline. This time neither Atkins nor any other Bear was near Unitas as he hit Moore for a touchdown and a 24–20 victory. That was the forty-fifth game in Unitas's amazing streak of forty-seven straight games with at least one touchdown pass.

"He'd wait in the pocket until the absolute last second, deliver the ball right on the money, and get smashed in the mouth," Berry recalled. "Then he'd call the same play again and hold the ball a little longer and get smashed in the mouth even harder. The bridge of his nose would be split. His mouth would be full of blood. Do you think he cared? John would have been a great middle linebacker."

Unitas had been forced out of two games in 1958 because of three broken ribs and a punctured lung, yet returned while wearing an awkward protector. He led the Colts the rest of the season and gave his most famous performance in a 23–17 overtime victory over the New York Giants in the NFL championship game.

"Quarterbacks are being paid to play, score touchdowns, and help win games," Unitas said. "They can't permit themselves to think of injuries, or they'll leave their game in the locker room. Once a game starts, a good athlete will tend to forget minor hurts and sometimes even major ones and concentrate on doing his job."

If Unitas could shrug off vicious hits, Parker took them personally. Parker protected Unitas's blind side at left tackle from his rookie year, 1957, until he moved to left guard when Shula replaced Weeb Ewbank in 1963. Few defenders got by Parker, though Atkins had more luck than most.

"I considered myself the best guard [and tackle] of this century, and I played against some mean ones, but I never met anyone meaner than Atkins," Parker said. "After my first meeting with him, I really wanted to quit pro football. He just beat the hell out of me. He rammed me back there so hard, the only thing I could do was wave to Johnny as I went by. It was awful. Finally, my coaches convinced me not every pro player was like Atkins."

Facing Parker was no picnic for Atkins, either. He called Parker the best blocker he ever faced. "You had to hit Jim full speed and sometimes that still didn't budge him," Atkins said. "He was good, but I could get to him. I'd call him 'a big so-and-so,' and he'd get so mad, I'd go around him and get Unitas. Finally, Unitas jumped him and said, 'Quit listening to that guy and keep him away from me.' Most of the time, he did."

Parker never forgave himself for the time in Chicago when he didn't.

#9
MUSIC CITY MIRACLE
TITANS' PLAYOFF GAME-WINNING RETURN
JANUARY 8, 2000

FOR THE TENNESSEE TITANS, it was the "Immaculate Reception" and "Stanford Band" play rolled into one. With one remarkable kickoff return, the Titans turned an impending playoff loss into a 22–16 victory over the Buffalo Bills and took a big step toward playing in their first Super Bowl.

The Titans ended each Saturday walk-through practice of the 1999 season with a variation of "Home Run Throwback," a razzle-dazzle kickoff return saved for desperate situations. The return man waits until the tacklers are almost on him, then laterals to a teammate who picks up blockers and runs down the left sideline.

Titans special-teams coach Alan Lowry borrowed the play from Southern Methodist, which used it for a 91-yard return that defeated Texas Tech in 1982. That return was overshadowed that year by a wacky kickoff return, aided by illegal forward passes, which California used on the final play to beat Stanford. The Stanford band was lined up in the end zone, and one of its members was knocked down on the play.

NFL players seldom expect these trick returns to work. But the Titans had no other option when Steve Christie's 41-yard field goal gave the Bills a 16–15 lead with twenty-two seconds left in Nashville. An uplifting 13–3 season for the Titans, highlighted by eight straight wins in their new stadium, seemed about to end with a thud.

"When the ball went through the uprights, I turned, and Alan was right there," Titans coach Jeff Fisher recalled for nfl.com.

"At the same time, we both said the same thing: 'Home Run Throwback.' We had to give ourselves the chance to push the ball upfield and give us a shot from field-goal range."

Tight end Frank Wycheck was supposed to field the kickoff, then lateral to wide receiver Isaac Byrd, who could keep the ball or pitch to a trailing player. But fullback Lorenzo Neal fielded the high kick at the 25-yard line and handed off to Wycheck near the right hash mark.

For the Titans, the short kickoff proved the key to victory. These tricky returns seldom work, partly because opponents anticipate a handoff and lateral and usually smother the second man to touch the ball. The Bills, consequently, overreacted to Neal's handoff and had eyes only for Wycheck as he ran to his right. That left wide receiver Kevin Dyson uncovered on the left sideline when Wycheck pivoted and threw halfway across the field. Dyson caught the ball and romped 75 yards for a game-winning touchdown. Officials reviewed the play to make sure that Wycheck's pass was a lateral and not an illegal forward pass.

"Frank threw it over there and all of a sudden everything opened up," Neal said. "It was like, 'OK, Kevin, get in field goal range.' And then it's 'Oh! Forget the field goal. Get a touchdown!'"

The crowd erupted into celebration, then became hushed as referee Phil Luckett reviewed the video. A national TV audience was led to believe the lateral was illegal when announcers pointed out that Wycheck had one foot over the 25-yard line while Dyson had one foot on the line and the other behind. In fact, the ruling depended only upon the flight of the ball, and an official standing on the 25 determined the ball remained parallel to the yard line. The review confirmed that call, though folks in Buffalo differ to this day. Bills coach Wade Phillips and his players sarcastically called the play, "Home Run Throw Forward."

"The loss to the Titans was the most devastating defeat I've ever experienced in football," said Ralph Wilson, owner of the

Bills since 1960. "I've never felt worse after a game, and I've seen lots and lots of games through the years."

Titans owner Bud Adams, one of Wilson's fellow AFL charter owners, could easily pick out his own most devastating loss. When the Titans were the Houston Oilers, they blew a 35–3 lead in a January 1993 playoff game at Buffalo and lost 41–38 in overtime. "It was poetic justice," Adams said. "The devastation the Bills felt after the kickoff return was the same devastation we felt after that comeback game."

Dyson never expected to make the return, much less score. He was a last-second fill-in for that role. Wide receiver Derrick Mason was out with a concussion, and his backup, cornerback Anthony Dorsett, was out with cramps.

"I was getting my mind right for the last couple of Hail Mary plays, and I heard Coach Fisher call my name, and I thought, 'What's he calling my name for?'" Dyson recalled. "As we were running on the field, they were trying to explain to me the gist of the play. It was basically a desperation play, and we were certainly desperate at the time."

That play shook up the Bills in more ways than one. Special-teams coach Bruce DeHaven was fired, even though he warned his coverage unit to look for a gimmick play. The Bills cleaned house and released fifteen players, including the remnants of their Super Bowl teams. They began sliding the next year, partly because of poor special-teams play.

The Titans followed up their huge win with upsets at Indianapolis and Jacksonville before a 23–16 loss to the St. Louis Rams in the Super Bowl.

"I really believe that play catapulted us to the Super Bowl," said Gregg Williams, then the Titans' defensive coordinator. "It made believers out of us. The next week, we went out and won another close game. That was a direct result of pulling out that Buffalo game."

Williams, ironically, became the Bills' head coach in 2001. Back in Nashville, he'd hung a framed photo of "Home Run Throwback" in his family room. He put it in a closet when he got to Buffalo. And when he was introduced as the Bills' new coach, Wilson kiddingly asked him if Wycheck's pass had been forward or not.

Williams replied, "As of today, my thinking is that, yes, it was a forward pass." That may have been the first time anybody in Buffalo got a big laugh out of the play.

#8
SWANN LAKE
STEELER'S BALLET DOMINATES SUPER BOWL
JANUARY 18, 1976

WHEN JERRY RICE, the greatest wide receiver of all time, was a teenager, there was one NFL player who set the bar for him.

"Lynn Swann was an idol," said Rice, who shattered the NFL's major career receiving records. "It would amaze me how he could fly through the air and make those catches. I'll never forget the one versus Dallas. It was the greatest catch I've ever seen."

Which one? When Swann had finished turning the Super Bowl into his own ballet recital, the only questions were: Which of his catches deserved to be ranked highest? And for which catch that day would he be best remembered?

The answer to the second question is simple. His 64-yard touchdown catch down the middle of the field is best remembered because it gave the Pittsburgh Steelers the clinching touchdown in a 21–17 victory over the Dallas Cowboys. It also clinched the game's MVP Award for Swann.

Yet of his four catches for 161 yards, Swann's touchdown catch was actually his third-most impressive reception. That merely showcased his blazing speed as he beat cornerback Mark Washington at the 5-yard line before taking Terry Bradshaw's pass into the end zone.

"I thought I could beat Mark Washington because I'd been beating him all day," Swann said. "The safetymen didn't give Washington any help. Washington played a pretty good game, but I made a couple of pretty good catches on him in the first half."

Pretty good? What set Swann apart from other top receivers was his leaping ability, body control, and great hands. His first two catches against the Cowboys were proof of that.

Bradshaw threw down the right sideline for Swann in the first quarter. Washington had him covered, and it was questionable if the ball could be caught in bounds. Swann leaped, caught the ball, and while in the air turned his body away from the sideline stripe before landing with both feet in bounds for a 32-yard gain. "It seemed to boost me," Swann said. "I never had a day in my life when I felt so loose."

In the second quarter, Swann made a 53-yard catch known as the "Levitation Leap." It required him to be part ballet dancer, part acrobat, and part juggler. It was the most spectacular catch of his Hall of Fame career.

Covered again by Washington, Swann leaped and got his hands on the ball but bobbled it. For a mere mortal of a receiver, that would've been an incomplete pass. Swann, though, displayed his uncanny knack for seeming to hang in the air and freeze time, as though he were in a slow-motion replay. The ball was still in the air as Swann began to fall, and he practically had to defy gravity to keep the play alive. He seemed to levitate to keep the ball within his grasp and made the catch as he landed on his back.

As tough as it was to make those three catches against the Cowboys, it was even tougher for Swann just to get on the field. Because of his 5-foot-11, 180-pound frame, some defenses tried to batter Swann. Oakland Raider safeties Jack Tatum and George Atkinson gave Swann a concussion in the AFC championship game, and he spent two nights in a Pittsburgh hospital.

He was listed as doubtful when the Steelers arrived in Miami a week later for the Super Bowl. Swann didn't go through any hard workouts. A day before the game, he was still struggling to concentrate and kept dropping passes. Physicians told Swann he could decide whether to play but that he risked permanent brain damage if he took another hard shot to the head. Swann made up his mind when Cliff Harris, the Cowboys' ornery safety, challenged his pride.

"I'm not going to hurt anyone intentionally," Harris said. "But getting hit again while he's running a pass route must be in the back of Swann's mind. I know it would be in the back of my mind."

Swann read that and said, "He was trying to intimidate me. He said I'd be afraid out there. He needn't worry. He doesn't know Lynn Swann. He can't scare me or the team. I said to myself, 'The hell with it, I'm gonna play.'"

Harris, of course, didn't have to worry about covering Swann. That unenviable task fell to Washington, the left cornerback. Because the Steelers had John Stallworth, another future Hall of Famer, on the other side, the Cowboys couldn't easily double-team either wide receiver. Washington was beaten by Swann on each of his three big catches, and the third one was the bomb that gave the Steelers a 21–10 lead.

"I reached for the ball but missed it," Washington said. "You feel some pressure when the safety blitz is on, and you're out there by yourself. Nobody can cover Swann adequately under those conditions."

The blitz by Harris and linebacker D. D. Lewis did, however, put Bradshaw out of the game. He managed to duck under Lewis and throw, but then Harris flattened him and knocked Bradshaw unconscious. He was revived and helped off the field but didn't know he'd thrown a touchdown pass until he was brought into the locker room.

So Bradshaw never saw Swann's touchdown catch. But he'd already seen a couple of catches that day that few quarterbacks are lucky enough to see in a career.

#7
SIX-PACK
GALE SAYERS'S RETURN CAPS A RECORD DAY
DECEMBER 12, 1965

ANYBODY WHO WANTS to fantasize about how great a career Gale Sayers might have had if he had stayed healthy should watch his 85-yard punt return for his sixth touchdown of the day on a muddy field in Chicago. Sayers, nicknamed the "Kansas Comet," was a Bears rookie running back and kick returner who, despite miserable playing conditions, showcased the brilliance that surgeries on both knees would diminish.

"I scored six touchdowns that day; I probably could've scored eight if they'd let me play because we were scoring that well," recalled Sayers, a first-round draft choice from the University of Kansas.

Nobody involved in the Bears' 61–20 victory over the San Francisco 49ers that day would argue with Sayers, who was rested once his team built a huge lead. "I never saw such a thing in my life!" Bears coach George Halas said. "It was the greatest performance ever by one man on a football field."

Hall of Fame linebacker Dave Wilcox likes to poke fun at himself by telling people that he was among the 49ers trying to contain Sayers that day. "He was the quickest and fastest person," Wilcox recalled. "I never did meet Barry Sanders, and they talk about how quick he was. But Gale Sayers was playing in mud and quagmires, and if he could have played on that same [artificial] stuff . . . holy cow!"

An early-morning rain turned the Wrigley Field turf into a mess, which kept getting muddier with each Sayers touchdown.

"I actually didn't like playing in that kind of weather," he said. "So many things can happen—you can slip, pull a muscle, tear a hamstring."

And did he mention that it's no small feat to field a slippery, waterlogged ball? On his famous punt return, Sayers appeared to be running on a carpet while everybody else was trudging through a swamp. He made sharp cuts while pursuers fell down running straight at him. Only two 49ers as much as grazed him. This was a video game in which only Sayers held the joystick. When he came to a stop near the middle of the end zone, his return route had formed almost a perfect "S."

Sayers fielded the punt on his 15-yard line, near the right sideline, with blocker John Arnett in front and to his left. Sayers darted outside Arnett to the sideline and easily avoided a defender who made a desperate dive at his ankles. Jack Chapple was the only 49er with a decent angle on Sayers, but a blind-side block took him out of the play.

Now Sayers had an alley to his 40-yard line, and it would take a great open-field tackle to bring him down. That wasn't going to happen. Wilcox was blocked toward the sideline and couldn't get close. Elbert Kimbrough was partially blocked and stumbled toward Sayers, who then deftly cut to the middle. Ed Beard fell down before he could get near Sayers, and Matt Hazeltine went sliding by as though he were on ice.

Now Sayers made one final cut, to the left sideline, and left the weary and fallen pack in his wake. He began looking back and trotting before he reached the San Francisco 30-yard line. When he scored, he casually flipped the ball in the air.

"I probably had to work hardest on that run than any other run [that day]," Sayers said. "That was, unquestionably, a very muddy field. To do the things I did on that particular run took a little effort and a little balance.

"I caught the ball on the right side of the field. I made a couple of moves, and everybody was flying by me. But it seemed to me the field was dry. They were sliding by, but Gale kept on going. You don't teach those moves, you don't practice those moves. You feel those moves within yourself. You feel people around you and make a move. It can't be taught. It's a God-given instinct."

With that return, Sayers tied the NFL record for most touchdowns scored in a game. It also gave him twenty-one touchdowns, an NFL single-season record that both he and Jim Brown of the Cleveland Browns achieved in 1965.

Sayers scored his first touchdown of the day on a screen pass from Rudy Bukich that he took 80 yards. He scored next on runs of 21 and 7 yards. Then came a spectacular 50-yard run on which he weaved through the 49ers' defense. His fifth touchdown came on a 1-yard plunge.

"Back then nobody cared about records," Sayers said. "I didn't even know I'd tied the six-touchdown record until after the ball game. We won, and that was the most important thing at the time."

It also was important to Sayers and his teammates to turn the tables on the team that had beaten them 52–24 in the opener, which started a three-game losing streak. The Bears had won eight of their next nine games and were trying to catch the leaders in the Western Division. "We were on a roll of sorts, and we wanted revenge," Sayers said. "The Forty Niners had killed us in the first game, and we had something to prove."

A knee injury knocked Sayers out of the last five games of the 1968 season, and he hardly played in 1970 or 1971 before he was forced to retire. Bears fans can only dream of the success they might have enjoyed if Sayers and legendary linebacker Dick Butkus, also a rookie in 1965, could have enjoyed full and healthy careers. Sayers was a first-ballot Hall of Famer, anyway. He probably locked up that honor after making one of the greatest punt returns of all time, a climax to one of the greatest days of all time.

Hall of Fame quarterback Y. A. Tittle was an assistant coach for the 49ers that day and said, "I just wonder how many that Sayers would have scored if we hadn't set our defense to stop him."

#6
MIRACLE OF THE MEADOWLANDS
HERM EDWARDS NEVER GIVES UP
NOVEMBER 19, 1978

WHEN HERM EDWARDS was coaching the Kansas City Chiefs in 2006, he was asked whether he was worried that his team had ruined its chances to win by committing too many blunders before beating the Seattle Seahawks in the last few minutes.

"I don't think about that," Edwards replied after the win. "Until the clock says: 'Zero, zero, zero,' you have a chance to win. That's the way I feel. I was involved in a game with twenty-six seconds left, and everybody was walking out of the stadium. . . ."

Nobody had to ask Edwards which game he was talking about. He was referring to the "Miracle of the Meadowlands"— his touchdown return of a fumble recovery that gave the Philadelphia Eagles one of the unlikeliest victories in pro football history. Edwards, the right cornerback, and his teammates were running out of time and hope because the New York Giants simply had to take a knee at their 29-yard line to finish off a 17–12 victory. The Eagles had no time-outs left.

But offensive coordinator Bob Gibson, to the dismay of his players, called for "Pro 65 Up," a run by fullback Larry Csonka over left guard. Gibson was trying to avoid a repeat of a fight on the previous play, when quarterback Joe Pisarcik took a knee only to see linebacker Bill Bergey bulldoze center Jim Clack. Pisarcik was chewed out by Gibson for changing a play the week before and wasn't about to try it again.

But the Giants had dawdled in the huddle, and Clack, trying to avoid a delay-of-game penalty on third down, snapped the ball before Pisarcik was ready. The quarterback bobbled the snap and put the handoff on Csonka's right hip. The ball fell to the ground. Edwards was at the line of scrimmage, opposite running back Doug Kotar, who didn't see the loose ball. Edwards did, however, and scooped it up on one bounce. He returned it 26 yards for a touchdown with twenty seconds left, and the 19–17 victory eventually would allow the Eagles to make the playoffs.

"It was a gift," Edwards said. "I was at the right place at the right time. As a little kid, you always dream about making the play to win the game, and that was one of those deals. I go into the end zone, and Giants Stadium is quiet. I'm looking around, going, 'What happened?' And everybody's wondering, 'What happened?'

"Everything got real still. You're almost so afraid, you don't know if it's really true. Did this really happen, or is this a flash to your brain? All of a sudden, we're whooping and hollering."

Eagles coach Dick Vermeil assumed the game was over and wasn't watching the play. "It dawned on him when he noticed people running by him," Edwards recalled. "He said, 'What are you doing?' And someone said, 'Herman ran it in for a touchdown!' He never saw it until he watched the tape."

Vermeil is among the few people Edwards runs into who will admit to not having seen the famous return. "There are two versions of the story," Edwards said. "One is, 'I was at the game.' And that can't all be true because there weren't enough people at the game for all the times I've heard it. The second is, they know where they were. They'll tell you, 'I was in a mall, standing in front of the TV,' or, 'I was in the parking lot. I turned the radio on and heard what happened.'"

That play benefited both franchises, though it helped the Eagles a lot sooner. They finished 9–7 to reach the playoffs for the first time since 1960. Edwards contends that near-miraculous victory gave the Eagles the winning attitude that propelled them to four straight playoff berths, including a Super Bowl appearance in the 1980 season. That play also forced a long-overdue overhaul for the Giants, who had regressed from the league's most glamorous to most dysfunctional franchise.

Gibson was fired the next day. Coach John McVay and the remaining assistants were fired after the season. Coowners Wellington and Tim Mara patched up their family feud long enough to hire, at Commissioner Pete Rozelle's urging, general manager George Young. His second head coach, Bill Parcells, guided the Giants to two Super Bowl championships.

Edwards's "miracle" earned him a legacy for life. "It's a nice deal, but it's kind of a bad deal," he said, explaining he'd prefer to be remembered as an overachieving and undrafted free agent who played 135 straight games for the Eagles. "I guess my mark will be that play. Fifty years from now, they may still be showing that play."

The "miracle" also reinforced a valuable lesson that's served Edwards well as an NFL assistant and head coach of the New York Jets and Chiefs. He's habitually told his players they need to make the most of opportunities once they arise.

"There's going to come a time in your life when the door's going to open, and hopefully you're ready for what's on the other side," Edwards said. "I try to make my players understand that. You never know what play is going to win the game, and you never know when it's going to come."

#5
BEAUTY AND THE BEAST
CHUCK BEDNARIK DECKS FRANK GIFFORD
NOVEMBER 20, 1960

CHUCK BEDNARIK can look up from the telephone in his Coopersburg, Pennsylvania, home and study the photograph of the most famous tackle ever made in professional football.

Bednarik, the Philadelphia Eagles' middle linebacker, is pumping his right fist in celebration after forcing the fumble that wrapped up a pivotal 17–10 victory over the New York Giants in 1960. Frank Gifford, who'd caught a pass from Charlie Conerly, is on his back, unconscious after getting nailed by Bednarik. Gifford, one of the most popular Giants ever, suffered a severe concussion that would sideline him until 1962.

Bednarik, unaware of how badly he hurt Gifford, went into a victory dance as soon as he saw linebacker Chuck Weber recover the fumble. The Yankee Stadium crowd, assuming Bednarik was gloating over Gifford's injury, became incensed. Bednarik has always insisted he was celebrating the victory, not the injury, and has felt no need to apologize for a clean, if vicious, hit.

"I have that picture right here, and you know what?" Bednarik asked. "I sell about a thousand of those a year. People request it. I send it autographed. I'm standing over him. He's out like a light, and I saw the recovery. With a clenched fist and my eyes closed—and it happened to be where he was laying—I said, 'This . . . game is over.'

"I had no idea where Frank Gifford was when I turned around and simultaneously made a gesture. The picture makes it look like I'm standing over him, gloating. I wasn't gloating. I had no idea he was there."

The play is famous for its ferocity but also because of the stars involved. Gifford and Bednarik were future Hall of Famers, but their demeanors could not have been more different. Gifford's matinee idol looks were as impressive as his running and receiving skills. As a marquee player in New York, Gifford was an early Joe Namath without the roguishness. After he retired, Gifford's play-by-play announcing on *Monday Night Football* made him the most enduring personality in the history of prime-time television.

Bednarik was the personification of the NFL tough guy in a no-holds-barred era. Baltimore Colts rookie halfback Lenny Moore wondered if he could survive in the NFL after getting a good look at Bednarik in his first exhibition game. "I couldn't believe what I was seeing," Moore said. "Chuck Bednarik and another Eagles player didn't just tackle Alan Ameche out of bounds. They carried him out of bounds and slammed him against a table behind the bench."

A center and linebacker, Bednarik was pro football's last true two-way player and played more than fifty minutes in three games during the Eagles' NFL championship season of 1960. He was a heavily decorated air force gunner during World War II and was nicknamed "Concrete Charlie" because he sold concrete in the off-season. People could be excused for thinking he got that nickname because of his hit on Gifford. The Eagles led 17–10 with fewer than two minutes left, and the game was crucial to the outcome of the Eastern Division race. The Giants had the ball, and Gifford was a dangerous runner after the catch, which is why Bednarik was waiting for him.

"It's a shot that people dream about," he said. "If you go down the field, doing a down and in, and you're coming across, you have to look at that quarterback throwing the ball, and at the same time I'm coming straight across. That's dangerous. That's like a Volkswagen going down a one-way street and a Mack truck is coming the opposite way.

"It's a head-on collision, and I happened to get that forearm out and hit him high on the chest. That's when he flipped. It snapped his head back like a boxer. He never saw me. The ball came out of his hands, and he's unconscious."

Though Gifford, a 6-foot-1, 195-pound halfback, was sturdily built for his era, he appeared small and vulnerable while lying at the feet of the 230-pound Bednarik. "I thought Bednarik killed him," recalled Giants Hall of Fame linebacker Sam Huff.

Gifford seldom discusses the tackle. He maintains it was clean and that too much has been made of it. He and Bednarik since have bumped into each other in more peaceful circumstances, such as Hall of Fame functions.

"He said to me, 'I made you famous, didn't I?'" Bednarik said, laughing.

"If you do anything big, do it in New York. It happened to be in New York, and since it happened to a revered guy like Frank, it'll never die. If that tackle was against anybody else, in any other city, it would have been forgotten."

#4
THE CATCH
DWIGHT CLARK STARTS 49ERS DYNASTY
JANUARY 10, 1982

THE CHAMPIONSHIP-LADEN RUN of the San Francisco 49ers in the 1980s and 1990s began with "The Catch." Joe Montana was just an up-and-coming quarterback who was surrounded by a so-so supporting cast.

When Dwight Clark snared a Montana pass in the back of the end zone to beat the Dallas Cowboys 28–27 in the National Football Conference title game, he put the 49ers in their first Super Bowl and coauthored the first chapter of the Montana lore.

Montana wasn't throwing to Jerry Rice or John Taylor back then. Nor was he handing off to Roger Craig or Wendell Tyler. His top runner, Ricky Patton, gained only 543 yards in 1981. The 49ers had more stars on defense than offense, and Clark was Montana's only runner or receiver who would ever make a Pro Bowl.

"Montana has to be the key," said Cowboys coach Tom Landry after the 49ers' shocking victory at Candlestick Park. "There really is nothing else there except the quarterback."

Despite committing six turnovers, two of which led to Dallas touchdowns, the 49ers trailed only 27–21 when they took over with 4:54 left. "During the TV time-out before we started, I didn't know if we'd have time for it," Clark told the *San Francisco Chronicle*. "I guess I thought we could do it, but man, I looked down that field, and it was a long way away."

Montana had made a reputation at Notre Dame for leading wild comebacks. But this was the NFL and he was facing the Cowboys, still a perennial playoff team. The 49ers were just an upstart, even if their 13–3 record had earned them home-field advantage in the NFC playoffs. Montana needed thirteen plays to move his offense 89 yards for a touchdown, but few remember much about the first twelve plays. The 49ers faced third-and-3 from the Dallas 6-yard line with fewer than ninety seconds left. Coach Bill Walsh called for "Sprint Right Option," the same play that had produced a touchdown pass to Freddie Solomon in the first quarter.

Solomon slipped coming off the line, however. Meanwhile, defenders Ed "Too Tall" Jones, Larry Bethea, and D. D. Lewis were beating a path to Montana's door. So Montana rolled to the right sideline and bought time while Clark got open. He threw at the last possible instant, off his back foot. The pass was so high that most teammates assumed Montana was throwing the ball away and began walking back to the huddle.

Not Clark. He leaped and his outstretched hands formed two sides of an inverted triangle. He caught the ball with his fingertips. Cowboys rookie cornerback Everson Walls was beside and then behind Clark and helpless to make a play.

"The play was designed so that by the time he throws it, the ball either goes out of bounds or is caught," Clark said. "When people say he was trying to throw the ball away, I just say, 'No, it was a spectacular throw, made under duress.' It was thrown exactly where it needed to be thrown. When Joe threw the ball, Walls had to think it was going out of bounds."

Walls, actually, said he thought Clark might have gone out of bounds. "I still can't believe how high he got, and how he managed to grab it with four fingers," Walls said. "Joe rolled to my left, and the play took so long. He went inside me and danced around the back of the end zone, and when I turned around to look for him, the ball was already up. Maybe it was wishful thinking, but I thought he went out of the end zone before he made the catch. It's not the best catch I ever saw, but it was the most important one."

Though the 49ers, losers in Walsh's first two seasons, were the new kids on the block, their rivalry with the Cowboys was fierce. The Cowboys pounded the 49ers 59–14 during 1980. When the 49ers returned the favor with a 45–14 win in 1981, several Dallas players claimed the real Cowboys hadn't shown up.

The 49ers hadn't achieved much since winning NFC West titles from 1970–1972, and in each of those three seasons they lost playoff games to the Cowboys. All the pent-up frustrations of 49er fans seemingly were released in a raucous, emotional explosion when Clark made his catch.

"At the time, I didn't have any idea what it would come to mean," Clark said. "Nobody did. I didn't realize how bitter the San Francisco fans were toward the Cowboys. I didn't pay attention to what had happened in the early seventies. I think that whole season was the end of the bad old days."

That play signaled a changing of the NFC's guard. The Cowboys would never get so close to another Super Bowl for the rest of the Landry era. And though the 49ers won four Super Bowls in a decade, who's to say their dynasty would have started without "The Catch"? That play will live on in the hearts and memories of San Francisco for as long as Clark seemed to hang in the air, which is, to say, forever.

#3
THE HORSE MAKES HISTORY
ALAN AMECHE PLUNGES INTO A NEW ERA
DECEMBER 28, 1958

IT WAS THE SIGNATURE PLAY of the "Greatest Game Ever Played." With a 1-yard plunge after 8:15 of overtime, fullback Alan "The Horse" Ameche gave the Baltimore Colts a 23–17 victory in the NFL championship game. He also pushed professional football front and center on America's sporting stage.

In the early 1950s, America's best-loved sports were Major League Baseball, college football, boxing, and horse racing. But dusk was falling on the pretelevision era, and the future of any sport in America would depend upon a partnership with television. The National Football League's popularity accelerated during the mid-1950s, thanks partly to the New York Giants—a marquee team in the nation's biggest TV market.

The 1958 title game between the Colts and Giants in Yankee Stadium was watched in 10.8 million homes, which was at that time the largest TV audience ever for an NFL game. Additionally, TV and radio dominated local pregame coverage because of a newspaper strike that shut down New York's nine dailies.

The star-studded matchup, featuring the Giants' dominating defense and the Colts' record-breaking offense, forced the NFL into America's sports consciousness. The Colts and Giants, who between them had seventeen future Hall-of-Famers, made the most of that exposure, and Ameche's plunge closed the sale. The game wouldn't be nearly as memorable had it ended with a routine field goal—and it easily could have if Colts quarterback John Unitas played it safe on the final drive.

On second-and-7, Unitas lofted a pass to tight end Jim Mutscheller at the 1. Reporters asked Unitas why he'd risk an interception. "When you know what you are doing, you are not intercepted," Unitas replied. "The Giants were jammed up at the line and not expecting a pass. If Jim had been covered, I'd have thrown the pass out of bounds. It's just that I would rather win a game like this by a touchdown than a field goal."

The Giants knew what was next. "We all knew the next play was going to be a run, and that Ameche would be carrying, but it didn't do much good," middle linebacker Sam Huff recalled.

The Giants' defense was worn out by a 73-yard drive that ended with Steve Myhra's 20-yard field goal, which made the score 17–17. The ball was snapped with just seven seconds left, and for the first time ever an NFL championship game would be decided in sudden-death overtime. The Giants won the coin toss but failed to get a first down, and their exhausted defense was under siege. The Colts started at their 20 and scored in thirteen plays. Unitas masterfully mixed passes and runs by Ameche to keep the ball moving and keep the Giants off balance.

Ameche might have ended this game with a longer run when he tried a draw five plays earlier. The Colts let right tackle Dick Modzelewski barrel in on Unitas, which left a big hole for Ameche once Huff dropped back to cover wide receiver Raymond Berry. Ameche ran for 23 yards to the Giants' 21-yard line, causing Berry to immediately regret not carrying out his blocking assignment.

"If I hadn't loafed on that play, Ameche might've scored," recalled Berry, whose catches kept burning the Giants. "My job was to get to the safety, and my excuse was that I was dragging and worn out. That play never breaks for more than 2 or 3 yards, anyway."

It's probably just as well that Ameche didn't score on that play, given the confusion that ensued. Colts fans in the Yankee

Stadium crowd of 64,185 were shaking the bleachers so hard that they disconnected a TV cable on the sideline and knocked the game off the air for two-and-a half minutes. Had the game ended then, NBC would have faced the onslaught of angry phone calls and controversy that it faced a decade later when it pulled the plug on the New York Jets and Oakland Raiders in the *Heidi* game.

The picture came back in time for the Unitas pass to Mutscheller and the climactic play, designated in the Colts' playbook as "16 Power." Mutscheller blocked linebacker Cliff Livingston, and running back Lenny Moore got a piece of safety Emlen Tunnell as Ameche scored untouched.

"We got the halfback [Moore] blocking ahead of Ameche with a double team on the tackle," Unitas explained. "When I slapped the ball in Al's belly and saw him take off, I knew nobody was going to stop him. They couldn't have done it if we needed 10 yards."

The Giants nearly had the game wrapped up when they led 17–14 with 2:22 left. On third-and-3, halfback Frank Gifford was tackled by end Gino Marchetti near the first-down marker. After a delay, caused by defensive tackle Big Daddy Lipscomb falling on Marchetti and breaking his ankle, the referee shocked Gifford by spotting the ball short of a first down. Don Chandler punted, and the Colts took over at their 14-yard line with 1:56 left.

"I said to myself, 'Well, we've blown this ball game,'" Berry recalled. "The goal post looked a million miles away."

Not after Unitas went to work in a no-huddle offense. He passed to Moore for 11 yards and to Berry for 25 to reach midfield with only 1:05 left. Two more passes to Berry moved the ball to the 13 for Myhra's kick. The goalpost sat on the goal line back then.

Ameche's run sits at the start of a striking timeline. Barely a year later, Pete Rozelle was elected NFL Commissioner and moved the league office from Philadelphia to New York. That same day, January 26, 1960, Lamar Hunt was elected president of the fledgling American Football League. Both leagues, under visionary leadership, would merge in 1966 and create the Super Bowl.

Unitas, who was twenty-five when he starred in the 1958 championship game, rode the early waves of the game's dramatic growth. But he declined an invitation to appear on a live telecast of the *Ed Sullivan Show* the night of the big win over the Giants. Ameche went instead and was paid three hundred dollars. He was happy to take the handoff from Unitas and not for the first time that day, either.

#2

"RUN IT! AND LET'S GET THE HELL OUT OF HERE!"
BART STARR'S SLIPPERY SNEAK
DECEMBER 31, 1967

BART STARR'S 1-YARD quarterback sneak in the most famous foul-weather game of all time was a testimony to his shrewdness, leadership, and guts under the most uncomfortable conditions imaginable.

There's good reason that the 1967 NFL Championship game between the Dallas Cowboys and Green Bay Packers is remembered as the "Ice Bowl." At kickoff in Lambeau Field, the temperature was 13 degrees below zero with the wind chill at minus 46. By the time Starr and Packers coach Vince Lombardi agreed on a play that would bring them a 21–17 victory, the players would've been better off wearing ice skates.

The Cowboys led 17–14 when the Packers took over at the Green Bay 32-yard line with 4:50 left. Starr guided his offense to third-and-goal at the Dallas 1 and called his last time-out with sixteen seconds left. He went to the sideline and told Lombardi he wanted to run between center Ken Bowman and right guard Jerry Kramer. The high-percentage decision would have called for a short field goal that would have sent the game into sudden-death overtime. Had a run failed, it's doubtful the Packers could have gotten their field-goal unit on the field before time expired.

Lombardi's decision raises widespread speculation about his motives. Was this the ultimate example of his motto, "Winning isn't everything, it's the only thing"? Or was this the arrogance of a proud coach accustomed to willing the result he wanted? Or was Lombardi just so cold that he dreaded the thought of shivering through overtime?

Starr explains he and Lombardi simply made a sound football decision. "Our lead play on short yardage going into the game was a wedge play," he said. "We already tried it twice in the game and knew it would work. Our linemen did an excellent job getting under the blockers. Jethro Pugh was a great tackle, [but] he was a little taller coming in on his charge, so you could get underneath him.

"I took time out and asked the linemen, 'Could you get your footing for one more wedge play?' They said they could. I said, 'Coach, there's nothing wrong with the play. The backs are slipping, though, to get to the line of scrimmage. I can shuffle my feet and just lunge in.'

"All he said, which was so typical for this man, was, 'Run it! And let's get the hell out of here!' I'm going back to the huddle at this brutally cold time, and I'm actually laughing."

Starr called "Brown Right, 31 Wedge," which told the 3 back, fullback Chuck Mercein, to run through the 1 hole, between Bowman and Kramer. Because the Packers' playbook didn't have a wedge play for Starr, he called it for Mercein but didn't tell anybody that he actually was going to keep the ball. Starr figured this ploy would work because he'd used it in a 20–7 victory over the San Francisco 49ers the year before.

Kramer found a soft spot in the ice and dug in with his right foot. At the snap, he got underneath Pugh so quickly that Pugh said he thought Kramer jumped offside. Bowman knocked Pugh into a linebacker, and Pugh fell on Kramer, leaving a hole for Starr. Mercein was focused on taking the handoff and told Lombardi biographer David Maraniss, "I'm psyched, I want this thing to go right. I'm taking off and lo and behold, Bart's not giving me the ball. He's kept it, and he's in the end zone."

Now, Mercein's only worry was that he might run into Starr's back and get penalized for pushing him into the end zone. So he threw up both arms to show he wasn't assisting Starr in a gesture that was widely interpreted as him signaling a touchdown.

Despite his disappointment, Mercein was a major player in this historic drive. He ran 7 yards for the drive's initial first down. He caught a 19-yard pass that was thrown high and behind him, then ran to the Dallas 11 before going out of bounds. On the next play, Mercein ran to the 3 on a fake sweep. Donny Anderson barely got the first down and carried twice more. But he couldn't crack the end zone.

The winning play provided the climax to *Instant Replay*, a best seller by Kramer and Dick Schaap that made Kramer the most famous offensive lineman in America. Years later, Bowman complained bitterly that he'd acceded to Kramer's request to downplay Bowman's role in the double-team block.

"The older I get, the more it bothers me," Bowman said. "I was young and stupid, and he patted me on the shoulder as he went up to the [television] podium after the game and said, 'Let an old man have his moment in the spotlight. You've got ten, twelve more years.' What I didn't realize was that blocks like that come along once in . . . hell, it's been two decades now."

Over in the losers' locker room, meanwhile, pro football's broadcast future was being shaped. Frank Gifford, the former New York Giants star, was part of the CBS television crew and had gone to the Cowboys locker room, expecting to interview the winners. Instead, he got an interview with losing quarterback Don Meredith that was so passionate and eloquent that Meredith became a national celebrity. When ABC executive Roone Arledge tried to hire Gifford as the color man for *Monday Night Football* in 1970, its debut season, Gifford decided to honor the last year of his CBS contract and recommended Meredith, instead. Meredith, Gifford, and Howard Cosell eventually became the most famous trio in sports-broadcasting history.

The Ice Bowl was pivotal to Meredith's retirement. He was weary of being the fall guy for the Cowboys' postseason short-comings and stayed around only one more season. That opened the door for Craig Morton to take the Cowboys to a Super Bowl and for Roger Staubach to turn "Next Year's Champions" into "America's Team." Starr's sneak also paved the way for the Lombardi era's last hurrah, a 33–14 Super Bowl victory over the Oakland Raiders.

Had Starr slipped on the ice, the Cowboy dynasty would have started a few years earlier. And the Packer dynasty would have died on a frozen field.

#1
THE IMMACULATE RECEPTION
FRANCO HARRIS'S INCREDIBLE SCORE
DECEMBER 23, 1972

IT WAS, DEPENDING UPON YOUR POINT OF VIEW, a magnificent effort by Pittsburgh Steelers rookie Franco Harris or a half-hearted effort that was rewarded by a stroke of incredible luck. It was, depending upon your point of view, a touchdown play correctly officiated under difficult circumstances or a miscarriage of justice against the Oakland Raiders.

Most of us can agree, however, that the "Immaculate Reception," was the most unforgettable play in the history of professional football. Even owner Al Davis, who has always insisted a playoff victory was stolen from his Raiders, described Harris's touchdown play as "one of the great moments in National Football League history."

Steelers fans at old Three Rivers Stadium were watching the first playoff game in franchise history and seemed on the verge of more heartbreak when reserve quarterback Kenny Stabler scrambled 30 yards for a 7–6 Raiders lead with 1:13 remaining. Just twenty-two seconds were left when the Steelers faced fourth-and-10 at their 40-yard line. They called the "66 Circle Post," and it began to develop with little promise.

Quarterback Terry Bradshaw's blocking broke down, and defensive linemen Tony Cline and Horace Jones each got a hand on him. Bradshaw, a 6-foot-3, 210-pounder, used his strength and speed to avoid the rush and threw a bullet 25 yards down the middle for running back John "Frenchy" Fuqua. Fuqua collided with safety Jack Tatum, and the ball boomeranged to Harris. The rookie fullback made a shoestring catch at the Oakland 42 and sprinted to the end zone with five seconds left for a 13–7 victory. Defensive back Jimmy Warren was the last Raider to get a hand on Harris before the stadium erupted in pandemonium and confusion.

Bradshaw was as confused as anybody because he was buried by the pass rush before he could see the play. Once he got up, he was puzzled to see the officials huddling to determine if Tatum had touched the ball. A completion then wasn't legal if the ball was tapped from one offensive player to another without a defensive touch in between.

"I didn't know what happened," Bradshaw recalled. "I just saw a black jersey [Fuqua's] going to the post, gunned the ball, and got waylaid. The next thing, I heard this incredible roar, and I knew it wasn't a first-down roar. I know it's a touchdown, and I'm wondering, 'Who scored, and who did I complete it to?' Then you kind of go, 'That's cool. I put that bad boy in there, and I'm a hero to millions.'

"Then there's that humbling part. You walk over, and they tell you, 'The ball hit Frenchy, and there's a question if Tatum hit it, too.' And I'm going, 'Huh? Come again on all of this?' I had no clue."

After conferring with his crew, referee Fred Swearingen went into the baseball dugout and phoned Art McNally, the league's supervisor of officials. Swearingen finally signaled a touchdown, and fans swarmed the field. It took fifteen minutes for officials to clear the field for Roy Gerela's extra point. The game was finally over, but the controversy was just warming up.

The play received its famous name when Steelers fan Michael Ord stood on a chair during a postgame celebration with friends and family and announced, "From here on, this day will be forever known as the Feast of the Immaculate Reception." Ord's girlfriend, Sharon Levosky, phoned sportscaster Myron Cope and asked him to use the nickname on the local newscast that night. That nickname has been on the lips of Pittsburghers ever since.

Though nobody can say for sure who touched Bradshaw's pass first, it's safe to say the play could not have been reversed by today's instant-replay rule. A decision can be reversed only when the referee has "indisputable visual evidence" of a wrong call. No such evidence exists on the game's telecast, though it appears that the force of Tatum's swat helped drive the ball to Harris.

"The last thing we said in the huddle was, 'Look, we got this game won, all we got to do is knock the ball down,'" recalled Raider safety George Atkinson. "And guess what happens? Tate went for the big knockout."

The ball carried 7 yards, to where Harris was trailing the play. He looked like an outfielder scooping the ball just before it hit the grass. Harris in his Hall of Fame career would never make a play quite so dramatic again.

"Going into the huddle, I was thinking how great a year it had been, and if this was going to be the last play, I was going to play it all the way out," Harris said years later. "Unfortunately, the play that was called didn't really involve me at all. I was supposed to stay in and block a linebacker if they blitzed, but they didn't.

"I knew Brad was in serious trouble, so I went downfield in case he needed me as an outlet receiver. I was always taught to go to the ball, so when he threw it, that's what I did. The next thing I knew, the ball was coming right to me. The rest has always been a blur. It happened so fast. It was all reaction. My only thought was to get to the end zone. It's amazing to me that this play has stood the test of time."

Steelers coach Chuck Noll, who was just starting to rev up a dynasty that would win four Super Bowls in six years, said, "Franco made that play because he never quit on the play. He kept running, he kept hustling. Good things happen to those who hustle."

Such praise wasn't forthcoming from Raiders linebacker Phil Villapiano. He claimed Harris actually loafed on the play, which is debatable, and that tight end John McMakin clipped him, which is not. McMakin's foul was flagrant.

"Bradshaw drops back," Villapiano told NFL Films. "I look at him, I look at Franco. Franco's doing nothing. He missed his block. Bradshaw scrambles, Franco comes jogging down the field, half speed. He's my man, I'm going half speed with him. I saw Bradshaw throw the ball. I shot over to help make the tackle. Meanwhile, Franco had drifted right over there—it was going right to him.

"Had I been as lazy as Franco, that ball would've come to me waist high. Now I spin around, I can still make the play. Their tight end, a smart player, dives at my legs. What's he got to lose? They're going to lose the game, anyway. [It was] the biggest clip ever. I remember laying on the ground, watching Franco run down the sideline. I couldn't believe it was happening."

Villapiano's teammates, to a man, claimed they were robbed. "Frenchy was between me and the ball," Tatum said in 2002. "So if the ball hit me, it would have had to come through him or over the top of him, and that didn't happen. It's thirty years later, and it doesn't really matter, but I never thought the ball hit me."

That play would matter to Davis a hundred years from now. "I think we got taken," he said. "The word is stronger than that. We should've had that football game, but we didn't get it. To his credit, Mr. [Steelers owner Art] Rooney got it. He was in an elevator, he didn't even see the play. He was going down to congratulate his guys for having a great season. He thought they lost, which they should've. But there was nothing we were going to do to prevent it. It was a mistake. I guess it was an honest mistake. Fuqua knows he hit it and it should have been our game."

If Fuqua knows that, he isn't telling. He has too much fun continuing to torment the Raiders.

"I can tell you what happened on that play, but instead I'm going to tell you what happened was truly immaculate," he said.

"Don't listen to any of those Raiders; they are still shell-shocked. That's something that happened in their lives they'll never recover from. I don't think any of them have regained their sanity since that play, and that includes [then coach] John Madden.

"Now I've become obsessed with it. I've been offered money to tell. But there's something about having something you know and no one else in the world knows. Frenchy's going to take it to the grave with him."

ACKNOWLEDGMENTS

I could have researched and related the Xs and Os of these one hundred plays without speaking to a human being. But I couldn't have made any of them come alive.

These plays aren't really about the Xs and Os. They're about the people who called them and made them. And these people can give you nuggets about these famous plays that have never been told or have been long forgotten.

How could I know that Colts fullback Alan Ameche should have scored several plays before his famous plunge, had I not talked to Raymond Berry? How could I know that Alan Page told his teammates he was going to block Chester Marcol's kick, which turned into a Green Bay touchdown, were it not for Packers quarterback Lynn Dickey?

How could I know how indignant Dolphins coach Don Shula remains over the snowplow play had he not said that even today he still wishes he'd thrown himself in front of the tractor that cleared a spot for a New England field-goal try? How could I know why Hank Stram was so cocksure of calling "65 Toss Power Trap," were it not for Chiefs quarterback Len Dawson?

I want to express my gratitude to them and every other ex-player and ex-coach who took the time to share his memories of modern pro football's greatest plays. Every interview was a treat and usually included a sidelight I was hearing for the first time.

I also want to thank some of the household names in pro football media that made my research as thorough as it needed to be.

NFL Films proved invaluable in providing detailed looks at these great plays, as well as interviews with many of the players who made them. *Pro Football Weekly* was kind enough to send me their 1998 list of "The 100 Greatest Plays Ever," which brought to my attention some deserving plays I might have otherwise overlooked.

As usual, the staff at the Pro Football Hall of Fame came through to help me locate people and materials that hold the keys to half-buried football treasures. I want to thank the hall's vice president of communications, Joe Horrigan; librarian Chad Reese; and researcher Matt Waechter.

This book never would have materialized were it not for Gene Brissie, associate publisher at Lyons Press, who suggested the idea. Editor Rob Kirkpatrick helped add muscle to the manuscript, and the rest of the Lyons team once again lent extraordinary skill and support. I also want to thank literary agent Ed Claflin for his role in contract negotiations.

I especially want to thank my wife, Barbara, and son, Steven, for not complaining when I deserted them in the evening to go back to my laptop. Without their support, I could have never met my tight deadline. I also want to thank my older children, David and Danielle, for their sustained support of my writing.

BIBLIOGRAPHY

Allen, Marcus, and Matt Fulks. *Road to Canton.* Champaign, IL: Sports Publishing, 2003.

Allen, Marcus, and Carlton Stowers. *The Autobiography of Marcus Allen.* New York: St. Martins Press Paperbacks, 1998.

Bosworth, Brian, and Rick Reilly. *The Boz: Confessions of a Modern Anti-Hero.* New York: Doubleday, 1988.

Callahan, Tom. *Johnny U: The Life and Times of John Unitas.* New York: Crown Publishing, 2006.

Daly, Dan, and Bob O'Donnell. *The Pro Football Chronicle.* New York: Collier Books, 1990.

Day, Chuck, and Don Weiss. *The Making of the Super Bowl.* New York: Contemporary Books, 2003.

Dienhart, Tom, Joe Hoppel, and Dave Sloan, editors. *Complete Super Bowl Book.* St. Louis, MO: The Sporting News Publishing, 1994.

Freedman, Lew. *Game of My Life: Chicago Bears.* Champaign, IL: Sports Publishing, 2006.

Izenberg, Jerry. *No Medals for Trying.* New York: Ballantine Books, 1990.

Knox, Chuck, and Bill Plaschke. *Hard Knox.* New York: Harcourt Brace Jovanovich, 1988.

Levy, Marv. *Where Else Would You Rather Be?* Champaign, IL: Sports Publishing, 2004.

Liu, Randall, and Matt Marini, eds. *Official 2006 National Football League Fact & Record Book.* New York: National Football League Books, 2006.

MacCambridge, Michael. *America's Game.* New York: Random House, 2004.

Madden, John, and Dave Anderson. *One Knee Equals Two Feet.* New York: Villard Books, 1986.

Maraniss, David. *When Pride Still Mattered: A Life of Vince Lombardi.* New York: Simon & Schuster, 1999.

Montana, Joe, and Dick Schaap. *Montana.* Paducah, KY: Turner Publishing, 1995.

Newhouse, Dave. *The Ultimate Oakland Raiders Trivia Book.* Rochester, NY: American Sports Media, 2001.

Owens, Terrell, and Jason Rosenhaus. *T. O.* New York: Simon & Schuster, 2006.

Pluto, Terry. *When All the World Was Browns Town.* New York: Simon & Schuster, 1997.

Raible, Steve, and Mike Sando. *Steve Raible's Tales from the Seahawks Sideline.* Champaign, IL: Sports Publishing, 2004.

Ryczek, Bill. *Crash of the Titans: The Early Years of the New York Jets and the AFL.* New York: Total Sports, 2000.

Shamsky, Art, and Barry Zeman. *The Magnificent Seasons.* New York: St. Martins Press, 2004.

Stabler, Ken, and Berry Stainback. *Snake.* New York: Doubleday, 1986.

Stallard, Mark. *Kansas City Chiefs Encyclopedia.* Champaign, IL: Sports Publishing, 2002.

Stallard, Mark, and Otis Taylor. *The Need to Win.* Champaign, IL: Sports Publishing, 2003.

Taylor, Jean-Jacques. *Game of My Life: Dallas Cowboys.* Champaign, IL: Sports Publishing, 2006.

Tobias, Todd. *Charging Through the AFL: Los Angeles and San Diego Chargers Football in the 1960s.* Paducah, KY: Turner Publishing, 2004.

Whittingham, Richard. *The Bears.* Dallas, TX: Taylor Publishing, 1994.

Winklejohn, Matt. *Tales from the Atlanta Falcons Sidelines.* Champaign, IL: Sports Publishing, 2005.

Wyatt, Jim. *Tales from the Titans Sidelines.* Champaign, IL: Sports Publishing, 2004.

Zimmerman, Paul. *The New Thinking Man's Guide to Pro Football.* New York: Simon & Schuster, 1984.

INDEX